THE SEASIDE

The author would like to thank the following for their kind and generous donations to The Ibis Trust

Mrs Margaret Fenston
Mr Charlie Watts
Mr Charles Wilson

Mr & Mrs Anthony Andrews
Mr & Mrs Robert Leigh

Mr & Mrs Alan Elliot
Sir Peter & Lady Hunt
Mr & Mrs Andrew Huntley
Mrs Jenny Lesslie
Sir Henry & Lady Rumbold
Mr & Mrs James Vernon

Mr Adrian Biggs
Mr & Mrs Richard Walton

And last but by no means least the Hon. Robin Finch Hatton who spent so much of his valuable time organising the advertisements.

THE
Seaside Gardener

RICHARD MORTIMER

BEELINE
Alderney and London

First published in 1997 by
Beeline Publishers Ltd,
7 Le Bourgage, Alderney
Channel Islands

First published in Great Britain in 1997

ISBN 0–9530860–0–3

Designer: Caroline Archer

Production: Keith Ireland

Typeset by Dorwyn Ltd, Rowlands Castle, Hants

Printed and bound
by Kyodo Printing Co., Singapore

RICHARD MORTIMER

is the pen name of a London medical practitioner who was educated at Malvern, Cambridge and Bart's, none of which is the least bit relevant to this book. However, he has had a life-long interest in gardening since growing radishes and lettuces in his sand pit, which he considered much more interesting than whatever else he was meant to be doing there. Following this unwitting contribution to the war effort, he has struggled unremittingly to establish gardens on other unpromising plots like shady, damp London courtyards, and, for the past 30 years, on a windswept, sandy and rocky site on the edge of the sea. It is the latter experience, along with the development of another courtyard, this one in Alderney, that moved him to write this book, which is dedicated with sympathy to all other gardeners sharing the same battles against wind and usually drought.

The snapshots in this book were all taken by the author

Oh, Adam was a gardener, and God who made him sees
That half a proper gardener's work is done upon his knees,
So when your work is finished, you can wash your hands and pray
For the Glory of the Garden, that it may not pass away!
And the Glory of the Garden it shall never pass away!

from *'The Glory of the Garden'*, RUDYARD KIPLING

Contents

I

A Beginning

One spring day thirty years ago there could have been an equinoctial gale blowing off the Atlantic with awesome ferocity. Monumental rollers could have been running in from the grey horizon to cascade in furious foam over pernicious rocks. Icy rain could have been lashing across the island in harsh sheets.

As it was the Heron rumbled to a stop on a landing strip ankle deep in a closely knit patchwork of wild flowers luminous in the pellucid afternoon light. It would have been hot but for the lightest of airs which barely stirred the wind sock.

The small green island had floated into view awash in an azure sea disturbed by nothing more than the rivulet currents of a turning tide.

From the low moorland of the north to the high cliffs of the south, Alderney basked in still and green benevolence.

Herivel and Hoskins, Estate Agents – the only estate agents – had arranged lodgings as the Grand Hotel – the only hotel – was not yet open for the season. The rooms were in Ruth Herivel's farm house on the edge of the Blaye, the ancient communal grazing land. Ruth was one half of Herivel and Hoskins.

Commander Ronnie Hoskins, ex-colonial policeman, ex-square rig sailor, ruddy face complemented by a snow white goatee beard and venerable boater, was the other half. It was he who conducted our tour of the island, spiced with tales of piracy, wrecking and plunder.

The objective was to find a home for my parents on my father's retirement.

Ronnie showed us with some pride a number of large and undeniably elegant Victorian and Georgian granite built houses on the cobbled streets of the town of St. Anne. The formality of our forebears and the stygian gloom of their interiors did not suit the sparkling mood of a bright blue day. Ronnie, no doubt aware of our restiveness, drove us into the countryside where nobody much had been foolhardy enough to live since the 17th century when the old harbour in Longis Bay had finally been abandoned.

There it was: a small white house standing bolt upright on the moor, a hundred paces from the sea.

It faced east across seven miles of tidal race to Cap La Hague, the coast of Normandy, protected from heavy seas by shallow water, but nevertheless exposed to the fiercest gales. Bracken, furze and bramble held tenaciously to the sand and rock.

The house had been built by the Ministry of Works quite recently to replace a family home elsewhere on the island destroyed during the German occupation. The previous owners had been far too busy to bother with the frivolity of garden making. The site, however, had the mesmeric magic of sea and skyscape, granite and maram – a wild and vivid beauty which proved totally seductive on that spring day thirty years ago.

Later, much later, after a new generation had been born into our family, we acquired one of the oldest granite houses in Alderney, close to the ancient thoroughfare of the town. It had been a farm house and the island's dairy. Ruth Herivel's husband had been born in one of its diminutive bedrooms. Between times it had suffered vicissitudes and neglect. Brambles, nettles and rubble obscured the walled farm yard no more than thirty feet by forty feet. We inherited two small apple trees, a bay tree, an unhappy lilac and four flourishing blackberry bushes.

So, over a period of thirty years, we have cultivated two very different gardens: the first large and as near to the sea as you can get without falling in; the second a small courtyard in the town, in the highest area of the island. Both are exposed to strong salty winds, but the town garden benefits from warm walls and better soil. The other common denominator is lack of water. A hosepipe ban has been in effect for three years as the island's water supply is dependent upon run off into "reservoirs" formed by the quarrying of granite used to build the 19th century fortifications. Until recently rain has been so minimal that these reservoirs have at times been almost empty. Nothing is watered except during planting.

Everything that is planted has to survive these conditions. Anything which fails to thrive is discarded. On the moor we also have myxomatosis-proof rabbits to contend with, which have put paid to most plants of rabbit height: new plants are now carefully corralled behind netting.

If one believes in "the greenhouse effect", these arid conditions are here to stay. Certainly a new dimension has been added to coastal gardening, and it is now imperative rather than important to pay due consideration, no matter whether you live in Yorkshire or Cornwall, to the tolerance of your plantings to heat and drought as well as to wind and salt.

Many plants which have been traditionally used in the Channel Islands fulfil these criteria, but until recently the list has been somewhat restricted. Far-sighted nurserymen, however, are now hunting for suitable species to extend choice and colour range. A modicum of reading and some knowledge of the characteristics which give plants natural tolerance – adaptation – will be of enormous help to coastal and dry gardeners. I hope this book will offer some guidance in circumventing the problems we all share.

2

Trials and Errors

A lot of gardens I know are like old style cottage hospitals with hard pressed part-time staff running around tending sickly plants whose tenuous hold on life is entirely dependent on a never ending rote of feeding, dosing, watering and minor surgery.

Like most amateur gardeners, we are certainly part-time, and cannot aspire to the cultivation of flower show blooms from species which would be happier in a Peruvian rain forest. For most of the time our plants have to fend for themselves. Even if watering was allowed, we would not be there to do it.

When we first started there was an appalling casualty rate among new plantings. We were almost totally ignorant about how to tackle the all too obvious enemy of heavy salty wind blowing over light sandy soil. It was not until we were introduced to Christine Kelway's *"Seaside Gardening"* (1962) and *"Gardening on Sand"* (1965) that we discovered some tricks of the trade. Immediately we had notable successes, and to this day these crusading books are a mine of felicitous facts.

Unfortunately they are long out of print and now somewhat out of date. However, the principles Miss Kelway propounded are still totally valid, and she would surely envy the vastly enhanced choice of plants commercially available to coastal gardeners today. In that far off time we had to rely on fellow gardeners' recommendations and their generous donations of cuttings; on trial and error and on local knowledge based on a long tradition of shared battles against hostile elements.

Unless suitably briefed a new seaside gardener can spend ill-affordable time and money re-inventing several dozen wheels, and not enjoying the process.

It was not until the appearance of Beth Chatto's *"The Dry Garden"* in 1978 that the reasons for Christine Kelway's success began to dawn on me. Miss Kelway recognised, of course, the importance of adding humus to sandy soil, of windbreaks and of careful planting. Her choice of plants, however, was dictated by tradition and trial and error. Mrs. Chatto describes so well the revelation of seeing garden plants growing in their native wild habitats. There, of course, is the blindingly obvious answer: match plant and environment with sufficient accuracy and the gardener need do little more.

The penny having dropped, the rest was relatively easy. Gone were the protracted cachectic deaths of the recently imported infants who looked so enticingly healthy in the garden centre. Almost.

A superficial glance at any uncultivated stretch of British seaside moorland will prove the point that it is not host to any notably exciting flora, apart from the smallest wild flowers growing as flat as the proverbial pancake. There might be the occasional gathering of grizzled gorse, but that is the extent of it.

The reasons are obvious if you live there rather than visit on a baking summer's day. Ocean gales are not easily ignored. Their unremitting primeval ferocity is literally staggering. Along with the wind comes salt from the sea and probably sand. This lethal admixture scours skin from the face and buds from the plants. No wonder they lie flat out of the way, it is tempting to do the same yourself.

Dig a spit down and you are likely to find pure sand. Dig another spit or two and you will probably hit bedrock.

Apart from the indisputable fact that sand will not hold moisture, rain running off will also carry away the small quantities of nutrients that may have accumulated. Add to this frequent periods of drought during the summer and the apparent increasing heat due to the greenhouse effect, and there is a compound of factors which many plants, no matter how vigorous, will be unable to surmount.

All, however, is not despair and despondency.

The sandy soil is warm and well aerated. Periods of sunlight are long. The air is humid and copious dew falls after the hottest day. This moist air holds salt in solution, and is in more or less perpetual motion, discouraging the formation of air and ground frost. Snow falls rarely, and when it does usually settles for a short period only.

To take advantage of these benefits windbreaks are essential. If constructed from the toughest plant material known to man, they will withstand incredible exposure to the elements.

Behind the windbreaks the most surprisingly tender plants can burgeon. There are still strict limitations on choice, but at least the major enemy is under some control.

Mulching in order to conserve moisture in the soil, to suppress competitive weeds, and to provide material for humus production is the vital second step.

Finally, before giving serious consideration to your choice of plants, analyse the soil to establish whether it is alkaline, neutral or acid. Much sandy soil is alkaline due to the presence of crushed shells: it is a terrible waste of time and money to attempt to grow on it acid-loving species such as ericas, rhododendrons and azaleas. Constructing and maintaining peat beds in a desert of alkaline sand is a task which would have made Hercules doubt his sense of commitment: conserve your energies!

Later I will describe plants which have proved their worth in seaside conditions. A large part of the enjoyment of gardening, however, at least for me, is to make discoveries rather than slavishly follow lists of recommendations all the time.

Of course you will have failures, some heartbreaking. For many years a plant may flourish and flower spectacularly, only to perish in an unusually cold winter. More often than not, however, the warm sandy soil will have protected the root system, and it will spring up the following summer. The rule is never to uproot and discard anything until a full year has passed.

A knowledge of the characteristics of plants which give them tolerance to wind and drought is very helpful. More often than not these are obvious in tough leathery leaves or grey or white foliage; in long whippy stems or thick coverings of spines.

Always take particular note of the wild origins of plants. Careful matching of your conditions to those prevailing in a plant's natural habitat will almost guarantee success. For instance many garigue and maquis plants from the Mediterranean seabord will do well, being perfectly attuned to poverty stricken sandy soil, long summer drought and comparatively warm short winters. Parts of Australia and New Zealand have similar conditions, and contain a largely untapped wealth of material, although there is an increasing interest. Warm, arid areas of the United States, such as California, and of South America, such as Chile, provide many other possibilities. South Africa occasionally offers reasonably hardy plants.

When making a start on your seaside site, have a good look at what is prospering in your neighbours' gardens. Gardeners are usually a friendly lot so ask advice, and, very politely, beg cuttings. Certainly that is how we started on our bare moorland. Luckily a neighbour's windbreaks had survived the depredations of the German occupation, and we were given copious cuttings of *Olearia traversii*, tamarisk and euonymus. Another neighbour had nurtured a fine collection of perennial "mesems" on his dry stone walls, and kindly gave us cuttings of these. Rather an eclectic selection, but it was soon extended through purchases from the local nursery run by Bill and Jessie Parmentier, who had the advantages of a Kew training and knowledge of a long tradition of gardening in the Channel Islands. With their patient help, more mature specimens were added to our rows of infant cuttings. To bolster our windbreaks in came *Pittosporum crassifolium*, *Eleagnus x ebbingei*, white poplar, Monterey pine, *Escallonia macrantha*, Holm oak and tree lupins. They also introduced us to the then new *Cupressocyparis x leylandii* which has proved its worth at the forefront of the windbreaks.

Today, many years later, these tough trees and shrubs have fused into lofty and impenetrable green and grey banks. Behind them the heaviest gale is but sigh and sussuration.

Having provided adequate protection for your plants and an improved soil, the aim is to establish a garden which you can enjoy with the minimum of labour. Never plant anything which cannot look after itself once established, other than occasional help in appropriate dead-heading and cutting back in the interests of prolonged flowering and neatness.

3
Soil and Plants

Your soil is almost inevitably going to be sandy in a garden by the sea. The sand will have been blown from beaches, or will have been left behind by ancient land upheavals or changes in coastal configuration. The presence of pulverized shells in sand will usually have given the soil a degree of alkalinity through the presence of calcium carbonate, an effect which is greatly magnified if the soil overlies chalk or limestone.

If your soil is seriously alkaline there is little sense in trying to make it acid for the sake of trying to cultivate rhododendrons, azaleas and ericaceous plants. No amount of additives will have a permanent effect. As always it is much easier to go along with nature and grow plants which positively enjoy the conditions.

When you take over a garden, or the site which you intend to make into a garden, an essential first step is to establish what type of soil you have inherited. To do this you can buy yourself a soil testing kit which will tell you the answer quickly and easily. The kit works on the principle of a chemical colour reaction to acidity or alkalinity, and measures the "pH" of the soil. pH is a logarithmic scale running from 1 to 14, the range of soil pH being from 4 to 9. Neutral is 7, acid from 6.5 to 4.5, alkaline from 7.5 to 8.5. Being a logarithmic scale, do not forget that 8.1 is ten times more alkaline than 7.1.

Take soil samples from several well dispersed points even in a small garden, as there can be a surprising variation of pH over small distances. Also remember when testing a virgin site to take your samples from beneath the top growth of grass and wild flowers.

This topmost layer will be more acid due to the presence of decaying plant matter.

We have touched upon the effect of mulching with peat or bark in conserving moisture through cutting down evaporation and suppressing weed growth. There are two other important effects a mulch will have. The first is to add humus to the soil, humus being the sponge-like organic content of soil which absorbs and holds water. Sandy soil is obviously seriously deficient in humus, and has no capacity to hold moisture; rain runs off quickly and carries with it soluble nutrients and trace elements vital to the health of plant life.

The second effect is to add a degree of acidity to the soil through the intrinsic acid property of decaying plant material.

Apart from peat and bark there are two other practical sources of mulching material available to coastal gardeners. One is seaweed. It is heavy and smelly, but is free. The smell can be cut down by digging it in. It does not have great nutrient value, but is rich in trace elements and potash, and is excellent in the provision of humus. It is poor in phosphates, but this can be rectified by the addition of "super phosphate". For hundreds of years seaweed, *"vraic"*, has been a highly valued perk for Channel Islands farmers, being there for the taking on beaches at high water mark after heavy seas.

The second source of a mulch is the dreaded compost heap. Much is written today about compost heaps. I don't like them. They entail a disproportionate amount of work with the grave risk that you will end up putting back on to your soil the seeds of weeds that you have so recently laboriously uprooted. We do have one — so called: it is really a rubbish tip, and nobody has seriously suggested using it for any purpose other than rotting down garden waste. It certainly harbours uninvited guests: a member of the family picked up what she thought was a slow worm only to find a large brown rat attached to the other end. Both parties were considerably surprised!

Personally I much appreciate the relatively expensive but convenient bag of nicely sterile peat or pulverised bark.

When using peat it is not necessary to dig it in, worms will do the work for you. In any case, if you do dig it in, it will lose its weed suppression property. You must, however, wet it before applying otherwise it will quickly blow off. Do this thoroughly as peat holds up to 16 times its own volume of water. Remember peat does not provide nutrients of any sort, only humus.

Pulverized bark has recently become easily available, and is probably a much "greener" material to use than peat. The massive demand for bagged peat is apparently endangering the countryside from which it is cut. Bark is laid on the soil about 2" deep, and has much the same usefulness as peat although it rots down much more slowly to form humus, and is obviously not water retentive in its original state. It does, however, last longer in suppressing weeds if it remains undisturbed, and effectively prevents evaporation of water from the soil.

One of the main disadvantages of alkaline soil is its property of "locking up" trace elements such as manganese and iron, making them unavailable to the root systems of plants. The lack of availability of iron can cause certain plants to develop chlorosis – a yellowing of the leaves – especially evident in roses, hydrangeas, ceanothus and chaenomeles. Simply adding iron compounds to the soil does not work as these too are quickly "locked up". Iron must be chelated so that it is soluble in water and easily available to roots. Proprietary products are sold under the names *Sequestrene* or *Sequestered Iron*, and these often contain added magnesium and manganese. An annual treatment, following the instructions on the packet carefully, is all that is usually required.

If you have a sloping site, remember that the soil will be thickest at the bottom, and that rain run off will have carried nutrients and trace elements away from the top. Trying to grow anything on the top of a slope where the soil is thin, starved and windswept is an almost impossible task apart from some very specialised plants such as the succulents, "mesembryanthemums" and small sedums.

After you have given your new plants a good start with bone meal added to peat in the "puddling-in" process (described later), no more fertilizer need be given. Indeed to feed drought adapted plants with a concentrated fertilizer is to invite disaster: the leggy, weak growth induced by freely available nitrogen spoils the appearance and character of some plants, and certainly can make them fatally vulnerable to lack of water. Mulching is all they need to help them along.

Although you may regret not being able to grow plants which must have moist soil to thrive, your sandy soil does have its advantages. It is warm, well aerated and easy to work. Root systems of suitable plants spread easily, and suckering plants are so delirious they positively rampage. We have a bank of white rugosa roses fully ten yards deep, and still going strong, throwing forward suckers into the seaside moorland. I wonder how they can be stopped when the need arises! Elsewhere healthy new offspring of the white poplars appear yards away from their parents; wall flowers seed everywhere; daffodils move in slow drifts downwind into adjacent land; plants which rightly belong to arid desert, such as agaves and yuccas, perform to perfection.

4

Weather and Plants

Growing plants on sandy coastal soil might have its problems, but these are severely exacerbated by the almost constant desiccating effect of wind. There is rarely a day when the coastal air is not in movement, and many days in any season when gales tear in from the sea.

These strong winds always carry salt, and will occasionally even pick up fine sand. The mixture is highly abrasive, and susceptible leaves will invariably suffer from excoriation. Apart from this sandpaper effect, deposited salt is also damaging to unadapted foliage: the highly osmotic property of salt crystals draws water through the thin outer membrane of a leaf causing burn.

The chill factor induced by wind, especially in winter, is also a threat to tender plants. In early spring all these malign influences will combine together to kill exposed, newly-forming buds. The sculpting effect of gales is demonstrated when trees and shrubs look as though they have been streamlined, leaning away from the direction of the prevailing wind although shoots to leeward develop relatively normally.

Wind also accelerates the evaporation of water: transpiration from leaves is increased dramatically in the "good drying weather," and moisture is carried away from bare earth.

Obviously root systems need to be developed adequately, especially in dry sandy soil, in order to support foliage. Deciduous trees and shrubs are not quite so vulnerable, but you are always taking a chance if you plant large new specimens of evergreens in spring when increasing warmth, diminishing rainfall and strong winds are likely to overcome the ability of roots to deliver water to the foliage. Autumn planting must be preferred with thorough preparation of the soil (see "Planting").

Wind also rocks plants. This is not a particular problem with small bushy plants, but the effect is damaging in taller single stemmed specimens when the leverage exerted above ground is transmitted to newly developing roots causing them to tear. Adequate staking, without completely stopping natural flexing, is vital.

Heat could well become a more significant factor in the garden if prognostications about the green house effect are fulfilled. Certainly the past few summers in the south of England and the Channel Islands have been blistering. Well established, fully adapted plants do not appear to have suffered, but hose pipe bans will have spelt disaster to spring plantings. Wind and salt adapted plants are also well equipped to cope with heat, no doubt due mainly to their thick leathery leaves preventing excessive transpiration. White or grey leaves, often hairy or heavily felted, are equally heat resistant. Unadapted herbaceous plants will not survive heat and drought without copious summer watering.

Severe cold is more problematical as many wind and salt resistant species have their origins in a Mediterranean type habitat where the mean February temperature is within a range of 40°F to 50°F. European species should be able to withstand lower temperatures for short periods, but valuable coastal plants from New Zealand, such as the hebes and olearias, are vulnerable to particularly cold snaps. Luckily these more tender species are protected beneath ground when growing in warm sandy soil, and will often regenerate if cut back. It would be unwise to rely on this, however, in the colder areas of Britain.

The mechanism of cold damage is through the formation of ice crystals within the cellular structure of the plant. All tissue above ground is susceptible. When thawing takes place the cell membrane ruptures in much the same way as a pipe bursts after a freeze.

The Channel Islands are particularly favoured with comparatively warm winters, but the severe cold spell in 1986, the worst recorded this century, changed the landscape dramatically, if only temporarily. Many windbreaks and hedges had been almost exclusively constructed from *Olearia traversii* and *Hebe* "Blue Gem". These were reduced to pathetic skeletons. The olearias regenerated, but the hebes were a permanent loss. The Australian cordyline "palms", which give the islands their well-recognised tropical look, were cut to the ground; these are now well on their way to recovery looking considerably bushier for their "pruning". Surprising plants were unscathed such as the yuccas and agaves: this could be due to their inherent capability of withstanding the bitterly cold nights of their desert habitat in Mexico and the south western area of the United States.

South African species are the most at risk from cold weather. Mesembryanthemums, which range in size from small rockery specimens to the massive "Hottentot figs", have heavy thick leaves full of water. The thin membrane of the leaf absorbs moisture and carbon dioxide to feed, the roots having little other purpose than anchorage. These characteristics, which make them so well able to withstand heat and drought, prove fatal in icy conditions. These plants are so attractive and useful that it is always worth taking the precaution of over-wintering some cuttings under glass. Indeed any valued tender plant should be treated this way.

Fortunately, whether your coastal garden is in a cold area or not, the protective effect of salt dissolved in constantly moving moist air will usually prevent the formation of deep frost. Close planting and mulching is also helpful as the blanket effect traps heat in the soil, and prevents chill penetrating to the roots.

Paradoxically close planting and mulching is also helpful in hot dry weather as the humid micro-climate created reduces transpiration through the leaves, and conserves moisture below ground.

It is worthwhile recapping the visible characteristics which give rise to heat, drought and/or wind tolerance: thick, leathery leaves (eleagnus, euonymus, olearia); white or grey leaves (senecio, santolina, perovskia); spines (gorse, *Genista hispanica*); small leaves (rosemary, lavender, *Iberis sempervirens*); felted leaves (*Stachys lanata*,

Ballota pseudodictamnus); needles (all the pines); succulent leaves (mesembryanthemum, lampranthus); the sticky leaves of cistus, and any of these in various combinations. The wind resistance of trees and shrubs with long, whippy stems is evident in *Lavatera olbia*, white poplar, tamarisk, *Buddleia davidii* and the brooms.

Of course, there are numerous other examples, many of which you will hopefully be able to find in the classified lists of plants in this book. However, much pleasure can be found in experimenting with your own "discoveries", and there must be plenty of scope with new varieties, and indeed species, which are being introduced continuously to the commercial market.

5
Planting

When to plant is a source of endless debate. Spring or autumn, that is the question. Whether 'tis wise to risk the drought of spring or by refuting choose to face the rigours of an icy winter, aye, there's the rub.

Seriously, I do believe the argument must fall in favour of autumn planting: the soil is still warm, there is still some growing to be done, especially in southern areas, and reasonably regular rain can be guaranteed. If you are not at hand to water spring plantings in dry weather, unacceptable casualties will be incurred; both expensive and annoying. I am sure more plants are lost to drought than any other cause.

SIZE

Losses of new plants can be minimised by deliberately choosing small specimens, especially of trees and shrubs. It is very tempting to buy a large plant on the supposition that it has a head start. The fact is that the larger the plant, the greater are the effects of wind and drought. The root system cannot develop quickly enough to support a large head of leaves. Deciduous plants suffer less from this effect.

Measured in time a small plant will soon catch up with a larger one of the same species, which, if it has managed to survive, will certainly have suffered several checks.

There are exceptions to this rule such as *Rhododendron ponticum*, the hebes and euonymus, all of which have compact fibrous root systems. These plants can be moved around the garden more or less at will, and the heavy investment in large new specimens can be worthwhile.

CONTAINERS

When selecting a plant to buy which has been grown in a pot, examine the base carefully. If roots are appearing in any quantity through the holes it is likely to be "pot bound", the roots having grown round in circles. Plant this and the roots will continue their merrygoround pattern of growth, unable to spread in search of moisture.

Trees sometimes will arrive from nurseries with roots and accompanying earth in a hessian bag. The temptation is to undo the bag before planting when the soil will promptly drop away. What you are meant to do is to plant the whole thing, bag and all. The hessian soon rots in damp soil and the roots will remain undisturbed.

"PUDDLING-IN"

Having chosen the position for your new plant, the next important task is to prepare its permanent home. The aim is, of course, to make life as easy as possible for a fragile infant that has so far received scientific cossetting in the nursery, protected from the elements and given every possible advantage. This spoilt brat that you have adopted at enormous cost will undoubtedly fail to thrive if not thoroughly gratified from the moment that you tip it out of its cradle pot. So measure the pot and dig a hole twice the depth and twice the width, being careful to make two distinct piles of the excavated soil – one pile consisting of the nutrient rich top half, the other of the underlying subsoil. Fill the hole three quarters full of moss peat enriched with a handful of bone meal (or use instead a proprietary potting compost), and add water until a puddle forms which fills it to the brim and stays there for five minutes. Whilst you have been doing this, the pot should have been standing completely immersed in a bucket of water for at least as long as it takes for the bubbles to have stopped rising from the compost (this may take up to an hour). Tip the pot upside down and shake the plant gently into your other hand. If it does not slide out easily, squeeze the pot if it is plastic. If this does not work, you will have to cut or break the pot away. The aim is always not to disturb the root system which will inevitably be exposed and fragile.

After this hopefully adroit bit of juggling, carefully drop the root ball into the puddle so that the top is an inch or two below the rim of the hole. Holding the plant in place with one hand, start filling the gap around with the first pile of soil from the uppermost layer. Firm the area with your hand, fill some more and gently tamp down with your feet. The result should be that the plant resides in a slight depression which should help to catch any rain that subsequently falls. Discard the second pile of soil.

What you have achieved is a thoroughly moist and nutritious environment to encourage fast root growth, and to sustain the plant in its first vital few months. Thereafter an annual mulch is all that it should need.

This process is known as "puddling-in" — neglect it at your peril!

PROTECTION

Having generally attended to every conceivable need of the roots, the next task is to protect the growth above ground. Enemies abound – wind, rabbits, dogs, cats, slugs, snails, mice – in any number of combinations.

First the wind. If the plant, be it tree or shrub, has a single main stem, support it. The rocking effect of wind will be transmitted to the newly developing tender root system and it will tear. A young tree must start life with a sturdy stake; a shrub with a substantial cane. Place the stake or cane on the side of the plant exposed to the prevailing wind. Tie the stem on to the support with garden string (not sharp-edged plastic or wire). Remember to loosen the tie as the plant grows, and replace string on sapling tree stems with proprietary plastic belts when they are sturdy enough. Check ties regularly; add new ones to growing tips, loosen old ones – they can be very effective tourniquets!

Bushy plants will put up with a certain amount of wind, deciduous ones better than evergreen, but nothing will survive the attentions of voracious rabbits if they happen to fancy the dish. Cats and dogs will like the surrounding loose soil for squatting or burying bones. Animal protection is effectively achieved with cylinders of plastic netting or chicken wire firmly tied with garden wire to stiff canes buried deeply. These cylinders will also help to diffuse wind.

Slugs and snails feed on emergent shoots, and liberal sprinklings of bait should be replaced frequently especially during rainy periods. Mice and their predilection for bulbs is another matter, and I have no suggestions – has anybody else?

SPACING

Ignore recommended planting distances. A windy site is rarely the place for isolated specimens, which become totally vulnerable to everything the elements can throw at them. The idea is to allow plants quickly to join ranks and interlace their branches. In this way many advantages to growth are created.

Close coverage of bare soil cuts down on evaporation and suppresses weed and grass growth. Rain and dew is trapped, and a beneficent humid localised micro-climate forms which wind cannot entirely disperse. Heat cannot effectively penetrate dense foliage, and root runs are consequently cooler and more moist. Conversely, during cold snaps, the soil is insulated by foliage, and heat is thereby conserved, thus discouraging the formation of ground frost locally.

When planting trees or large shrubs mass grouping is a good idea. Group the plants in triangles of threes rather than rows if space allows. The apex of the triangle should face into the prevailing wind.

This apical plant will bear the brunt of the wind, and will protect the two behind.

Inevitably there will be bare ground in the early days of a new planting. Mulching is vital in mimicking the effects of foliage until the plants join together. For long life bark cannot be beaten. Seaweed is good as long as you can stand the smell. Peat is fine but worms bury it quickly.

Recently mulching new plantings with black polythene has had much publicity. This sounds like a good idea. Of course, polythene does not help with humus formation, but it will most certainly retain moisture in the soil and suppress weeds. The technique is to cut out a circle of material 3' in diameter, cut a slit in the middle large enough to allow you to slip the plant through, lay the material on the clean soil around the plant, and tuck the edges well into the earth. If you do not like the look of the black polythene, cover it with a thin layer of earth or bark. *"Gardening from Which?"* has run a trial which is most convincing in demonstrating a rate of new growth better than that achieved with any other material (November 1990).

Where gaps are larger in plantings of trees, expendable, short-lived shrubs are useful. Attractive ones are *Lavatera olbia* and tree lupins. These will last for a few years, can be propagated easily from cuttings and seeds, grow with great rapidity, and have bags of intrinsic charm with colourful blooms over a long flowering period, not minding wind and sandy soil one bit.

Of course, there is one distinct disadvantage of close planting. Sooner or later some plants will start to dominate their neighbours, and decisions will have to be made about what to move, and, even harder, what to scrap. Some plants move easily, for example those with compact fibrous root systems such as *Rhododendron ponticum, Griselinia littoralis,* euonymus and the hebes. Others with tap roots or long searching root systems simply will not tolerate disturbance – the brooms, romneyas. It is as well to bear these characteristics in mind at the planning stage, and place unmovable key plants carefully having considered their likely eventual spread and height.

Do not forget that the usual speed of development and dimensions of many plants will be considerably modified in an exposed coastal garden. Only totally adapted maritime species will behave as predicted by an ordinary reference in a catalogue or book. Wind will have a constant pruning effect through destruction of early bud formation. Poverty of nutrients and lack of moisture in sandy soils will retard growth. Trees, for instance, with a mature stature of 60' in an inland garden will struggle to top half that height, and will take at least twice as long to do it.

6

Windbreaks

If you have not acquired an established garden, you cannot afford any delay or error in establishing windbreaks. Nothing can be achieved without them. As we have already discussed, wind is the seaside gardeners' greatest enemy – it desiccates, abrades, chills, tears and rocks. Only very particular plants will put up with its unmitigated hostility.

Luckily all the hard work of trial and error has been done for us very many years ago. In the days before imported plant material was generally available, farmers growing crops in exposed areas had to contend with the problem using anything suitable and freely available. Fields were small and enclosed by excavated banks reinforced with rubble and stone as seen still in Cornwall and Devon and the *"bocage"* of Normandy. The banks were topped with diffusing screens of tough shrubs and small trees such as tamarisk and hawthorn, pussy willow and stunted sycamore. Later, when gardening fever gripped the monied classes in the 19th century, these techniques were studied and adapted. The wealthiest gardeners in windy areas built miles of high dressed stone walls behind which they established tall-growing trees. Others with less money to expend, such as Augustus Smith in the Scilly Island of Tresco, built his shelters as from 1843 of oaks, poplar, elm and sycamore. As foreign species became commercially available, he added Holm oak from the Mediterranean seabord and *Cupressus macrocarpa* and *Pinus radiata* from California. Before his efforts the land, which now supports the most luxuriant of gardens, grew nothing higher than gorse.

Since these early times there have been many tough and useful introductions from Australasia and the Far East as well as hybrids of more recent origin.

Very few of us nowadays have access to the capital necessary to build long stretches of high stone walls, even if the labour and skill were available to do this. As it happens solid barriers have been shown to be disastrous to new plantings: the accelerated forces created by eddies in the lee of a solid obstacle can literally lift plants out of the ground.

Having established the direction of the prevailing wind in your area, the first task is to erect instant artificial diffusers. Forget about larch lap or hessian; it will be blown flat. Suitable materials are small mesh plastic netting or plasticised chicken wire (or split hazel hurdles if you can find them). Attach the material to well buried, creosoted stakes at suitable intervals. The height of these barriers should be about four feet.

This first line of defence will be sufficient to break the full force of strong winds, and allows the natural permanent second line to establish itself.

The construction of the second line should be carefully designed and planted as a whole. The tallest elements can be a mixture of the most vigorous evergreen and deciduous trees that you can find. As these grow the developing branchless trunks will allow the wind in. To preempt this, plant to windward a supplementary barrier of lower growing shrubs which will provide ground level protection for the future.

Attempting to establish low protection later will be impossible, as the roots of the large trees will have commandeered the soil.

Spacing when planting is worth giving some thought to. Obviously, when using material purchased from nurseries, expense is a prime factor, and the temptation must be to spread out your plants as much as possible. To do so to excess is a mistake as the success of a windbreak is dependent upon mutual support being created through the interlacing of branches. Do not forget that the height, and to a lesser extent the spread, of trees especially is heavily influenced by the strength of the winds they are exposed to, the quality of the soil they are growing in and the rainfall. A further important factor is the inherent adaptation of the individual plant to the conditions it is grown in. Sycamore in an inland area growing on water retentive soil will reach 100': grown by the sea in sandy soil, and exposed to gales, it will rarely exceed 20' in height. *Pittosporum crassifolium*, however, is well adapted to wind, salt and drought, and given a warm seaside site, will quickly grow to its fully mature height of 15'.

Spacing, therefore, is not a matter of hard and fast rules, and you must make calculated judgements according to the species you are using and the conditions prevailing in your garden. On a typically windy coastal site, it would be reasonable to halve the usually quoted spread of an individual specimen, and space at the resulting distance. Halve this distance again if constructing a hedge. However planting *too* closely will create its own problem of root competition.

As the windbreak develops it will be sculpted by the wind into a streamlined bank. It will not be an object of great beauty, much of it to windward being burnt and brown in patches. Viewed from inside it will be more attractive, especially if you vary the colour and texture of the foliage imaginatively.

It is important to plant well, to stake firmly, and to use quick growing material. The gardener's life is all too short and be blowed to posterity!

Be careful to take scale into consideration. If your site is small you will have to be content with shrubs of neat and modest habits – avoid suckering plants whatever you do! There are plenty of choices listed below.

DECIDUOUS TREES FOR WINDBREAKS

N.B. Trees which come into leaf early will suffer the effects of spring gales: leaves will inevitably look tatty for the rest of the season, having been torn when young and tender.

Acer pseudoplatanus ("Common Sycamore")
Seeds too freely, rank in growth, leaves quickly torn and brown early, but fully hardy and withstands heaviest winds although badly stunted by them. Can tolerate dry conditions. Mix with evergreens. Protected will reach 100', lucky to achieve more than 20' in exposed position. Only for periphery of a large site.

Betula pendula ("Silver Birch")
Used for shelter in north of Scotland. Small leaves, twiggy growth, slim silver white trunk, graceful. Comes into leaf late avoiding too much wind damage. Protected height 20–30': 15' on exposed site.

Crataegus monogyna ("Common Hawthorn", "Quick", "May")
Thorny, densely branched, glossy small green leaves, scented white flowers in May, clusters of small crimson haws in autumn. Protected height 15–20': 10–15' on exposed site.

Fagus sylvatica ("Common Birch")
Hardy, gale tolerant, likes well-drained soil with high lime content, good autumn colour. Protected height 40': ± 25' on exposed site. Can be trimmed as hedge.

Fraxinus excelsior ("Common Ash")
Survives fiercest conditions if planted closely, late coming into leaf so less torn than equally tough sycamore. Does not object to clay and heavy soils. Quick growing; wide spreading surface roots so do not plant near buildings. Can reach 100': ± 30' on exposed site.

Populus alba ("White Poplar")
Fast growing, suckers freely, well clothed low branches. Leaves grey-green above, white and woolly beneath, branches whippy, pendulous catkins. Totally wind tolerant, thrives on sand. Do not plant near buildings. Height ± 30'.

Salix caprea ("Pussy-willow")
Fast growing, small leaves, whippy branches, ovoid catkins. Height ± 20'.

Salix alba ("White Willow")
Fast growing, grey-green tapering leaves, stalked catkins in May. Height ± 25'.

Sambucus nigra ("Common Elder")
Pinnate leaves with ovate, sharply toothed, mid-green leaflets, cream white flowers in June, round shiny black berries in September. Good undergrowth. Height ± 10'.

Sorbus aria ("Common Whitebeam")
Young leaves silver-white and downy, later upper surfaces dark green; russet and gold in autumn. Cream-white flowers in May and June, scarlet globular fruits in September. Likes lime. Height ± 15'.

Sorbus aucuparia ("Rowan", "Mountain Ash")
Leaves mid-green with grey undersides, yellow and orange from October. White flowers May and June, globular orange-red berries from August. Short-lived in shallow alkaline soils. Height ± 20'.

Ulmus glabra ("Wych" or "Scots Elm")
Mid-green leaves turn yellow in October. Successful in coldest, windiest position. Height ± 25'.

Ulmus stricta syn. *Ulmus carpinifolia* 'Cornubiensis' ("Cornish Elm")
One of the most wind and salt resistant of deciduous trees, late in leaf (May). Conical shape, glossy elliptic mid to deep green leaves, gold in autumn. Height ± 25'.

EVERGREEN TREES FOR WINDBREAKS

Cupressus macrocarpa ("Monterey Cypress")
Gaunt when mature, suffers badly from blast but makes quick windbreak. Largely superseded by its hybrid *Cupressocyparis x*

leylandii (qv). *C.m.* 'Lutea' ("Golden Macrocarpa") much superior, slower growing, better (but not great) tolerance of gales.

Cupressocyparis x leylandii

Hybrid of *Chamaecyparis nootkatensis* and *C. macrocarpa* with best qualities of each. Hardy, salt resistant, better tolerance of gales, fast growing. Protected height 50': 25–30' on exposed site. Columnar habit.

Four forms: 'Haggerston Grey', plumose shoots with dark grey-green scales; 'Castlewellan', plumose with pale yellow new growth; 'Leighton Green', long pinnate sprays of rich green; 'Hyde Hall', dwarf form.

Plants 18–24" tall are easiest to establish, but large specimens transplant if well staked.

Griselinia littoralis

In its native New Zealand grows to 60' but only achieves 20' in UK. Thick, yellow-green leaves unusual and impervious to salt and wind. Resents close planting, failing to thrive if not given plenty of elbow room. Can be moved when quite large therefore excellent for quick results. Moderately hardy.

Olearia traversii

Attractive leaves, green above, silver-white beneath, totally impervious to wind and salt. Grows quickly on poor sandy soil to 30'. Despite New Zealand origin, surprisingly hardy by the sea. Cut down by prolonged icy conditions but mostly regenerates rapidly. The most useful of all large windbreak material in a mild area.

PINES

Mostly prefer well-drained acid soil and will tolerate drought when established.

Pinus contorta contorta ("Lodgepole Pine")

Tough and ugly, from British Columbia and Alaska. Very quick growing to maximum 45'. Dislikes drought. The two other geographical varieties, *P.c. latifolia* and *P.c. murrayana*, are slow-growing.

Pinus mugo ("Mountain Pine")
Native of Central and SE Europe, gnarled appearance and bushy. Grows fast in dry, poor soils to maximum 15'. Used in N Scotland as windbreak close to Atlantic.

Pinus muricata ("Bishop Pine")
From the Californian seabord therefore more suited to south and west. Handsome but scorched by more vicious winter gales, usually recovers in late spring. Protect to windward with deciduous trees. Quick growing to maximum 40'.

Pinus nigra maritima, syns. *P.n. calabrica, P. laricio* ("Corsican Pine")
Tall, very quick growing to 40', does well on shallow, poor soil tolerating lime. Does not move well, plant when small in groups for mutual support against wind. Not liked by rabbits.

Pinus pinaster ("Maritime Pine")
From the Mediterranean seabord; does well on very poor sandy soil growing to maximum 45'. Tall bare trunk a disadvantage.

Pinus radiata ("Monterey Pine")
Beautiful bright grass-green needles on a Californian native which grows quickly to maximum 50' remaining well clothed to ground. Prefers milder areas, but highly wind-tolerant to all except most vicious salt-laden gales. Tolerates some lime.

Pittosporum crassifolium
Leathery, obovate leaves, dark green above, off-white felted beneath. Maroon flowers in April/May followed by white, ovoid seed capsules. Wind and salt resistant and used as windbreaks in the Scillies and Cornwall. Reasonably hardy, but was killed in the Channel Islands in the bad winter of 1986 (the worst this century). From New Zealand, grows to 15'. Happy on alkaline sandy soils. Increased easily from seed or cuttings. Tolerates drought.

Quercus ilex ("Holm Oak", "Evergreen Oak")
From the Mediterranean, it prefers warmer regions but is hardy. Small, ovate, dark green, glossy, leathery leaves, grey beneath. Grows slowly to 20' or more, and in windy position on poor soil, remains bushy to ground for many years. Excellent in a mixed planting, impervious to wind and salt. Tolerates drought.

SHRUBS FOR WINDBREAKS

Atriplex halimus ("Tree Purslane")
Evergreen with silver-grey, dusty leaves, quick growing, hardy, wind tolerant. Grows on dry, sandy soils to 4'. Good informal hedge.

Elaeagnus x ebbingei
Evergreen from Japan, vigorous with ovate leathery leaves, glossy green above, dull white beneath. Silvery flowers in October/November, sometimes followed by small, oval, red or orange fruits. Grows well on poor, sandy, alkaline soils to 15'+. Tolerates drought and can be clipped to shape as tall hedging. Impervious to wind and salt.

Escallonia macrantha
Evergeen from S America, only hardy in south and west. Small, ovate, glossy, rich deep green leaves with rose-crimson flowers from June to September. Excellent hedging, growing to 10', impervious to wind and salt. Tolerates drought when established.

Euonymus japonicus ("Spindle Tree")
Evergreen from Japan, densely leafy, leaves leathery, glossy, mid-green with green-white flowers in May/June. Slow growing to 15'. Impervious to wind and salt. Tolerates drought. Excellent hedging and can be clipped to shape. Hardy in south and west.

Hebes (formerly included in genus *Veronica*)
These are ideal maritime shrubs ranging in height from 6" to 5', many with highly decorative flowers borne over a long period.

They are generally half-hardy, but are rarely killed completely near the sea: this only happened in the Channel Islands in 1986 when the cold was prolonged. Otherwise they are wind and salt resistant, and are perfectly happy on the driest sandy soils.

Hebe x franciscana 'Blue Gem'

Evergreen and almost hardy, it is the toughest plant for low hedging, reaching 4' with rounded rich green leaves and bright violet flower spikes 3' long borne intermittently throughout the year. A real winner. Strikes easily from cuttings.

Hippophaë rhamnoides ("Sea Buckthorn")

Deciduous shrub from Europe and temperate Asia. Brown-scaled, spiny branches clothed with linear silvery leaves. If male and female plants are grown together, females bear masses of small, round, bright orange berries in autumn and winter. One male will pollinate six or more females. Thrives on coastal sand, growing to 10'. Hardy.

Rosmarinus officinalis ("Common Rosemary")

Evergreen from S Europe, Asia Minor, grows quickly to 7', less on sandy soil in full exposure. Gnarled and untidy after a number of years, but excellent for quick results as a hedge. Mauve flowers in March/April and sporadically until September. Strikes easily from cuttings.

Senecio 'Sunshine' syns. *S. greyi, S. laxifolius*

Evergreen from New Zealand with oval grey green leaves, densely white felted beneath, growing to 3'+. Bright yellow daisy-like flowers in clusters from June to August. Almost hardy. Strikes easily from cuttings.

Tamarix pentandra syn. *T. hispida aestivalis* ("Tamarisk")

Deciduous shrub from S E Europe with fine oval shaped leaves growing to 15'. Lax in growth but long slender stems good wind diffusers. Feathery heads of tiny rose-pink flowers in August. Variety "Rubra" has deep rose-red flowers. Used as windbreak from ancient times. Said not to be lime-tolerant, but certainly puts up with alkaline sandy soil in Channel Islands. Strike from cuttings.

Ulex europeaus **'Flore Pleno'** ("Double-flowered Gorse")

Evergreen spring shrub from W Europe. Superior to common gorse in every way, more compact in habit, lasts longer in flower but does not set seed. Dazzling golden-yellow pea-like flowers in April/May. Only happy on hungry, dry soil in full sun. Impervious to salt and wind. Strikes from cuttings.

FILLERS FOR WINDBREAKS

Whilst waiting for larger windbreak material to join ranks, fill in the gaps with easy, short lived, quick growing, expendable, but decorative shrubs which are easily propagated. Sturdy examples are:

Lavatera olbia rosea syn. *L. thuringiaca* 'Kew Rose'

This is *not* the "Tree Mallow" *(L. arboreus)*, and you *must* obtain the superior variety "rosea" which bears really good large, single, mallow flowers of bright rose-pink in great profusion from June to November. It very quickly makes a 10' + bush with whippy stems on dry, poor, sandy soils.

Lupinus arboreus ("Tree Lupin")

A shrubby species from California but naturalised in Europe. Grows very quickly from seed to 4' in poor sandy soil and full exposure. Too lax in rich soil. Typical lupin flowers, fragrant, cream to yellow mostly, but possible to find shades of lilac and purple to blue. Terrific.

7
Propagation

The expense of furnishing a new garden can be daunting – especially a larger one! You should not economise when constructing your initial windbreaks, if at all possible: you need a flying start, and cuttings take time to reach a useful size. But you can thicken out nursery purchases with plants raised from cuttings, and you can certainly use this method to provide a supply of choice specimens for the garden proper.

Neighbours, of course, are the obvious source for obtaining material from particularly desirable species. Ask, and it will be given – hopefully!

On acquiring a well grown bushy specimen from a nursery, the healthy plant will not mind giving up some of its peripheral branches, and so always take the opportunity, during autumn planting, of taking four or five cuttings. (This will not be a popular suggestion with nurserymen!)

Remember that seeds are not a reliable source for regeneration of hybrids: they will not necessarily come true, and reversions will inevitably occur. Cuttings must always be preferred.

Once you have a good plant growing vigorously always take a few cuttings, especially if it is tender. Should the following winter be clement, and you do not need them, somebody will always be grateful for them; your favourite charity's bring and buy sale committee, for instance.

HARDWOOD CUTTINGS

This method is the simplest and easiest for the majority of hardy trees and shrubs, and should be done in late autumn or early winter.

"Hardwood" is the vigorous one year old growth which has had time to become hard and woody with a thin bark. The stem will have buds along its length ready to shoot the following year. The exact timing of taking the cuttings varies somewhat from species to species, but October is a good compromise.

The stem should be cut off near its base with sharp secateurs in all but the most vigorous species. Ideally the cutting should be 8" to 10" long, and so a long stem will provide two or more pieces. Do not use the weak tip of the stem. Look for the buds, which will be more or less obvious, and cut below and above a bud. The new roots will develop from the lower bud. Remove all the leaves from the bottom half of the cutting and the larger leaves from the upper half. If all the leaves are large on the upper part, cut them in half with a razor blade to reduce transpiration.

If the bark looks particularly tough, slice off two thin layers on opposite sides of the stem.

Dip the bottom end of the cutting in a general purpose rooting powder, and carefully knock off any coagulation – too much hormone can be counterproductive.

Now for what to do with those carefully prepared bits.

Find a site sheltered from wind and designate it "the cuttings bed". The soil should be sandy. If it is not, dig the area over and work in some coarse sand: the soil must be sharply drained and well aerated. Make a slit in the soil by sticking in a spade the full length of the blade and working it backwards and forwards. Fill the bottom half of the slit with sand. Lay the cuttings on one edge of the slit with their bottoms resting on the sand 6" apart. Close the slit using your foot, making sure that it is firmly shut: air pockets are not much good for developing roots. Finally, water the area well.

This is all you need do for twelve months – apart from removing competitive weeds. At the end of this period carefully dig up the plantlets, and puddle them into their permanent homes.

During prolonged dry spells it is better to water occasionally in case top growth defeats the capability of the developing root system to provide moisture. A belt and braces approach, especially with evergreens, is to reduce transpiration from the leaves by spraying with liquid plastic ('S600').

CUTTINGS FROM TENDER TREES AND SHRUBS

Proceed by taking cuttings as described above.

Fill a 5" pot with a mixture of potting compost and sand in equal parts up to the ledge below the rim. Soak the mixture thoroughly with water.

The pot will contain between five and eight cuttings depending on their size. Make holes with a length of cane around the periphery, one third the length of the cuttings. Having applied rooting powder, insert the cuttings and firm down. Water again to eliminate any air pockets.

Stand the pots out of direct sunlight and wind, and water occasionally during dry spells. In cold weather remove the pots to a warmer environment under glass.

SEMI-HARD CUTTINGS

Some trees and shrubs will not root readily from hardwood cuttings, such as actinidia, aucuba, caryopteris, choisya and lavandula.

Semi-hard wood is the current year's growth which is maturing at its base, but is still soft and growing vigorously at the tip. The time to take this material for cuttings is in August, or earlier if the summer is hot: they will need shade from the sun, and more watering than hardwood cuttings.

When rooted, the cuttings can be potted on if from tender species, and kept under glass over winter, or, if from hardy species, planted out in the protected cuttings bed. It may be two years before they are sturdy enough to transplant to their permanent positions.

The cutting itself roots better if taken with a "heel". To do this pull down the selected stem, about 6" long, away from the direction of growth: the side shoot will come away bearing a sliver of tissue from the parent branch. Trim the heel to $1/4$", and then cut out the growing tip. Strip the leaves from the lower half of the cutting, dust with rooting powder and pot as usual. Water generously.

The semi-hard cuttings will need humidity to encourage rooting. Achieve this by covering the pot with polythene. The best material is a freezer bag, being rather stouter than ordinary household polythene. Support the bag with stiff garden wire: cut two lengths 12" long, bend into U-shapes, and insert the ends in the edge of the pot so that the two U's cross at the top. Slip the bag over the pot, and secure with painters' masking tape.

Rooting will usually have started after three weeks. At this stage start the "hardening off" process by punching a few holes in the bag to let the air in. A week later increase the number of holes. After a further week, remove the bag altogether, and, after yet another week, pot on. At no time should the cuttings be in direct sunlight — they will broil – but they do like warmth, and the rooting process can be enhanced by applying bottom heat, best provided by an electrically heated propagating unit. This is by no means always necessary, however.

TIP CUTTINGS FROM PERENNIALS

Tender perennials can be treated in a similar way. The only difference is the method of taking the cutting. Choose a non-flowering side stem, and cut off the top 4" making sure you have at least three leaf joints. Having settled the cuttings in pots, pinch out the growing tip. Cover with polythene, and, after three weeks, harden off as usual.

WARNING – Propagating cuttings can become an obsession, being an infinitely satisfying process. Try not to be too enthusiastic; nurturing a host of potted cuttings at various stages of development can be akin to running an overlarge and unruly kindergarten, with the added complication of inviting an unacceptable rate of fatalities!

8

Choosing Plants

Before investing in any permanent perennials or shrubs for your new garden, give some thought to the effect you wish to achieve. It will be impossible to create the appearance of a traditional inland garden. Tall herbaceous plants, which are still the mainstay of the formal border, simply will not survive; drought and wind are fatal to them. Modern bush roses fail through the poverty of sandy soil and its lack of humus.

Apart from the obvious factors such as wind, salt and drought, there are other more subtle influences at work. The climate of a coastal area is essentially maritime temperate, in other words winters are generally mild and summers relatively cool. Rainfall will be higher in the west and lower in the east of Britain, but this variation is somewhat negated by the lack of humus in sandy soil and evaporation caused by seaside winds. Extreme summer heat, which would be oppressive in inland areas, is mitigated by the cooling effect of these same winds.

The plants which are going to be happy within windbreaks are essentially those which can withstand drought. Not quite so obvious will be their willingness to accept comparatively little temperature variation between seasons. A number of plants are ill-attuned to temperate conditions. High alpine plants will miss their long periods of chill, despite their adaptation to poor soil and summer drought. Plants with a natural distribution in Siberia or northern China will be equally displeased.

Choice of plant material can be extended by taking risks at the hot end of the temperate range. Most Mediterranean species will appreciate it, and will tolerate short colder periods, but to draw upon species from Australasia, South Africa and appropriate parts of South America is to invite fatalities in an untypically cold winter. In my opinion these risks are worth taking in view of the wonderfully exotic creatures that are then within grasp.

Take careful note of the pH of your soil, and resign yourself to not being able to grow limehaters ("calcifuges") if you are gardening on alkaline sand.

Drought and heat adapted species are dominated by those with white or grey foliage. After all this is how they have come to terms with these conditions. Plants with white or grey foliage tend to bear yellow or blue flowers. Any species you can find to relieve the monotony is very welcome. Amongst shrubs the hebe and escallonia varieties are outstanding in this respect with their rich deep evergreen foliage and variety of flower colour. Recent introductions from South Africa, such as varieties of osteospermum (dimorphotheca) and of *Argyranthemum frutescens* from the Canary Islands, extends the range of pink and purple flowers. Varieties of *Penstemon hartwegii* from Mexico are now much more readily available, and provide crimson and scarlet in the spectrum.

Whilst waiting for permanent plants to develop, enormously colourful bedding displays can be obtained from the pelargonium family and F_1 petunia varieties. Both revel in hot sunshine and drought. They are ideal for containers where they require very little attention apart from dead-heading. Too much water and they will turn to leaf.

The bright clear days of a seaside summer demand bright clear colours. What might appear somewhat loud and tasteless inland looks perfectly at home against a backdrop of vivid azure sky and emerald sea. Subtle colours have little place, and are effectively masked out by the strong light.

Garish gazanias, purple petunias and pelargoniums, scarlet salvias – you can really let yourself go without restraint. Nobody is going to dub the result "naf".

Very soon you will forget all about the cartwheel clematis whose shoots would be whipped off and whose roots would not find moisture – the hostas – the tradescantia – the lupins – the delphiniums – the astilbes – the asters . . .

What exactly you do eventually choose to grow, and in what combination, is such a matter of personal preference that I hesitate to offer any advice whatsoever. Whether you are a plantsman or an "exterior decorator", you will derive huge pleasure from the challenges and spectacular successes of a seaside garden. Certainly the end result will look more or less exotic.

However, within your windbreaks it is always wise to establish key shrubs, preferably evergreen, which will be totally reliable, and will offer additional protection to more tender plants. I always think of a garden along the lines of the female anatomy: the windbreaks are the tough long bones and muscles; key shrubs, the smaller parts of the skeleton; all supporting the much more decorative and vulnerable parts such as well-groomed hair, manicured and brightly polished finger nails, luscious lips, etc, etc . . . !

Reading is an essential part of the process of acquiring a working knowledge of plants. I have already mentioned Beth Chatto's *"The Dry Garden"*. A reference book valuable for identifying the origin of plants and their cultivation requirements is the Reader's Digest *"Encyclopaedia of Garden Plants and Flowers"*. The periodical *"Gardening from Which?"* is a source of endless information. W.J. Bean's monumental *"Trees and Shrubs Hardy in the British Isles"* is totally definitive, as is the new *"RHS Dictionary"* (if your local library can afford it!). Armed with access to these, and anything else in print which looks appropriate, you should be equipped to plant out your unforgiving parcel of seaside. It is even worth exploring books about areas which may initially appear irrelevant. Ronald King's *"Tresco, England's Island of Flowers"* and Hugo Latymer's *"The Mediterranean Garden"* will certainly provide plenty of ideas for gardeners in the south of England and the Channel Islands. An indispensable resource for all gardeners is *"The Plant Finder"*, which accurately tells you names of the nurserymen who can supply your specialist plants.

Also invaluable are the check lists of local flora often available. Our *"Flora of Alderney"* was first published in 1838, and has been revised and extended many times. It now records 80 trees and 783 plants (1988). Careful note is made of the habitat of plants and the frequency of distribution. Garden escapes are usually included in these lists, and they will give clear indications of the basic species which will thrive on your particular site.

What will be abundantly clear from your reading is the miraculous legacy which has been passed on to us by our gardening forebears. Investment in hard cash, and indeed lives, was made in hunting for new species on a scale which is almost incomprehensible today. Discoveries of new continents stimulated an insatiable interest in foreign flora, and entrepreneurs soon appreciated that the obligatory appendage of a botanist to an expedition reaped dividends of a more tangible nature than purely scientific. By the 17th century the Dutch bulb growers had squeezed every possible guilder from hybridising the Turkish tulip: by the late 18th century English enthusiasts had exhausted the show potential of the alpine auricula, and rose breeders had ground to halt for want of the China species. With the development of the Wardian case for reliable transportation of growing material and fast steam ships, the 19th century witnessed a flood of new plants from every corner of the globe, which found an immediate and well-primed market eager to snap up every novelty.

A glance at the Tresco Abbey plant catalogue shows the astonishing variety that one man, Augustus Smith, had managed to amass between 1831 and 1872; 111 species from 74 genera from Australasia, Japan, China, South Africa, South America, Canary Islands, Himalaya, Sikkim and Persia. By 1960 succeeding generations of Smiths had increased the collection to 4000 species, a large proportion of which came from the southern hemisphere. 129 years previously the bleak island of Tresco, a fistful of miles south west of Lands End, had contained "only a wind-swept upland covered by brambles and a close-growing mat of furze."

'There it was: a small white house standing bolt upright on the moor, a hundred paces from the sea'.

Thirty years later the enlarged house is surrounded by tough windbreaks impervious to salty gales.

I was glad to be behind the harbour's breakwater during this ferocious spring gale.

The next day's calm. There is no damage to the 'Tree Lupin', *Lupinus arboreus*; leaves of the *Phormium tenax* are a little burnt.

Lavandula stoechas, 'French Lavender', is an aromatic small bush from the Mediterranean for the warmest, driest position.

The deceptively delicate looking *Hebe* 'Youngii' bears masses of vivid flowers from June.

The evergreen *Ceanothus arboreus* flowers twice a year against a neighbour's warm wall.

As with all the 'Rock Roses', *Helianthemum* 'Alice Howorth' has diminutive flowers which open in sun and are at their best in May and June.

One of the most drought and wind resistant shrubs, *Brachyglottis [Senecio]* 'Sunshine' has attractive evergreen foliage and masses of flowers in high summer.

Comparable great gardens were being developed in other favourable maritime areas such as Logan on the south-westerly tip of Scotland; Inverewe, on the Scottish north-west coast, 60 miles from Cape Wrath; Abbotsbury, on the Dorset coast, where the camellias are thought to be at least 200 years old and there is a *Pittosporum tenuifolium* 50' high; Caerhays in Cornwall, famous for rhododendrons, azaleas and magnolias which thrive behind high windbreaks.

Plentiful, cheap labour made these achievements possible, along with substantial capital wealth. Today we cannot aspire to grow anything other than a fraction of this inheritance; we can but stand back and wonder.

But what matter? We have a pair of hands, some tools, a bag of potting compost and a strong back. Christine Kelway in the 1960's was proud to boast that every plant in her Cornish garden had been grown from a cutting. Thirty years later we have a host of specialist nurserymen to help us, and no less intuitive heads to give us inspiration. Achievement surely is not simply a matter of grandiose scale? It must lie in the pleasure and satisfaction of contributing to a great and infinitely enjoyable tradition, and even, perhaps, giving succour in our warm, safe havens to scarce and threatened species.

9

The Plants of the Garigue and Maquis

I was a very lucky child and teenager: I spent every summer holiday in the South of France. My parents had a small villa on the Cap d'Antibes, purchased in the days before the Second World War when this very particular part of the Côte d'Azur had been imbued with a raffish glamour by American and English litterateurs such as Somerset Maugham, Scott Fitzgerald and Ernest Hemingway together with their respective acolytes. Latterly the Duke of Windsor and Mrs. Simpson had made it their home.

I really cannot admit to having properly appreciated these associations at the time: I was six when I first travelled there. Neither could I, when younger, savour the definitely hedonistic attractions of the smart beach that we walked to every day at Juan-les-Pins. What I did enjoy enormously was collecting butterflies, moths and insects in the mornings and evenings. In those days, before the area had become a densely populated tourist destination, the insect life was brilliant. I explored every inch of the surrounding lanes, fields and allotments, armed with a Watkins and Doncaster kit of net and chloroform bottle. Nothing was safe from my pins and setting boards.

Our own garden contained self-reliant plants and trees, which I remember more than anything else for their marvellous acrid, resinous smells. This was because I usually had my nose in them. The santolina bushes contained the most horribly fascinating praying mantises. I would watch mesmerised as the females devoured the males after mating. I climbed the mimosa trees to paint the branches with a syrup of molasses which made huge hawk moths drunk and catchable. I swiped with my net at the beautiful Scarce Swallowtail feeding on diminutive flowers – it was usually far too fast and wily for me.

I now know that the tough, prickly and sticky, low growing and highly aromatic undergrowth I plunged through in pursuit of my quarry was "maquis".

Before the days of intensive cultivation by man, the shores of the Mediterranean were covered by dense woods of evergreen Holm oak and pines. Gradually trees were destroyed for fuel and the undergrowth exposed. These lower plants took over, and now constitute the maquis. In themselves they provide many commercially useful products such as gums, resins, charcoal, brushwood, tannings, fibres and dyes.

The maquis is characterised by dense thickets of aromatic, stiffly twiggy plants many with small, dark green, leathery leaves, the whole a blaze of colourful flowers in spring, but becoming dormant in the blistering heat of summer. Many hundreds of species contribute to this shrubby mélange, but those which dominate are cistus, rosemary, juniper, genista, lavender, tree heathers, Spanish broom, Jerusalem sage. This dry, crisp, impenetrable jungle gave its name to the "maquisarde" – the Maquis, the French resistance fighters who used it to great effect as a refuge during the German occupation.

Garigue is the vegetation growing on more impoverished soil where the activities of men and domesticated beasts have reduced the land to a more or less eroded rocky desert. It is characterised by low-growing, scattered bushes. These tend to be spiny or have small leaves, often hairy or heavily felted. As well as maquis species, herbs abound, and the garigue is home to kitchen necessities such as thyme, sage, savory, hyssop, garlic and rue. Also in abundance are many tuberous and bulbous plants familiar to the gardener in tulips, crocuses, irises, grape hyacinths, fritillaries, Star of Bethlehem and allium species.

In the United States the Californian "chapparal" corresponds to the Mediterranean garigue and maquis, and supplies us with romneya (tree poppy), zauschneria and artemisia. In Central Asia similar areas are found in Afghanistan and Russia.

All these plants are adapted to long, hot, dry summers and short, relatively warm winters with occasional frosts; ideal subjects to try in our coastal gardens.

10

Sub-tropical Plants

Although maquis and garigue plants will provide the major part of your plantings, it will be possible in milder areas of the south and west of England and Scotland to take acceptable risks with considerably more tender species. However, always remember to "garage", like any practised gambler, a small supply of cuttings overwintered under glass to replace any losses (if the plants are amenable to this treatment; otherwise germinate seeds).

Australasia is a bountiful source of plants adapted to maritime conditions. Nearly all of them must be classified as tender, and cannot be considered as at all suitable for inland gardens unless grown in an exceptionally warm and protected site. The range of commercially available trees and shrubs is formidable, and covers everything from impressively wind tolerant species, such as the olearias, to the delicate and exotic scarlet bottle-brush flowered callistemons.

South America contributes a number of useful and decorative species. The wind and drought tolerant escallonias from Brazil are the most prominent whilst *Eccromocarpus scaber,* from Chile, is an impressive evergreen climber with orange tubular flowers that appear in abundance from June to October: it may be cut down by a cold snap, but usually grows again from the base. The abutilons from Brazil, Guatamala and Chile are worth risking for their brightly coloured funnel-shaped flowers. *Solanum crispum* (the Chilean potato-tree) is an almost hardy evergreen scrambler with delicate purple blue star-shaped flowers for a warm wall. The tuberous alstroemerias, also from Chile, have given rise to the half-hardy Ligtu hybrids, 2' high, in a wide range of colours including white, pink, scarlet, orange and yellow.

South Africa also gives us many tender but brilliantly colourful flowering plants such as agapanthus, arctotis, *Aster pappei*, gazanias, gerberas and osteospermum and pelargonium varieties. It is also home to the "mesembryanthemums" – "mesems", "mezzies", "mesmerisms" – ranging from the hugely spreading, very large leaved and flowered "Hottentot fig", *Carpobrotus edulis*, to the fabulous cascading lampranthus varieties for the dry wall. Bulbs are also well represented for colour in the varieties of crocosmia (montbretia); pale pink *Nerine bowdenii* and *Nerine sarniensis* (Guernsey lily) with a range of colour from pink to red; *Amaryllis belladona*, pink or white.

II

Trees and Shrubs

The plants in the following list are all suitable for a seaside site. Some require wind protection, and this is noted along with any other significant factors such as soil preference and hardiness. The list is not necessarily exhaustive, certainly as regards varieties of some super-abundant species, but it will give a clear indication of much reliable material which should keep you busy for a year or two!

Needless to say I have not grown every plant mentioned myself: it will probably be fairly obvious from the entries those which I have. However, each and every recommendation is justified by somebody, somewhere, having succeeded with them on the coast.

The letters and symbols after each entry give a quick idea of the plant's characteristics:

LT = large tree (height dependent on growing conditions)
MT = medium tree (height dependent on growing conditions)
ST = small tree (15' to 30')
LS = large shrub (more than 10')
MS = medium-sized shrub (5' to 10')
SS = small shrub (3' to 5')
DS = dwarf shrub (1' to 3')
PS = prostrate shrub
D = deciduous
E = evergreen
SE = semi-evergreen

O   =   requires full sun to succeed
◗   =   prefers or tolerates part shade
●   =   requires or tolerates full shade
I   =   date introduced to this country
C   =   date first cultivated in this country

AWARDS

The awards noted in the text are those given by the Royal Horticultural Society, and are an excellent indication of a plant's worth.

AGM = Award of Garden Merit
First awarded in 1921 but the AGM Committee reviewed all previous awards between 1982 and 1984. All AGM's awarded before 1984 are therefore now not noted. The Committee has made no awards since 1984.

AM = Award of Merit
Awards are made on the basis of judging specimen plants. Founded in 1888.

AMT = Award of Merit (Trials)
Awards are made after trials at the RHS Gardens at Wisley.

CORY CUP The Reginald Cory Memorial Cup is awarded to the horticulturist who raises the best hybrid in any year.

FCC = First Class Certificate, first awarded in 1859.

FCCT = First Class Certificate (Trials)

ABELIA X GRANDIFLORA MS – SE – O

Abelias are mostly too tender to survive a really cold winter, but the hybrid *A.x grandiflora* is hardier and more vigorous than either parent *(A. chinensis* and *A. uniflora),* and is recommended for its brilliant green leaves and abundant white funnel-shaped flowers tinged with pink from July to October. Not fussy about type of soil, and easily propagated from cuttings in autumn. Raised in Italy before 1866. AGM 1984.

A. x g. **'Francis Mason'** has dark green leaves with gold margins; variation develops best in dry soil. New Zealand. AGM 1984.

A. **'Edward Groucher'** *(x grandiflora x schumannii)*, raised in Maryland, U.S.A., has darker-coloured purple-pink flowers. Smaller than *A. x grandiflora*, good for small gardens.

ABUTILON VITIFOLIUM ls – d – o

Abutilons are tender and may need more moisture than offered by very sharply drained sandy soils. *A. vitifolium* from Chile is the hardiest, and withstands wind if well staked when young. Large, grey-green, downy leaves and profuse, beautiful pale purple-blue mallow-like flowers from May to July. Easily raised from seed. Short-lived. I 1836. FCC 1899. AGM 1984.

A.v. **'Album'** – snowy white flowers. AM 1961.

A.v. **'Veronica Tennant'** – pale lavender to almost purple flowers according to soil.

ACACIA

A. dealbata. "Silver Wattle" ls to st – d – o
Tender, dislikes direct wind; the "mimosa" of the South of France and a florists' favourite. An Australian with silvery, fern-like leaves and profusely borne, small, fluffy, fragrant, yellow flowers in late winter, early spring. Intolerant of alkaline soils. Good with protection of wall or windbreak. I 1820. AM 1935. FCC 1971.

A. rhetinoides st – d – o
Tender, needs wind shelter. Willow-like grey green leaves and large, loose panicles of yellow, fragrant flowers from July to

January. One of the most lime-tolerant of acacias. Tasmania.
I 1871. AM 1925.

ALOYSIA TRIPHYLLA (LIPPIA CITRIODORA) MS to LS − D − O

The "Lemon Verbena" is an excellent wall shrub especially near
doors as its lance-shaped leaves are highly aromatic. It bears profuse
small purple flowers in terminal panicles in August. It will survive
all but the severest winters in maritime areas as long as it is grown
in poor dry soil. Chile. I 1784.

ARBUTUS

A. andrachne ST − E − O
The beautiful Grecian "Strawberry Tree" has smooth red bark,
large, leathery, grey-green leaves and clusters of whitish flowers
in spring. Numerous small, rough fruits. Tender when young,
hardy in maturity. Lime tolerant. Its habitat in the wild is maquis, woods and thickets. SE Europe. I 1724.

A. x andrachnoides ST − E − O
Cross between *A. andrachne* and *A. unedo*. Cinnamon-red
branches and reasonably hardy. Flowers during late autumn and
winter. Found wild in Greece. C 1800. AM 1953. AGM 1984.

A. unedo ST − E − O
The "Killarney Strawberry Tree", although ericaceous, tolerates lime, and is gale resistant. Laurel-like leaves: globular rosy
red fruits and clusters of creamy, drooping, bell-shaped flowers
produced simultaneously in late autumn. Slow growing. A
maquis inhabitant widespread throughout the Mediterranean
region. Fruits edible − *"unedo"* means "eat one", i.e. one is
quite enough, thank you very much. The wood is used to

make flutes in Greece. Naturalised in SW Ireland. FCC 1933.
AGM 1984.

A.u. **'Rubra'** is a choice form with light pink flowers and
prolific fruits. C 1835. AM 1925. AGM 1984.

ATRIPLEX HALIMUS MS – SE – O

The hardy, grey-leaved and gale tolerant "Tree Purslane" is of no
great beauty, but a no-nonsense shrub, growing fast when established, making good low shelter. An excellent wind-stopper. S
Europe. C since 17th century.

AUCUBA JAPONICA MS – E – ● to ◗

Although the Victorians ruined its reputation, the quite remarkably
tough laurel is totally salt tolerant, and an excellent shrub for the
seaside especially in shade. Many forms are in cultivation, variously
variegated and spotted with gold.

A.j. **'Variegata'** with leaves speckled yellow was the first form
introduced from Japan in 1783. FCC 1865.

AZARA

A. *dentata* MS – E – O
A tender shrub for mild localities; dark glossy leaves, felted beneath
and clusters of fragrant yellow flowers from April to June. Requires
shelter from cold winds. From Chile. I about 1830.

A. *microphylla* TS – E – O
Hardier, grows in any soil. Tiny leaves in large sprays and
yellow flowers smelling of vanilla ice cream in spring – elegant.
Chile, Argentina. Also a variegated form. I 1861. FCC 1872.

BACCHARIS

B. halimifolia ("Bush Groundsel") LS – D – O
Not ornamental; grey-green leaves and dull white flowers, but females bear interesting thistle-like fruits in winter. Useful for windy seaside conditions. NE America. I 1683.

B. patagonica LS to ST – E – O
Another "useful" shrub for the seaside. Deep green, polished evergreen leaves; yellow-white flowers in May. Chile, Argentina.

BALLOTA PSEUDODICTAMNUS DS – SE – O

A small sub-shrub completely smothered, branches and leaves, with grey-white wool – very tactile. Small lilac pink flowers appear in July on new branches, which should be cut back in late autumn or spring. Tolerates very driest conditions. Mediterranean region. AGM 1984.

BERBERIS

The "Barberries" are a huge genus with more than 600 species, and present a wide choice of colour and size. In coastal conditions *B. darwinii* and *B. x stenophylla* do best, but require protection from the heaviest winds. They must be planted young from pots, and not disturbed. They thrive in sun or shade and any soil which is not too damp. Valued for showy berries and brilliant autumn leaves. The purple-leaved forms are superb as contrast with the grey-green foliage of many maritime plants. Consult Bean, Hillier and *"The Plant Finder"*. The three species described below bear spines.

B. darwinii MS – E – O to ●
One of the finest of all shrubs, discovered by Charles Darwin in 1835 on the voyage of the "Beagle". Dark, shining leaves, bright orange flowers in spring, plum-purple berries. Chile, Argentina. FCC 1967. AGM 1984.

B. x stenophylla MS – E – O to ●
A cross between *B. darwinii* and *B. empetrifolia*; long arching branches with profuse yellow flowers in April. C 1860. FCC 1864. AGM 1984.

Many forms of varying size down to prostrate, some with pink flowers (e.g. **'Pink Pearl'**).

B. thunbergii SS – D – O to ●
Compact with bright red berries and brilliant autumn leaves. Japan. I about 1864. FCC 1890. AGM 1984.

The atropurpurea group of this species have wonderful leaf variations from deep purple to variegations of grey, pink and gold. There are many distinguished named varieties such as **'atropurpurea nana'**, **'Harlequin'**, **'Red Chief'**, **'Rose Glow'**, all of which have an AGM.

BESCHORNERIA YUCCOIDES MS – E – O

Related to the agaves and much like the yuccas, it sends up 6' stems with exotic drooping racemes of bright green flowers with red bracts. For mild localities only and a protected position. Full sun and dry soil is essential. Mexico. I before 1859. AM 1933.

BRACHYGLOTTIS (SENECIO)

A large and complicated genus mostly from New Zealand, many previously classified as *Senecio*. Not very cold tolerant, but all species withstand drought and usually wind in full sun. All evergreen with yellow (occasionally white) daisy-like flowers, leaves mostly oval, white-felted beneath. Excellent seaside shrubs and infallible in warmer areas.

B. compactus SS – E – O
Compact as name suggests. Leaves oval with wavy edges. Flowers bright yellow.

B. elaeagnifolius MS – E – O

Stiff, many branched with elaeagnus-like leaves, glossy above, thick buff felt beneath and on young shoots and flower stalks. Flowers unimpressive, but a useful plant for exposed positions.

B. monroi SS – E – O

Domed shape. Leaves wavy margined. Flowers yellow.

B. reinoldii MS – E – O

Rounded habit. Typical leaves. Unremarkable yellowish flowers, but impervious to heaviest gales.

B. rependa LS – E – O

Tender; very large (up to 12" long) soft green leaves and large panicles of scented flowers. Tropical appearance. Leaves used by Maoris as primitive postcards. Requires protection from wind as the leaves will tear easily. The form **'Purpurea'** has leaves purple above, white felted beneath.

B. 'Sunshine' SS – E – O

Hybrid of *B. greyi* and probably *B. compactus*. Certainly the most decorative with silvery-grey young leaves and generous large showy corymbs of bright yellow flowers in summer. Kept neat by pruning. Wind and drought resistant. Often incorrectly labelled *S. greyi* or *S. laxifolius*. Really good. AGM 1984.

B. viravira MS – E – O

A beautiful tender shrub, silver-white, lax with finely divided pinnate leaves. Flowers whitish of no great distinction. Requires protection. I 1893. AM 1973.

BUDDLEIA

B. alternifolia LS to ST – D – O

A very beautiful, vigorous, weeping-willow-like shrub with long, narrow dark green leaves and masses of fragrant lilac flowers in June. Likes good loamy soil. Protect from strong winds to retain habit. China I 1915. AM 1922. AGM 1984.

The form 'Argentea' has leaves covered with silky hairs that give the whole a silvery sheen.

B. *auriculata* MS – D – O

An open shrub with leaves white-felted beneath and valuable for long panicles of very fragrant, creamy white flowers from September to January. Unless grown on a wall only reasonably hardy in mild areas. Happy on light, well-drained loamy soil. S Africa. AM 1923.

B. *davidii* MS – D – O

The best known buddleia from China and Japan does well by the sea, but the long racemes of colourful flowers all too soon turn a beastly brown. Cut back hard in March. Attracts butterflies. Many varieties: some of the best are **'Black Knight'**, very deep violet, AGM 1984; **'Dartmoor'**, magenta, FCC 1990; **'Peace'**, white, AM 1962; **'Royal Red'**, red-purple, AM 1950, AGM 1984; **'Pink Delight'** is a recent hybrid with bright pink flowers, AM 1988.

B. *globosa* MS – SE – O

Erect with handsome foliage and orange, ball-shaped inflorescences in June. Not everybody's favourite: certainly needs much trimming to keep tidy. Andes of Chile, Argentina and Peru. I 1774. AGM 1984.

The variety **'Lemon Ball'** has lemon-yellow flowers.

B. 'Lochinch' *(B. davidii x B. fallowiana)* MS – D – O

Bushy and compact with young stems and leaves initially grey, leaves turning glabrous green with white, woolly undersides. Flowers fragrant, rich lavender-blue. Cut back hard in March. Associates well with yellow Spanish Broom *(Spartium junceum)* which flowers at the same time. AGM 1984.

BUPLEURUM FRUTICOSUM MS – E – O

Excellent for exposed positions. Grows in any soil, but likes chalk. Beautiful blue-green foliage and small yellow flowers in summer which attract crowds of flies (so do not plant near the house!). Associates well with equally wind and salt tolerant grey-leaved *Atriplex halimus* and *Teucrium fruticans*. S Europe. AM 1979.

CALCEOLARIA INTEGRIFOLIA SS – D – O

Sage-like leaves and masses of large, bright yellow pouch-shaped flowers in late summer. Tender; best protected in dry soil at the bottom of a warm wall where it can attain 6'. Take cuttings to replace losses in a hard winter. Chile. I 1822.

The variety **'Angustifolia'** has narrower leaves. AM 1960.

CALLISTEMON

The Australian "Bottlebrushes" are magnificent, but only for the mildest areas in full sun, and not for shallow, chalky soils. Flowers during summer in cylindrical spikes.

C. *citrinus* 'Splendens' MS – E – O
Brilliant scarlet flowers for a long period and graceful form. Safe in the open in warm areas. "Citrinus" refers to the lemon scent when the leaves are crushed. AM 1926.

C. *sieberi* MS – E – O
The "Alpine Bottlebrush" is hardier than the type with pale yellow flowers.

C. *subulatus* SS – E – O
The hardiest of the red flowered varieties. Bright green leaves and crimson flowers in late summer.

CALLUNA

There are very numerous varieties of *Calluna vulgaris*, the familiar "heather" and "ling". All are easy in poor, dry, acid soil, and like full sun: heathers become leggy and unsightly in rich conditions. They appear not to mind wind and salt, but wind certainly keeps them dwarf. Flowering times vary according to the form, from July through to November. Trim off old flowers in March. Many cultivars have interesting coloured foliage. Refer to catalogues for your personal preference of flower and foliage colour, and to specialist books for detailed cultivation requirements.

CARPENTERIA CALIFORNICA MS – E – O

Not overly tender, but should have a sunny wall and well-drained soil to perform well. Truly the most beautiful of shrubs, the "Tree Anemone" produces fragrant, large white flowers with conspicuous golden anthers in June and July. Foliage bright green above, pale soft felt beneath. When happy can grow to well over 12'. Do not attempt to grow from seed: increase by layering. Associated with Gertrude Jekyll, for whom it first flowered in 1886. California. FCC 1888.

Two varieties with larger flowers are **'Bodnant'** and **'Ladham's Variety'**.

CARYOPTERIS X CLANDONENSIS SS – D – O

Arthur Simmonds, Secretary of the RHS, raised this hybrid in his garden in West Clandon in Surrey in the 1930's; a cross between *C. incana* and *C. mongolica*. Evergreen, aromatic, toothed leaves and bright blue flowers in September. Hardy and drought tolerant, it grows well on any light soil in full sun. Good on chalk. Prune hard in spring to encourage flowers on new growth. Protect from salt spray. It is variable: reject plants with weedy growth and insipid flowers. Buy named varieties:

'**Arthur Simmonds**' AM 1933. FCC 1941. AGM 1984.

'**Ferndown**', dark green leaves, deeper violet-blue flowers. AM 1953. AGM 1984.

'**Heavenly Blue**', more erect and compact, deeper blue flowers. AGM 1984.

'**Kew Blue**', slightly darker than "Arthur Simmonds". AGM 1984.

CASSIA (SENNA) CORYMBOSA MS – D – O

What you are buying, or should be buying, is *C. x floribunda*, a first-rate, vigorous but tender wall shrub with large, deep yellow flowers in terminal clusters from late summer to winter. The true *C. corymbosa* is less robust and has smaller, paler flowers. S America. C 1800.

CASSINIA FULVIDA SS to MS – E – O

"Golden Heather" is dense with small, closely packed dark green leaves with yellow, downy undersides and heads of white flowers in July. A good contrast for grey and glaucous plants, but otherwise of no great worth. New Zealand.

CEANOTHUS

The "Californian Lilacs" are a remarkable genus containing a wide variety of form from prostrate shrubs to small trees, evergreen and deciduous, all outstanding for the characteristic vivid blue flowers. They are ideal for coastal gardens, but need wall shelter in northern areas. Evergreen varieties are more tender than deciduous. They all require full sun and well-drained gritty and impoverished soil to flower well, but only the most vigorous will tolerate alkaline sand; some can become chlorotic. Evergreens should not be pruned hard as they flower on the previous year's growth: trim, if you must, immediately after flowering. Deciduous kinds can be more severely treated as they flower on the current year's growth. Being of such outstanding beauty, it is worthwhile giving considerable thought to their positioning: the developing flower buds of the more tender evergreens will be destroyed by cold spring winds, despite wall protection in warm areas; all varieties withstand cold better if planted in poor soil with restricted root runs. Remember they are natives of the Pacific coast where they form a large part of the "chapparal", the American equivalent of the Mediterranean "maquis".

All members of the genus must be worth trying, but the following have proved to be successful in coastal situations:

C. arboreus 'Trewithen Blue' LS to ST – E – O

Vigorous and large; an improved variety with big oval leaves and long panicles of deep blue, lightly scented flowers in spring. Raised in Trewithen Gardens, Cornwall. AM 1967. AGM 1984.

C. 'Autumnal Blue' MS – E – O

Hardiest evergreen hybrid; masses of deep sky-blue flowers in late summer and autumn, often in spring as well; bright glossy green leaves. AM 1930. AGM 1984.

C. 'Delight' MS – E – O

Another almost hardy evergreen; long panicles of rich blue flowers in spring. AM 1933. AGM 1984.

C. 'Gloire de Versailles' MS – D – O

Deservedly the most popular deciduous ceanothus; large panicles of powder-blue flowers in summer and autumn. Universally recommended for seaside planting. FCC 1872. AGM 1984.

C. 'Henri Desfosse' MS – D – O
Similar to *C.* "Gloire de Versailles" but with violet-blue flowers. AM 1926.

C. *impressus* MS – E – O
The "Santa Barbara Ceanothus" is near hardy with small leaves and deep blue flowers in spring. AM 1944. FCC 1987. AGM 1984.

C. *impressus* 'Puget Blue' MS – E – O
Raised in the University of Washington Arboretum, an improved variety with narrower leaves. AM 1971. AGM 1984.

C. 'Indigo' MS – D – O
Tender, but wind and salt tolerant in mild areas. Must be tried for true indigo-blue flowers in summer. AM 1902.

C. *thyrsiflorus* LS to ST – E – O
One of the hardiest evergreens; dark green leaves and bright blue flowers in early summer. I 1837. AM 1935.

The variety **'repens'** is vigorous, *prostrate* and hardy with Cambridge-blue flowers. AGM 1984.

CERATOSTIGMA WILLMOTTIANUM SS – D – O

Small bristly leaves on occasionally purplish stalks; small bright blue flowers in dense terminal heads on new growth, opening successively from July to October. Flowers are fairly sparse but useful for late season. Often cut down by frost: if not, prune back previous year's growth in spring. Grows well on dry chalky soil. Grown by Miss Ellen Willmott from seed sent by Ernest Wilson from the semi-arid Min River Valley in 1908. W China. AM 1917. AGM 1984.

CHOISYA TERNATA MS – E – O or ❱

The "Mexican Orange Blossom" is remarkably hardy in view of its origin, but more reliable against a wall in colder areas. Shiny, dark green trifoliate leaves with clusters of fragrant white flowers from late spring to early summer, repeat flowering usually in autumn. Protect from cold winds to preserve good dome shaped form. SW Mexico. I 1825. FCC 1880. AGM 1984.

'**Sundance**' is a new introduction of smaller form with vivid light yellow young foliage. '**Aztec Pearl**', a hybrid (*C. arizonica* x *C. ternata*) raised by Messrs. Hillier in 1982. A small shrub with bright green leaves and similar flowers to *C. ternata* but larger and buds flushed pink. AM 1990.

CISTUS

"Sun Roses" are natives of S Europe and N Africa, thriving on the Mediterranean seabord where they form an important element of the "maquis". Although they will not stand severe frost, they are ideal maritime evergreens, enjoying full sun and dry conditions and happy on chalk. They are remarkably wind tolerant, making excellent, decorative, quick and easily propagated material for new gardens by the sea. Most are small with white flowers resembling single roses in great profusion in June and July. There are pink forms and many hybrids more vigorous than their parents. Their popularity with gardeners since the 17th century peaked in the early 19th century when 112 species, varieties and hybrids were recorded: they deserve more attention today even if not genuinely hardy. They do not transplant well: propagate by cuttings in containers and plant small. The following is a selection of the hardiest and most decorative:

C. x aguilari '**Maculatus**' *(C. landanifer x C. populifolius)* SS
  Vigorous with very large white flowers blotched crimson. Spain and Morocco. AM 1936.

***C.* 'Anne Palmer'** *(C. crispus x C. palinhae)* SS
  Shoots bear long white hairs; wavy edged leaves and large pink flowers. Cory Cup 1960. AM 1964. AGM 1984.

C. x corbariensis *(C. populifolius x C. salvifolius)* SS
Almost hardy; densely bushy with smaller white flowers stained yellow at the base of petals. Vigorous: has survived deep frosts at Kew. Takes its name from Corbières in the South of France. AGM 1984.

C. x cyprius *(C. ladanifer x C. laurifolius)* MS
Fairly hardy; considered the most beautiful. Vigorous and bushy with elegant narrow leaves and medium sized white flowers with blood-red basal blotches. It grows to 8'. France, Spain. AMT 1925. AGM 1984.

C. x dansereaui 'Decumbens' DS
Survives the average winter; grows no higher than 2' and spreads twice as much. Flowers medium-sized, white with crimson basal blotch. Discovered as early as 1845.

C. 'Elma' *(C. laurifolius x C. palinhae)* MS
Vigorous and sturdy with deep green, polished leaves and very large, striking white flowers. AM 1949.

C. ladanifer MS
Tall and erect, almost hardy. Although of scrawny habit and requiring underplanting, has large white flowers with blood-red basal blotches. S Europe, N. Africa. I 1629.

C. laurifolius MS
Tall and erect; open habit. Medium-sized white flowers. Valuable as the hardiest cistus. Long, profuse flowering season from June to August and pervasive incense-like perfume on hot days. Withstands driest possible conditions. SW Europe. I 1731. AGM 1984.

C. palhinhae SS
Compact with dark green leaves densely felted white beneath and large, satin-white flowers in May and June. Very beautiful and proving hardier than expected. Happy on limestone. SW Portugal. AM 1944.

C. 'Pat' *(C. ladanifer x C. palhinhae)* SS
A hardy hybrid with very large white flowers with maroon basal blotches. AM 1955.

C. 'Peggy Sammons' *(C. albidus x C. laurifolius)* MS
Erect habit, grey-green downy leaves and delicate, feminine pink flowers. A new introduction described in "The Gardener" (Journ. RHS 1981), said to be better than 'Silver Pink'. AGM 1984.

C. *populifolius var. lasiocalyx* SS
One of the hardiest with large, wavy, white flowers, yellow stained at base of petals. S Spain, S Portugal, Morocco.

C. *x pulverulentus* *(C. albidus x C. crispus)* DS
Compact with wavy, sage-green leaves and vivid cerise flowers. SW Europe. C1929.

C. *x purpureus* *(C. creticus x C. ladanifer)* SS
Wavy dark green leaves and large, rosy-crimson flowers with maroon basal blotches and conspicuous clusters of yellow stamens. I 1790. AMT 1925. AGM 1984.

C. 'Silver Pink' *(C. creticus x C. laurifolius)* SS
One of the hardiest with long clusters of silver pink flowers. AM 1919.

C. *x skanbergii* *(C. monspeliensis x C. parviflorus)* SS
Fairly hardy with grey-green foliage and small, beautiful pale pink flowers. A rare natural hybrid from Greece. AGM 1984.

CLERODENDRUM TRICHOTOMUM LS – D – O

Vigorous with sweetly scented white flowers in August followed by unusual bright turquoise-blue berries in autumn. **C.t. var. fargesii** is said to be less tender: it suckers rather too freely but fruits more generously. Requires sunny, sheltered position and grows well on lime. May need too much watering to be of much use in dry soil. Takes a number of years to flower, but worth waiting for. **C. trichotomum**, China, Japan. C1880. FCC 1893. ***C.t. var. fargesii***, W China. I 1898. AM 1911.

CLIANTHUS PUNICEUS MS − SE − O

Too tender for all but warmest areas and there prefers a south or west wall where it can climb. Its name "Lobster's Claw" refers to the curious brilliant red flowers which appear in early summer. Leaves long and pinnate. N Island of New Zealand. I 1831. AM 1938.

Varieties include: **'Albus''**, white flowers. AM 1938; **'Flamingo'**, deep rose-pink flowers; **'Red Cardinal'**, brilliant scarlet flowers; **'White Heron'**, white flowers tinged with green.

COLLETIA

South American leafless shrubs with densely packed green spines and small fragrant flowers in summer and autumn.

C. hystrix *(C. armata)* MS − E − O
Vigorous with profusion of white flowers. Chile. N Argentina. AM 1973.

The variety **'Rosea'** has pink flower buds. AM 1972.

C. paradoxa SS − E − O
Very unusual, slow growing shrub with branchlets forming flat triangular spines. Profuse flowers in late summer and autumn. E Argentina, Uruguay, S Brazil. I 1824. AM 1959.

COLUTEA

The "Bladder Sennas" are useful shrubs for dry, poor sand where they thrive. Pea flowers are followed by unusual large seed pots. Leaves pinnate.

C. arborescens LS – D – O
Yellow flowers throughout the summer. Takes up a large space but can be cut back almost to old wood in February. S Europe, Mediterranean region. I 16th century.

C. buhsei LS – D – O
Vigorous and upright with large golden-yellow flowers from June to autumn. Introduced from N Iran in 1972 by Roy Lancaster and Mrs. Ala. AM 1987.

C. x media MS – D – O
Vigorous with grey leaves and bronze-yellow flowers. Garden origin. C1809. Variety **'Copper Beauty'** has blue-green leaves and profuse bright orange flowers.

C. multiflora MS – D – O
An arching shrub with purplish-red shoots and deep blue-green leaves. Small flowers brick-red turning to orange. Introduced by Tony Schilling from Nepal.

C. orientalis MS – D – O
Rounded shrub with glaucous leaves and copper-coloured flowers. Caucasian region. I 1710.

CONVOLVULUS CNEORUM SS – E – O

Tender, but more or less safe against a warm wall in dry sandy soil. Beautiful silky silver leaves and large, white pink-tinged funnel-shaped flowers in May and intermittently throughout summer. Resistant to salt. SE Europe. C1640. AM 1977. AGM 1984.

CORDYLINE AUSTRALIS ST – E – O

The New Zealand "Cabbage Palm", is not a palm at all but looks like one, growing erect even in most exposed positions. Eventually has a long trunk with branches after several feet, topped by dense heads of sword-like leaves. Large panicles of fragrant white flowers in early summer. A common but none the less impressively sub-tropical tree in warm areas. Cut to the ground in the Channel Islands in the coldest winter on record in 1986, but they have all recovered, and look bushier and healthier for their pruning. I 1823. AM 1953.

The form **'Purpurea'** has purple leaves.

COROKIA

Evergreen shrubs from New Zealand which are impressively wind hardy in mild areas. Characterised by small star-shaped yellow flowers and red or orange berries.

C. buddleiodes MS – E – O
The "Korokio" has whippy stems with dark willow-like leaves, white-felted beneath. Small flowers followed by dark red berries. C1836.

C. cotoneaster SS to MS – E – O
The "Wire-netting Bush" is dense and rounded with contorted, curiously curly branches and tiny flowers and orange berries. Almost hardy. I 1875. AM 1934.

C. macrocarpa LS – E – O
Attractive shrub with large lanceolate leaves, silvery beneath. Large red berries.

C. x virgata *(C. buddleioides x C. cotoneaster)* MS – E – O
Erect habit, leaves white beneath. Very generous in flower and fruit, making excellent hedging material as it survives most winters. I 1907. AM 1934. Varieties include **'Cheesemanii'**, very upright and dense, orange-red berries; **'Red Wonder'**, deep red berries; **'Yellow Wonder'**, profuse bright yellow berries.

CORONILLA

Shrubs with attractive pinnate leaves and umbels of bright yellow pea flowers. They withstand drought well, and thrive on alkaline sand being natives of the Mediterranean seabord. Easily propagated by cuttings or seeds.

C. emerus MS – D – O
Hardy. Seed pods like scorpions' tails. Flowers in May and again in autumn. Cultivated in England since 16th century. C and S Europe.

C. valentina subsp. glauca MS – E – O
Tender in cold areas but valuable in the south and south west for long and generous flowering. Withstands all except coldest winds but burnt by salt. Grows on any reasonable soil including alkaline. Flowers deliciously fragrant, reminiscent of peaches, borne from April to June, but in warmer areas blooms from autumn until late spring. Pinnate leaves glaucous. Pinch back tips of new shoots to retain bushiness. S Europe. I 1722. AM 1957. AGM 1984.

COTINUS

C. coggyria LS – D – O
The "Venetian Sumach" or "Smoke Tree" has smooth, round green leaves, well tinted in autumn, and profuse long plumes of inflorescences in June and July, initially fawn maturing to a smoky-grey colour. Europe. C1656. AGM 1984.
Varieties include:
C.c. purpureus, the "Burning Bush" has green leaves and large inflorescences of a purplish-grey colour. AM 1948. AGM 1984.
C.c. 'Royal Purple', leaves deep purple, translucent in bright sun. AGM 1984. 'Notcutt's Variety' is similar.
C.c. 'Velvet Cloak', leaves deep red-purple turning red in autumn.

C. 'Flame' (probably *C. coggyria x C. obovatus*) LS – D – O
A sturdier, more vigorous version of *C. coggyria* with larger leaves turning brilliant orange-red in autumn.

C. 'Grace' *(C. obovatus x C. coggyria* 'Velvet Cloak') LS – D – O
Vigorous with large, soft purplish-red leaves which turn scarlet in autumn and large purplish-pink inflorescences. AM 1983. Cory Cup 1984. FCC 1990.

C. obovatus LS – D – O
The American "Chittamwood" is a rare (and expensive) shrub with large leaves which turn quite the most brilliant colours in autumn – a mixture of shades of orange, red and purple. I 1882. AM 1904. AM 1976.

COTONEASTER

A large genus of evergreen and deciduous, hardy shrubs varying in habit from prostrate creepers to small trees. Profuse white or pink tinged flowers in June, liked by bees. Leaves and berries are brilliant in autumn. Tolerant of all soils, but seed freely in alkaline conditions. Some are wind resistant. Those mentioned below are good in maritime areas.

C. bullatus LS – D – O
One of the very best with large, corrugated leaves turning a rich colour in autumn when accompanied by large, bright red berries. Wind resistant. W China. I 1898.

C. conspicuus 'Decorus' DS – E – O
Excellent ground cover especially for banks. Free fruiting. FCC 1953. AGM 1984.

C. 'Cornubia' LS to ST – SE – O
Profuse, brilliant red berries weigh down branches in autumn but flowers can be stripped off by heavy winds reducing

performance, therefore protect. Raised at Exbury in 1930. AM 1933. FCC 1936. AGM 1984.

C. 'Exburiensis' LS − D − O

Almost the same as C. 'Rothschildianus' (AGM 1984). Valued for yellow fruits turning pink in winter. Both raised at Exbury in 1930's.

C. horizontalis DS- D − O or ❱

Spreading shrub with characteristic "herring-bone" branches. Richly coloured leaves and berries in autumn and winter. Excellent for shady walls and ground cover for banks. W China. Introduced by Père David in about 1870. FCC 1897. AGM 1984.

C. lacteus MS − E − O

Large, oval leathery leaves with grey wool beneath. Profuse clusters of small red berries lasting well into winter. China. Introduced by George Forrest in 1913. AM 1935. AGM 1984.

C. salicifolius LS − E − O

A graceful specimen shrub with profuse, small, bright red berries in autumn. China. I 1908.

The form **'Fructuluteo'** has yellow fruits.

C. pannosus MS − E − O

Long, arching branches with small sage-green leaves and late, deep red berries. Wind-resistant. W China. Introduced by Abbé Delavay in 1888.

C. rotundifolius SS − E − O

Vigorous, semi-prostrate shrub with long arching branches bearing small, glossy leaves and large rose-red berries. Wind-resistant. I 1825.

C. simonsii MS − SE − O

Erect growing and neat, suitable for hedging. Large, scarlet berries. Himalaya. I 1865. AGM 1984.

CYTISUS

"Brooms" are the ideal deciduous coastal plants, their long whippy stems withstanding wind well. Although they prefer poor fare and dry conditions, they do need deep soil for their long tap roots. The majority are lime tolerant, but *C. multiflorus* and *C. scoparius* cultivars and hybrids dislike extremes of chalky and acid soil: they do best on neutral or slightly acid soil. They all thrive in full sun. Careful siting is therefore important despite their vigour.

All brooms are easily raised from seed, but cannot be relied upon to develop the same colours as the parents: it is better to buy pot grown plants. They grow quickly but are short-lived. Being heavy seed bearers, shorten stems immediately after flowering has finished: this will keep them neat and tidy. However, the tall growing species will tend to become leggy despite judicious annual pruning, and so underplant with low growing shrubs.

Due to their long tap roots they do not transplant, and must be established when young. Never give manure.

There are very many named hybrids and varieties with colour variations of the usual yellow pea-like flower: those named below are only a representative selection of available species and hybrids. Consult catalogues for your personal preferences, remembering that the pure yellow flowers make much more of an impact at a distance than the fancy colour variations.

C. ardoinii DS

Small, mat-forming shrub for the rockery. Flowers bright yellow from April to May. Maritime Alps. I 1866. AM 1955. AGM 1984.

C. battandieri TS

Grey, silky leaves and pineapple-scented clusters of bright yellow flowers in July. Being long and leggy, it is ideal for high sunny walls, but sprawls happily in the open in all but the coldest areas. Morocco. I about 1922. AM 1931. FCC 1934. AGM 1984.

C. x beanii *(C. ardoinii x C. purgans)* DS
Flowers golden yellow in May. Garden origin 1900. FCC 1955. AGM 1984.

C. 'Burkwoodii' MS
Vigorous hybrid. Flowers cerise, wings deep crimson edged with yellow from May to June. AMT 1973. AGM 1984.

C. 'Hollandia' MS
Hybrid with pale crimson flower, wings cerise from May to June. AMT 1973.

C. 'Johnson's Crimson' MS
An erect hybrid with particularly good clear crimson flowers. AMT 1972. FCCT 1973. AGM 1984.

C. x kewensis *(C. ardoinii x C. multiflorus)* DS
Semi-prostrate with profuse cream flowers in May. Raised at Kew in 1891. AGM 1984.

C. 'Luna' MS
Large flowers with complex colouring; standard pale cream tinged red, wings rich yellow, keel pale yellow. C1959. AMT 1972. FCCT 1974. AGM 1984.

C. multiflorus MS
The "White Spanish Broom" will not tolerate lime. Prolific small white flowers in May and June. Spain, Portugal, NW Africa. C1752. AMT 1974. AGM 1984.

C. 'Porlock' *(C. monspessulanus x C. x spachianus)* LS
Unusual, quick-growing semi-evergreen with racemes of very fragrant, butter-yellow flowers which appear intermittently between autumn and spring. Almost hardy on a sunny wall. Raised about 1922. AM 1931. FCC 1990.

C. x praecox *(C. multiflorus x C. purgans)* SS
Compact plants with profuse flowers.

'**Albus**', white flowers.

'**Allgood**', arching sprays of yellow flowers. FCCT 1974. AGM 1984.

'**Gold Spear**', small deep yellow flowers. FCCT 1973.

'**Warminster**', masses of rich cream flowers. AGM 1984.

C. *purpureus* SS
The "Purple Broom" has lilac-purple flowers in May. C and SE Europe. I 1792. AM 1980. The variety '**Atropurpureus**' has deep purple flowers.

C. *scoparius* MS
The "Common Broom" bears its familiar butter-yellow flowers in May. It is the parent of many hybrids of which the following is a selection:

'**Andreanus**', yellow flowers marked with brown-crimson. Normandy. FCC 1890. FCCT 1973. AGM 1984.

'**Cornish Cream**', attractive cream flowers. AM 1923. FCCT 1973. AGM 1984.

'**Golden Sunlight**', strong-growing, flowers rich yellow. AMT 1973.

subsp. maritimus, a dwarf spreading variety with large bright yellow flowers. A rare wild plant on sea cliffs in the west of the British Isles. AM 1913.

DENDROMECON RIGIDA LS – E – O

The tender Californian "Bush-Poppy" is safe in mild maritime gardens in the shelter of a warm wall or hedge. The long succulent branches bear stiff, glaucous leaves and large, bright buttercup yellow flowers intermittently throughout the summer months. I about 1854 by William Lobb. AM 1913.

DESFONTAINEA SPINOSA MS – E – O

Spectacular South American shrub with small holly-like leaves and tubular crimson-scarlet flowers in late summer. Slow growing and only suitable for damp and mild coastal areas in rich acid soil.

ELAEAGNUS

Fast-growing deciduous or evergreen shrubs and small trees, ideal as maritime plants being wind and salt resistant. The insignificant flowers are profuse and scented. They are happy in any soil except very shallow chalk, but the silvery leaved species colour best in sandy soil in full sunlight. All species, however, tolerate partial shade.

The variegated evergreen varieties provide quite the most brilliant foliage colouring, and are exceptionally valuable for winter interest. They are most useful as a backdrop for brightly coloured flowers in summer.

They do not tolerate transplanting; the roots are very sensitive and so handle carefully when planting from pots. Propagation is easy from hardwood cuttings taken between February and March. Avoid buying grafted plants (obvious from the swelling on the stem just above the compost); they are not as long-lived.

E. *angustifolia* LS to ST – D
The "Oleaster" is spiny with silver-grey, willow-like leaves and yellow flowers in June followed by dull orange fruits. Excellent on sandy soils. Temperate W Asia, but widely naturalised in S Europe. C in England from 16th century. AM 1978.

The variety **'caspica'** has broader more silvery leaves. Caucasus.

E. *commutata* MS – D
The "Silver Berry" is a striking shrub with intensely silver, willow-like leaves and white flowers in May followed by silver fruits. Excellent on sandy soils. N America. I 1813. AM 1956.

E. x ebbingei LS to ST – E

One of the hardiest, quick growing shelter shrubs. Large grey-green leaves, silver beneath. Flowers in autumn: orange red fruits in spring. Can be clipped to shape in June and September. Garden origin 1929.

The very decorative variegated sorts are:

'Gilt Edge', green leaves edged gold. Smaller than parent. C1961. AM 1971. FCC 1987. AGM 1984.

'Limelight', green leaves splashed with gold. Tends to revert: remove shoots immediately. Upright habit.

E. macrophylla LS – E

Large, broad, roundish leaves, initially silvery on both sides but ageing to grey-green above. Autumn flowers better than type. Korea, Japan. I 1879 by Charles Maries. AM 1932.

E. pungens LS to ST – E

A vigorous, spreading, rarely spiny shrub making good wind shelter. Leaves shiny green above, dull white speckled with brown scales beneath. Autumn flowers white and fragrant. Japan. I 1830.

The very decorative variegated sorts are:

'Dicksonii', more slow-growing, erect. Leaves green holly-like with wide irregular margin of golden yellow.

'Frederici', slow-growing with mainly pale creamy yellow narrow leaves edged bright green.

'Goldrim', deep glossy green round leaves edged yellow.

'Maculata', leaves dark green with large central splash of gold. Very bright. Tends to revert: remove shoots immediately. FCC 1891. AGM 1984.

'Variegata', vigorous. Green leaves with thin cream edge.

E. umbellata LS to ST – D

Vigorous, spreading shrub of open habit with soft green leaves, silvery beneath, turning yellow in autumn when the branches are weighed down with small red fruits speckled with white. Flowers in May and June are strongly fragrant. Korea, Japan. I 1830. AM 1933.

ERICA

The "Heaths" thrive on sandy, acid soil. The exceptions to this rule are the winter flowering species and their cultivars such as *E. carnea, E. erigena, E. terminalis* and *E. x darleyensis*, which tolerate lime. Heaths are increasingly popular due to the year round flowering that is possible by planting appropriate species. They associate happily with the heathers, dwarf conifers and dwarf rhododendrons, if you like this style of garden scheme.

Consult catalogues for your preference in a wide range of leaf and flower colouring: the choice is vast!

Propagation is simplicity itself: lift a plant, replant some inches deeper, and sprinkle the centre with a mixture of peat and sand so that the young shoots protrude; these will have rooted independently in a year's time.

ESCALLONIA

Perfect evergreen seaside shrubs providing species and hybrids for windbreaks, some of sufficient decorative value to grow as specimens. All flower throughout the summer and on into autumn. They thrive in all types of well-drained soil in sun and are drought resistant.

Being natives of South America they are not entirely hardy inland, but only the coldest winds will damage plants in coastal areas. In general the smaller leaved varieties are hardier. Any damage repairs itself quickly in spring.

No species have large leaves or flowers. They grow to between 3' and 12' after a slow start. Never give manure when planting. Propagated easily by cuttings.

The toughest, most vigorous sort for windbreaks is:

E. rubra var. macrantha LS
Glossy, dark green leaves and rose-crimson flowers. Grows up to 12'. Chile. I 1848. AGM 1984.

All others make good hedges within gardens. The Slieve Donard Nursery in Northern Ireland has specialised in producing colourful and attractive varieties.

E. 'Apple Blossom' SS
Attractive, compact, slow growing with comparatively large soft pink flowers. AM 1946. AGM 1984.

E. 'C.F. Ball' MS
Erect, vigorous, larger leaves, good for hedges. Bright crimson flowers. Raised at Glasnevin about 1912. AM 1926.

E. 'Donard Beauty' MS
Large leaves and profuse rich rose-red flowers. Hardy. AM 1930.

E. 'Donard Brilliance' MS
Not a strong grower, but graceful with arching branches. Large leaves and remarkably brilliant rose-red flowers. AM 1928.

E. 'Donard Gem' MS
Compact with small leaves and large, pink, fragrant flowers. AM 1927.

E. 'Donard Radiance' MS
Compact, strong-growing. Large, shiny, deep green leaves and large, brilliant, soft rose-red flowers of chalice shape. AM 1954.

E. 'Donard Seedling' MS
Vigorous. Large leaves and white flowers, pink in bud. AM 1916.

E. 'Donard Star' MS
Compact, upright habit. Large leaves and beautifully formed large flowers rose pink. AM 1967.

E. 'Donard White' MS
Compact, rounded habit. Small leaves and white flowers, pink in bud, over a long period. Hardy.

E. 'Iveyi' LS
Stiff, vigorous growth with handsome glossy foliage. Large panicles of white flowers from August onwards. Named after head gardener who raised it at Caerhays. Tender in northern areas. AM 1926. AGM 1984.

E. 'Langleyensis' MS
Graceful, arching habit. Small leaves and rose-pink flowers wreathing branches. Associates well with E. 'Donard Seedling' as contrast. Hardy. Garden origin 1893. AM 1897.

E. 'Peach Blossom' SS
Similar in habit to 'Apple Blossom' but bears clear peach-pink flowers. AGM 1984.

E. 'Pride of Donard' MS
Large, dark green, shiny leaves with terminal racemes of bell-shaped, brilliant rose flowers from June throughout summer. Highly rated by the Slieve Donard Nursery – obviously justifiably. AGM 1984.

E. 'Red Elf' SS
Vigorous with dark green, shiny leaves and profuse deep crimson flowers. C1970. AGM 1984.

E. *rubra* 'Crimson Spire' MS
Erect, strong-growing with largish, dark green, shiny leaves and bright crimson flowers. Ideal for hedging. AGM 1984.

E. *rubra* 'Woodside' SS
Unique in being small and neat but spreading. Good for banks and large rock gardens. Small crimson flowers.

E. 'Slieve Donard' MS
Compact with small leaves and large panicles of light rose-red flowers. Very hardy.

EUCALYPTUS

The "Gum Trees" of Australia are good evergreens for a warm seaside position as long as their roots are in deep soil and given a good supply of humus on planting: they will not thrive on shallow, sandy soil. Having satisfied these requirements, they will be salt and wind tolerant, the hardier species only succumbing to the coldest strong winds. They grow remarkably quickly and require careful staking when young. On warm, damp coasts they can make immensely tall trees, but they can be kept small by severe pruning in early spring: this has the advantage of ensuring that the brilliantly coloured juvenile foliage is retained.

They benefit from the occasional dressing of bone meal on sandy soil, but on no account should they be given manure. They will tolerate thinner, drier soil when grown as shrubs for juvenile foliage and given a thick, generous mulch annually. Although eucalypts grow on most soils, they generally dislike chalk.

E. coccifera LT
   Surviving all but the hardest winters, the "Mount Wellington Peppermint" has outstanding glaucous adult leaves and stems. Tasmania. I 1840. AM 1953.

E. dalrympleana MT
   The "Mountain Gum" is one of the hardiest eucalypts; quick-growing, young leaves bronze becoming grey-green. The bark is a patch-work of cream, brown and grey. Most attractive. New South Wales, Victoria, Tasmania. AM 1953.

E. globulus LT
   Given a mild, damp climate this tender species, the "Blue Gum", will make an immense tree, but it is usually grown as a bedding plant for the silvery blue-green leaves. It can attain 6' in a single season. Tasmania, Victoria. C1829.

E. gunnii LT
   The "Cider Gum" is one of the hardiest and certainly the best known. Young leaves bright silver-blue and round: adult leaves

sage-green and sickle-shaped. Ideal to train as a bush, retaining juvenile foliage. Tasmania. C1853. AM 1950. AGM 1984.

E. parvifolia MT

Very hardy and tolerates chalky soil. Smooth grey bark and adult leaves narrow and blue-green. New South Wales.

E. pauciflora ST

Coming from mountainous regions, the "Snow Gum" is very hardy. White bark and adult leaves long and sickle-shaped. S E Australia, Tasmania. C1880.

Subsp. niphophila is slow growing with patchwork bark of green, cream and grey and grey-green leaves. AM 1977. AGM 1984.

EUONYMUS JAPONICUS LS – E – O to ●

As a hedging plant in the windiest, driest, sandiest position by the sea, in sun to shade, the leathery leaved and evergreen E. japonicus cannot be beaten. Initially slow-growing, it will eventually achieve 12' or more, forming a dense bush with mid-green leaves. It is easily propagated by cuttings, and tolerates transplanting when large due to its compact root system. It can be clipped to shape. AM 1976.

The following are good variegated and dwarf forms:

'Albomarginatus', young leaves pale green maturing to blue-green with a narrow white margin.

'Aureus' ('Aureopictus'), gold centres to leaves, broad green margin. Tends to revert: cut out shoots immediately.

'Latifolius Albomarginatus' ('Macrophyllus Albus'), conspicuous broad white margin to leaves. AGM 1984.

'Marieke' and **'Ovatus Aureus'** ('Aureovariegatus'), two very similar varieties, if not identical. Compact and slow-growing. Need sun to develop colour of leaves which are suffused and margined creamy-yellow. AGM 1984.

'**Microphyllus Variegatus**', similar in form to above with white-margined, green leaves.

EUPATORIUM LIGUSTRINUM MS – E – O

A dense, hemispherical bush up to 9' high and wide. Pale bright green evergreen leaves and delightfully fragrant flowers of a pinky-white colour on long stalks in late summer much resembling gypsophila. The "Mexican Incense Bush" is not reliably frost-hardy, but survives in warm areas. It has no fads as to soil, and is easily increased from cuttings. I 1867.

EUPHORBIA

A huge genus of shrubs, herbs and succulents with a wide distribution. Described below are the evergreen sub-shrubs suitable for dry seaside gardens. The perennial plants are listed later.

E. characias SS – E – O to ◗
Upright, unbranched, biennial stems bear linear, bluish-green leaves and terminal panicles with the typical conspicuous bracts being yellowish-green, the glands a reddish-purple. A striking plant especially during spring and summer. Mediterranean region especially where stony. AM 1961. AGM 1984.
   Varieties include:

E.c. subsp. wulfenii, glands yellowish-green. S E Europe. C1837. AM 1905. FCC 1988. AGM 1984.

E.c. 'John Tomlinson' larger, nearly rounded flower heads, bracts bright yellow-green. Collected in Yugoslavia in 1966. FCC 1977.

E.c. 'Lambrook Gold', flower heads columnar, bracts bright golden-green.

E. mellifera MS – E – O

A tender shrub from the Canary Islands only suitable for the mildest areas. Dense and rounded, the thick shoots bear narrow leaves and brown, honey-scented flowers in May. It can grow as high as 15' in Cornwall.

FABIANA IMBRICATA MS – E – O

Evergreen, heath-like shrub from Chile. Tender, but sufficiently beautiful to warrant trying on light, dry soil in a sunny, sheltered position. Juniper-like, grey-green foliage on dense branches covered in tubular flowers in June. I 1838. AM 1934.

Varieties are:

F.i. 'Prostrata', small and hardier. Feathery branchlets covered in pale mauve flowers in May and June.

F.i. violacea, similar to the type but more spreading and flowers lavender-mauve in colour. FCC 1932.

X FATSHEDERA LIZEI MS – E – ◗

A fascinating hybrid between *Fatsia japonica* (see below) and the "Irish Ivy", *Hedera hibernica*, this shrub has the spreading habit of the ivy and the large leathery, palmate leaves of the fatsia along with its spherical heads of white flowers in autumn. The long, floppy branches need support against a trellis or wall: they are not self-clinging and require tying in. Very useful for dark, shady corners, and distributes its favours lavishly when happy on well-drained soil. Good ground cover also. Hardy and wind tolerant. Garden origin 1910 – it is hardly likely to have come from the wild!

Varieties are **'Annemieke'** with leaves blotched with bright yellow-green, and **'Variegata'** with grey-green leaves having an irregular creamy-white margin.

FATSIA JAPONICA MS to LS − E − O or ◗

In a seaside garden *Fatsia japonica* looks like a geisha girl in "The Dog and Badger", but very surprisingly this highly ornamental, not to say elaborate, shrub with very large, glossy, dark green, palmate leaves withstands wind and salt incredibly well. Although absolutely hardy, it looks sub-tropical, having large terminal heads of milk-white flowers in October and November, followed by generous bunches of black berries. It succeeds on any soil as long as it is well-drained, in sun or semi-shade. Japan. I 1838. FCC 1966. AGM 1984.

The variety **'Variegata'** has white tips to the lobes of the leaves. FCC 1868. AGM 1984.

FREMONTODENDRON 'CALIFORNIA GLORY'
LS − E − O

Do not bother with its parents ***F. californicum*** and ***F. mexicanum***: this vigorous hybrid is dazzling with cup-shaped, waxy, glowing yellow flowers against a background of small grey-green lobed leaves. The flowers are abundant throughout the summer and persist into autumn. It is tender, and needs a warm wall in all but the mildest districts. Good on chalk. Never ever water it: if you do, it will die with remarkable speed. However, plant in the poorest soil with a restricted root run, do not feed it, and it will survive all but the hardest frosts. This total neglect will give you an entirely unwarranted reputation as a skilled plantsperson. Cut back leaders at any time during summer to encourage flowering. Originated in California in 1952. FCC 1967. AGM 1984.

FUCHSIA

Look up "fuchsia" in *"The Plantfinder"* and you will discover that you can take your pick from approximately 2,100 varieties: there are 115 under "A", starting at 'A1' and ending at 'Azure Sky'. This national fuchsia fascination is nothing short of phenomenal, and is reflected in the crowds surrounding the spectacular specialist stands at the Chelsea Flower Show. The amazing diversity of form and alluring boudoir colour combinations of the pendulous complex flowers are the obvious reasons for this obsession.

However, the seaside gardener need not panic. The huge majority of hybrids are not only very tender, but also require more moisture than is available in light sandy soil; they are only suitable as bedding plants. Few sorts are tolerant of dry conditions. If you live in a temperate area of high rainfall and deep rich soil, then you can experiment with a much wider variety. Fuchsias are generally voracious feeders, and need copious watering during the growing season: they are not exactly ideal, therefore, for a labour-free garden! The requirement for moisture can be ameliorated by planting in semi-shade. A great bonus is their virtually complete resistance to disease. They are easily propagated by cuttings. Give some protection from wind and blazing, midday sun. In the relatively hot, dry Channel Islands the following succeed without attention:

F. *procumbens* DS – D – O to ◗

A tender prostrate, scrambling shrub with wiry stems and oval leaves. Flowers have calyx tubes of a pale orange-yellow, reflexed sepals of purple and blue anthers. Fruits are magenta and decorative. A coastal plant of rocky, sandy areas. New Zealand. I about 1854. AM 1980.

F. 'Riccartonii' LS – D – O to

A vigorous, almost hardy sort attaining up to 6', but much bigger in areas of high rainfall. Lanceolate leaves and masses of small flowers with scarlet tubes and sepals and violet corollas. A good hedger which looks terrific from July onwards. Said to have been raised at Riccarton, Scotland around 1830. AMT 1966. FCCT 1977. AGM 1984.

GARRYA ELLIPTICA LS − E − ◗ to ●

The "Silk Tassel Bush" is an invaluable, vigorous specimen for a sunless wall. The male plant has long, grey-green catkins during January and February which are extremely decorative. The female has shorter catkins, but makes up for this by bearing long clusters of deep purple-brown berries. They benefit from pruning as soon as the catkins are over: this keeps them from becoming too bushy and obscuring the tassels and fruit the following season. Being natives of California they are perfectly happy on dry, well-drained soil (of all types); perversely they are surprisingly hardy. An ideal maritime species. I 1828 by David Douglas. AM 1931. AM 1975 (for fruit). AGM 1984 (male plants only).

The variety **'James Roof'** is a virile male with large leathery leaves and even longer catkins. AM 1979. AGM 1984.

GENISTA

As natives of the Mediterranean the genistas are happiest in hot, dry conditions on any sharply drained soil, being especially useful on chalk. They vary in form from small trees to prostrate rockery plants. Their whippy stems are exceptionally tolerant of wind and salt, and, although mainly deciduous, the young green branches give the impression of the plants being evergreen. The flowers are pea-like and of some shade of yellow borne in profusion during summer. Propagation by cuttings is not easy, but genistas grow readily from seeds. The species listed below are hardy and choice:

G. *aetnensis* LS − D − O
   The "Mount Etna Broom" is a spectacular tree-like shrub with long arching leafless stems of supreme elegance given sufficient space to develop. It bears a fabulous display of fragrant golden flowers in July and August. Sardinia and Sicily. FCC 1938. AGM 1984.

G. *cinerea* MS – D – O

The slender stems have a silky texture when young, and bear clusters of flowers in June and July. SW Europe, N Africa. AM 1924.

G. *hispanica* SS – E – O

The intensely prickly "Spanish Gorse" is said to have developed its formidable defence to protect itself against voracious goats (and perhaps vigorous gardeners!). It is densely mound forming making excellent ground cover on the driest bank, and is covered in flowers in May and June. Tough as old boots. SW Europe. I 1759. AGM 1984.

G. *lydia* DS – D – O

A very pretty, pendulous shrub with profuse flowers in May and June. Excellent for banks and large rockeries. E Balkans. I 1926. AM 1937. FCC 1957. AGM 1984.

G. *pilosa* DS – D – O

A dwarf native of the British Isles and Europe with brilliant golden-yellow flowers in May. The Dutch variety **'Goldilocks'** has more erect branches and flowers for a longer period. Good ground cover.

G. *tenera* 'Golden Shower' LS – D – O

A vigorous, arching bush with profuse, luminous yellow, fragrant flowers in June. AGM 1984.

G. *tinctoria*

The "Dyer's Greenweed" is a native of the British Isles and Europe and is distinguished by its long and late flowering season. The bright flowers are borne in long terminal racemes. The following varieties are choice:

G.t. 'Golden Plate', low growing and spreading. Good for ground cover.

G.t. 'Plena', dwarf and semi-prostrate with double flowers. .AGM 1984.

G.t. 'Royal Gold', small shrub with rich yellow flowers throughout summer.

G.t. var. virgata, upright, medium sized shrub.

GREVILLEA

These Australian shrubs are distinctly tricky but exceptionally beautiful evergreens: they are totally intolerant of alkaline conditions, shade and damp; and they are tender. Given the ideal situation, they will produce honeysuckle-like flowers – smaller but more showy. They are happiest in a hot garden against a south wall in the driest possible, light acid soil – a difficult combination to say the least!

G. alpina DS – E – O
A compact plant with grey-green needle leaves and red and cream flowers throughout summer. SE Australia. I before 1857. AM 1936.

G. junipera 'Sulphurea' MS – E – O
Bright green needle leaves and brilliant yellow flowers in terminal racemes in summer. New South Wales. AM 1974.

G. rosmarinifolia MS – E – O
The "Red Rosemary" has aromatic deep green needle leaves and crimson flowers in long terminal racemes from December to May. SE Australia. I about 1822. AM 1932.

GRINDELIA CHILOENSIS SS – E – O

A tender, evergreen sub-shrub, but survives a surprising amount of cold in very dry, sharply drained soil in full sun. Hoary, wavy narrow leaves and large yellow flowers like cornflowers borne singly on stout stems throughout the summer into autumn. Argentina. I about 1850. AM 1931.

GRISELINIA LITTORALIS ɪs – ᴇ – ᴏ

This handsome, decorative native of New Zealand should be easy in a seaside garden, but it does need richer living than thin dry sand, and would appear to resent close planting with other species. When fully gratified it is totally wind and salt tolerant, making excellent protective hedging. The leathery leaves are bright apple green. Not entirely hardy even on the coast. It will transplant well when large. I about 1850. AGM 1984.

G.l. 'Dixon's Cream'
A sport from Jersey with leaves mottled with creamy-white.

G.l. 'Variegata'
Leaves margined white. AM 1978.

X HALIMIOCISTUS

Attractive hybrid of halimium and cistus: they will survive cold winters in full sun and the driest soil – full sun is vital.

h. 'Ingwersenii' ᴅs – ᴇ – ᴏ
Spreading shrub with dark green, linear, hairy leaves and white flowers. Portugal. I about 1929.

h. *sahucci* ᴅs – ᴇ – ᴏ
Spreading with narrow leaves and white flowers throughout summer. S France. I about 1929. AGM 1984.

h. *wintonensis* ᴅs – ᴇ – ᴏ
Large flowers with yellow blotches at the base of white petals which are further delicately marked with maroon. Foliage grey. Originated in Hillier Nurseries. I about 1910. AM 1926. AGM 1984.

The variety **'Merrist Wood Cream'** is a sport found in 1978 with a basic flower colour of pale creamy-yellow.

HALIMIUM

These charming, low shrubs are Mediterranean plants mostly, and are demanding of hot, arid conditions in full sun when they will be relatively hardy. They have no objection to chalk.

H. alyssoides SS – E – O
A spreading mound former with tangled branches bearing small, grey, downy leaves and small bright yellow saucer flowers in terminal corymbs for a long summer period.

H. commutatum DS – E – O
A pretty small shrub with small narrow leaves, shiny above, hairy beneath and masses of mostly singly borne yellow flowers in June.

H. lasianthum SS – E – O
A totally hardy, widely spreading and very attractive shrub, the whole covered in grey-white down and hairs, and masses of bright, rich yellow flowers with brown-purple blotches near the base of each petal in May and June. An excellent ground cover for dry banks. I 1780. AM 1951.
The variety **'Sandling'** has crescent shaped red blotches.

H. ocymoides DS – E – O
An attractive erect shrub whose young shoots are covered with white down. Leaves small and pale grey; flowers bright rich yellow with brown basal blotches in May June. C1800. AGM 1984.

HALIMODENDRON HALODENDRON

An unusual shrub with attractive small, silver-grey leaves and abundant pale purple-pink pea-flowers in short racemes in June and July: very spiny. It is a native of Russian Central Asia and so is hardy. Known as the "Salt Bush", it grows in the sands bordering the Caspian Sea, the steppe region north of the Black Sea and the flood plains around the Aral Sea and Lake Balkash. It is perfectly happy, obviously, in a maritime position on pure sand. I by Dr. William Pitcairn in 1779.

HEBE

The genus *Hebe* ("Shrubby Veronica") contains about 100 species of evergreen shrubs and small trees, mainly natives of New Zealand. Some are tender, especially the hybrids, but generally they are ideal coastal plants, their leathery leaves imparting tolerance to wind and salt, and being well adapted to dry, sandy soil. They hybridise with gay abandon and spectacular results, the innumerable garden varieties having a wide range of colour of flower produced abundantly in terminal racemes over very long periods. They have no soil preference, but are hardier on poor soil in full sun. They are easily propagated by cuttings, and transplant well. There are approximately 370 species and varieties listed in *"The Plant Finder"*. The current Hillier catalogues lists 47 available for sale. All are worth growing, and so take your pick from an incredible variety of form and flower colour.

Those mentioned below are only a representative selection, chosen mainly for accolades awarded by the RHS and their diversity.

H. *albicans* DS
A dense, rounded shrub with glaucous leaves and white flower spikes throughout summer. Very decorative and hardy. I about 1880. AGM 1984.

H. 'Alicia Amhurst' SS
A beautiful tender *H. speciosa* hybrid with long spikes of deep purple-blue flowers in late summer. Raised by Veitch in 1911. AGM 1984.

H. x andersonii 'Variegata' MS
Vigorous with long leaves margined and splashed with creamy-white and long spikes of soft lavender-blue flowers fading to white from August to September. C1887. AGM 1984.

H. armstrongii (cf *H. ochracea*) DS
This is a "whipcord" species with tiny olive-green leaves tinged with orange at the tips on blackish stems and white flowers on short racemes in July and August. Unusual and hardy. AM 1925.

H. 'Autumn Glory' SS
A hardy shrub of open habit with vivid violet short flower spikes in late summer and autumn. C1900. AGM 1984.

H. buchananii DS
A rock garden sort with tiny round leaves and small white flowers in clusters of three or four spikes in June and July. AMT 1982.

H. 'Carnea' SS
Long racemes of rose-pink flowers fading to white from May throughout summer. C1881. AM 1925. The variety 'Variegata' has grey-green leaves margined white.

H. cupressoides SS to MS
Compact with long slender green or grey branches like a cypress bearing small pale blue flowers profusely in June and July. FCC 1894.
The variety 'Boughton Dome' is dwarf and rounded. FCCT 1982. AGM 1984.

H. 'Emerald Green' ('Green Globe') DS
A recent discovery from the Ruahine Mountains, New Zealand. A pretty little compact, globular shrub with upright branches densely covered in tiny, brilliant green, glossy leaves. Small white flowers in summer.

H. x franciscana 'Blue Gem' SS
Compact shrub with thick leathery leaves and profuse racemes of bright blue flowers. Hardy in all except the most severe

winters, and commonly used as a hedging plant. FCC 1869. AGM 1984.

The variety **'Variegata'** has leaves broadly margined with white and is less compact: deserves better than its usual treatment as a popular but transient inhabitant of a window box.

H. **'Great Orme'** SS
Lanceolate leaves and long tapering racemes of bright pink flowers. Excellent and comparatively hardy. AGM 1984.

H. **'Hagley Park'** DS
Upright shrub with toothed, red margined, glossy leaves and large panicles of rose-purple flowers in early summer. AM 1976.

H. hulkeana SS
Oval, dark green, glossy leaves on a shrub of open habit. Large panicles of pale lavender-blue flowers profusely borne in May and June. FCC 1882.

H. **'La Seduisante'** SS
Lives up to its name with large racemes of bright crimson flowers. Leaves dark and glossy, purple tinged when young. AM 1897.

H. macrantha DS
Tender but most unusual for very large white flowers. Leathery, toothed leaves. AM 1952.

H. **'Midsummer Beauty'** SS
Leaves light green, reddish beneath and long racemes of lavender flowers throughout summer. Very attractive. AM 1960. FCC 1974. AGM 1984.

H. **'Mrs. Windsor'** SS to MS
Purple leaves and bright blue flowers. Effective and reasonably hardy. AM 1978. AMT 1982. AGM 1984.

H. ochracea (cf *H. armstrongii*) DS
A "whipcord" species very similar to *H. armstrongii* but more pronounced old gold colour to leaves which are pointed.

White flowers in July and August. AMT 1982. AGM 1984.

The variety 'James Stirling' has thicker branches and brighter foliage but loses out on the elegance of the type. AMT 1982. AGM 1984.

H. 'Pewter Dome' DS
Dome shaped with grey-green leaves and short racemes of white flowers in early summer. AGM 1984.

H. *pinguifolia* 'Pagei' PS
Spreading, prostrate shrub with small glaucous-grey leaves and small but profuse white flowers in May. Tends to die off in centre with age, otherwise good ground cover. AM 1958. AMT 1982. AGM 1984.

H. 'Purple Queen' SS
Tender but choice with large racemes of purple flowers. AM 1893.

H. *rakaiensis* DS
Very hardy, dense and compact with small, pale green leaves and masses of short racemes of white flowers in June and July. Excellent ground cover. AMT 1982. AGM 1984.

H. *recurva* SS
Slender and of open habit with lanceolate, glaucous leaves and narrow racemes of white flowers. AM 1972.

The variety 'Boughton Silver' is dwarf and compact with vivid, silvery-blue leaves.

H. *salicifolia* MS
Bright green, willow-like leaves and long racemes of white or lilac-tinted flowers from June to August. Unusual and useful for its size and relative hardiness. AMT 1982.

The variety 'Variegata' has leaves margined creamy-white.

H. 'Simon Delaux' SS
Rounded habit with large racemes of deep crimson flowers. AGM 1984.

H. 'Spender's Seedling' SS
Very hardy with profuse white flowers throughout summer which are uniquely fragrant. AM 1954. AMT 1982.

H. 'Youngii' (*H.* 'Carl Teschner') DS
Compact and hardy with small lanceolate leaves and abundant short racemes of violet flowers with white throats in June and onwards. AM 1964. AGM 1984.

HELIANTHEMUM

These native of the Mediterranean region, the "Rock Roses" or "Sun Roses", are only suited to the hottest, driest spots in the garden. They are prostrate, evergreen and spreading, and absolutely require a sharply drained soil. In nature they usually occur on limestone. The small, brilliantly colourful flowers appear in May and June in great profusion with a lesser quantity throughout summer, but only open in sunshine and are at their best on hot afternoons. Each flower has a single day's life span. Easily propagated by cuttings, and they should be trimmed after flowering. The outstanding sorts are nearly all garden hybrids of three species; *H. appeninum*, *H. nummularium* and *H. croceum*. They have small, silver, evergreen leaves and double or single flowers in a great range of colour – through all shades of yellow to red; white, rose and scarlet. Try them all, but below is a small selection to demonstrate their potential.

H. 'Ben Nevis'
Green foliage and deep buttercup-yellow flowers with bronze-crimson centre zones. AM 1924. AMT 1924.

H. 'Fire Dragon'
Grey-green leaves and bright orange-scarlet flowers. AGM 1984.

H. 'Jubilee'
Green foliage and drooping, double, primrose-yellow flowers. AMT 1970. AGM 1984.

H. 'The Bride'
Silver-grey leaves and creamy-white flowers with bright yellow centres. AM 1924. AMT 1924. AGM 1984.

H. 'Watergate Rose'
Grey-green leaves and rose-crimson flowers with orange-tinged centres. AMT 1932.

H. 'Wisley Pink'
Grey foliage and soft pink flowers. AGM 1984.

H. 'Wisley Primrose'
Light grey-green leaves and primrose yellow flowers with deeper yellow centres. AMT 1970. AGM 1984.

H. 'Wisley White'
Narrow grey leaves and clear white flowers with golden anthers.

HELICHRYSUM

Marvellous white to grey leaved, evergreen plants for the seaside, revelling in the hottest, driest, poorest soil. Only one species is recognised as being sufficiently shrubby, i.e. woody, by Bean, the remainder being classified as herbs, but all worthwhile sorts are included here for convenience. Many of the species from New Zealand and Australia are now treated as a separate genus, *Ozothamnus*.

Propagation is easy by cuttings. Plants should be cut back hard in April, and trimmed in late summer to keep them neat and bushy.

H. italicum DS
A very attractive plant with small, narrow, silvery-grey leaves and long clusters of small, bright yellow flowerheads throughout summer. Mediterranean seabord.

H.i. subsp. serotinum *(H. angustifolium)* DS
The "Curry Plant" is distinguished by its strong aroma redolent of long, languorous summer afternoons; much more pleasing

than that emanating from the local "Star of India". Small, narrow, silvery leaves and relatively insignificant yellow flowerheads in summer. S Europe. AGM 1984.

H. petiolare PS

Long, trailing, woody white stems and oval, grey, woolly leaves with yellow flowers late in the season. Tender, but can survive a mild winter in very dry soil. Commonly used as a dispensable foil for bright flowering plants in a summer container. S Africa. AM 1987.

H. plicatum DS

Silvery-white with long, narrow, downy leaves and terminal clusters of bright yellow flowers in mid-summer. Tender. S Europe. I 1877.

H. splendidum SS

A distinguished, white-woolly shrub up to 6' in the wild, but usually only 3' in this country. Leaves linear, woolly on both sides and bright yellow "everlasting" flowers well into winter. Prune well to maintain globular habit. Remarkably hardy for its S African origin. AGM 1984.

HIBISCUS

Definitely plants for hot, dry gardens only, and painfully slow growers taking up to three years or more to settle in and flower. The late mallow-like flowers, single or double,in a wide range of colours, are very attractive and quite profuse in a hot summer in full sun, but for the rest of the year the 5' to 10' bushes are leggy with sparse foliage: surely "back of the border" shrubs where their skinniness is less apparent. Hardy, but they need a warm wall in cold areas to develop flowers. Deciduous. Propagation is easy from cuttings, and they do not have any soil preferences.

H. *sinosyriacus* MS

More vigorous and spreading than *H. syriacus* with larger leaves and flowers, otherwise very similar. China. Described in 1922.

Available varieties include:

'**Autumn Surprise**', white flowers with feathered cerise bases to petals.

'**Lilac Queen**', lilac flowers with garnet-red bases.

H. *syriacus* MS

Upright habit. Grown in England since the 16th century. From China and India via Syria.

Varieties include:

'**Blue Bird**', violet blue single flowers with darker eye AM 1965. AGM 1984.

'**Diana**', single white flowers with crimped petals. AGM 1984.

'**Red Heart**', large with flowers with prominent red eyes. AGM 1984.

'**Woodbridge**', strong growing; single, rose-pink flowers with crimson centres. AM 1937. AGM 1984.

HIPPOPHAË RHAMNOIDES MS – D – O

The "Sea Buckthorn" is an excellent wind-break in any soil. Leaves are small and narrow, silver-green on twiggy, spiny branches. The flowers are inconspicuous, but females bear profuse orange berries throughout the winter. Very decorative. Being unisexual, group planting is best at a ratio of six female to one upwind male as the pollen is air-borne. The magnificent fruits are not appreciated by birds. Propagation by seed or layering. Europe and temperate Asia AM 1944. AGM 1984.

The palm tree was planted in our French garden when I was born. Neither of us appear to be thriving: I survived, the palm didn't!

The appearance of the first water skiers I had seen, wearing the first bikinis, didn't impress me much: at that age I preferred chasing butterflies.

The 'Sun Rose' *Cistus palhinhae* from Portugal is hardy in the south in full sun, bearing its delicate flowers in great profusion in early summer.

The tender *Chrysanthemum frutescens*, 'French Marguerite', dons a dazzling display in high summer.

A powerful climber, *Rosa filipes* 'Kiftsgate' puts up with wind and drought.

Hydrangea macrophylla prefers the deep, well-cultivated soil of this old farm land but the stout 'Shasta Daisy', *Chrysanthemum maximum*, will thrive in poor conditions.

The 'Double Sea Campion', *Silene maritima* 'Flore Pleno', sprawls happily over a hot wall but requires adequate soil around its roots.

Poor, chalky soil suits the 'Mock Orange' *Philadelphus* 'Virginal' perfectly given enough sun, when it produces its richly fragrant double flowers in June and July.

Happy in dry shade, *Helleborus corsicus* has handsome, evergreen, pale leaves and bears massive panicles of yellow-green flowers in March and April.

HOHERIA

A beautiful genus from New Zealand which thrives on any soil, and tolerates a modicum of wind. They dislike dry soil, but produce leaves at the expense of flowers if it is too rich. If you can provide the right conditions they are quite the most spectacular shrubs with masses of star-shaped, white, fragrant flowers in July. Although quite hardy, they prefer to be warm. They are fast-growing and best increased from seed.

H. angustifolia ST – E – O
Columnar habit; dense and bushy when young with minute, oval leaves and profuse small flowers. Mature plants have long, narrow leaves. AM 1967.

H. glabrata LS – D – O
The "Mountain Ribbonwood" weighs down its branches with quite remarkable quantities of flowers in June and July. C1871. AM 1911. FCC 1946. AGM 1984.

H. 'Glory of Amlwch' LS to ST – SE – O
A hybrid (H. glabrata x H. sexstylosa) which flowers profusely, and is evergreen given a mild winter. AM 1960.

H. lyallii LS to ST – D – O
Also "Mountain Ribbonwood" with shiny juvenile leaves becoming densely hairy with maturity. Profuse, cherry-like flowers in July. AM 1955. FCC 1964. AGM 1984.

H. populnea LS to ST – E – O
A tender and quite spectacular plant, the "Lacebark" has broad oval leaves, and bears profuse clusters of flowers in late summer and autumn. AM 1912.
    Varieties include:

'Alba Variegata', creamy-white margined leaves. AM 1976.

'Foliis Purpureis', underside of leaves plum-purple. AM 1977.

H. sexstylosa LS to ST — E — O
Vigorous; similar to *H. populnea* but hardier and more upright. FCC 1924. AM 1964. AM 1984.

HYDRANGEA

Hydrangeas are generally poor plants for the seaside. As their name suggests they are moisture lovers, and deeply resent the dessicating winds and sandy soils of maritime areas. Given retentive soil and shelter, they would, however, appreciate the mild climate as long as their roots were protected from direct sunlight and drought. You may be lucky enough to be able to offer these prerequisites, in which case it would be worthwhile experimenting with the easier species and garden varieties of this wonderfully ornamental genus.

For most of us there is only one sort which succeeds: this is **H. macrophylla var. normalis**, the wild plant found on the coast and the islands near Tokyo. Strangely the first specimen arrived in Europe from China around 1788: it was given to Kew by Sir Joseph Banks, and identified and described by Sir James Smith in 1792. Apparently Chinese gardeners had long cultivated it, but it was little appreciated in its own country. It rapidly became popular in the milder parts of the British Isles, and Loudon in 1838 describes seeing a specimen "as big as a large haycock." It is this hydrangea, now named **'Sir Joseph Banks'**, that is still a familiar sight in many long-established seaside gardens.

H. macrophylla var. normalis grows up to 10' in the wild, but is usually no more than 4' to 6' in this country unless especially happy. It is the archetypal "mop-head" with the original flat corymbs of pink or blue flowers on stout branches which are pale green when young. The leaves are broad-ovate and 4" to 8" long, rather fleshy, and are retained throughout winter unless frosted. In shallow chalky soils it can be chlorotic: this is overcome by generous feeding and mulching. Alkaline soils give pink flowers; acid, blue flowers.

The variety **'Sea Foam'** is a small to medium-sized shrub with bluish-pink flowers and vivid green leaves.

Increase by cuttings. Cut off dead flower heads, and remove two to three year old flowered shoots at ground level to promote new growth.

HYPERICUM

Despised because they are good-natured and accommodating, the hypericums nevertheless have considerable intrinsic charm with highly ornamental, invariably yellow flowers in late summer and attractive foliage retained throughout mild winters. Although they thrive in any type of light soil, they do generally prefer moisture and acid conditions. They grow well in full sun or half-shade. Not plants for arid hot spots, but they usually tolerate drought if part shaded. Propagate by cuttings, but this can be difficult.

H. calycinum DS – E
The "Rose of Sharon" has large leaves and large golden flowers. Invasive if let loose, but excellent for clothing dry, shady areas. SE Bulgaria, N Turkey. I 1676. AM 1978. AGM 1984.

H. empetrifolium DS – E
A shrublet of some delicacy in appearance, the golden yellow flowers borne in erect panicles during summer. Unusual in its preference for hot, sunny, dry positions. Greece. I 1788. AM 1937.

H. forrestii SS – D
Typical, saucer shaped flowers profusely borne and rich coloured foliage in early winter. Introduced by George Forrest in 1906. SW China. NE Burma. AM 1922. AGM 1984.

H. 'Hidcote' MS – SE
A hybrid of *H. x cyathiflorum* 'Gold Cup' and *H. calycinum*, an excellent compact plant with typical profuse flowers in late summer and autumn. Deservedly popular. AM 1954.

H. kouytchense SS – SE

Rounded habit, compact with profuse large flowers having particularly long stamens. Bright red fruits. China. AGM 1984.

H. x moserianum DS – D

Arching stems and large flowers with reddish anthers. Good ground cover. A hybrid of *H. calycinum* and *H. patulum*. FCC 1891. AGM 1984.

The variety 'Tricolor' has white, pink and green variegated leaves. AM 1896.

H. olympicum DS – D

A sub-shrub with small, glaucous leaves and bright yellow flowers in terminal clusters in summer. Balkan peninsula, Turkey. I 1675. AGM 1984.

The variety 'Citrinum' has attractive pale yellow flowers. AGM 1984.

H. 'Rowallane' MS – SE

Quite the most distinguished of the breed, this graceful shrub needs all its preferences met to attain its potential; shelter, warmth, moisture and a light acid soil. If pleasured it will produce very large, bowl-shaped, rich gold-yellow flowers of beautiful form. It will be cut down by frost, but will regenerate from the base. It arose as a chance self-sown seedling at Rowallane, Co. Down. AM 1943. AGM 1984.

HYSSOPUS OFFICINALIS DS – SE

The Hyssop, the "holy herb", has been grown as a medicinal plant from biblical times: it is still to be found naturalised on the walls of Beaulieu Abbey where it was probably cultivated by the Cistercian monks in the 13th century. The "Ysope" was described in the *"Feate of Gardening"* before 1440, and was valued as a means of driving away "the winde that is in the eares, if they be holden over it", and as a "countrey people's medicine for a cut or greene wound, being bruised with sugar and applyed." It is also a vital constituent in the preparation of the monkish anodynes *Chartreuse* and *Eau de Cologne.* Being highly aromatic, it was one of the herbs strewn on malignly odiferous medieval floors, and survived in Tudor and Elizabethan times as an important plant in the knot garden. It remains an excellent, but undeservedly neglected shrub for a low, informal hedge.

It is a native of the Mediterranean region, appreciating warm, light, sandy soil, and is variable, but is generally an upright shrub with small linear leaves of a rich green and rough overall. The bluish purple flowers are borne in profuse terminal panicles, and open from mid-summer to September. Forms include:

H. albus, white flowers.

H. aristatus, smooth, bright green leaves and dense flower spikes.

H. purpurascens *(H. ruber),* red flowers.

Propagate by cuttings and trim in spring.

IBERIS

The shrubby, perennial "Candytufts" are evergreen miniatures for the most hostile positions; the drier and stonier the better, where they can be thoroughly baked. The early summer flowers are prolific and carried in flat, round terminal umbels. The leaves are small and linear, grey-green; typical of heat tolerant plants. They are happy on calcareous soils.

"Iberis" means the flower of Spain. "Candytuft" refers to another supposed country or origin, Candia – the ancient name for Crete. In fact they are indigenous to the whole of S Europe, spreading into W Asia..

They are easily propagated by cuttings and should be trimmed over after flowering.

I. gibraltarica DS

A spreading shrublet up to 3' in diameter. Flowers are white or reddish-lilac borne from May to July. Natives of S Spain and Morocco, including Gibraltar, where it grows in the scantiest soil on cliffs. I 1732.

I. sempervirens DS

Spreading, with white flowers freely borne from April to June. Narrower leaves. Remarkably hardy if in ideal conditions, and exceptionally neat and decorative. Cultivated as early as 1739 in the Chelsea Physic Garden, it derives its name from its Persian reputation for being totally impervious to hardship, being the symbol of indifference in the oriental language of flowers.

JUNIPERUS

The "Junipers" are an incredibly diverse race, ranging from prostrate to tall, columnar forms. All are evergreen and unfailingly decorative, having a wonderful array of foliage colour. These conifers are invariably slow-growing, and are valued in the small inland garden for this property, and for the compact and neat habit of many of the varieties. The dinky sorts are not suitable subjects for the rough and tumble of the windy seaside garden: in this situation the prostrate forms come into their own, and are ideal for covering dry sunny banks on alkaline soils where they are excellent substitutes for calcifuge heathers and heaths. They are universally hardy. The following species are representative of a wide choice.

J. communis subsp. depressa DS

The "Canadian Juniper" is wide spreading and dense with yellowish to brownish-green foliage with silver backs turning bronze in winter. The following varieties are choice:

'**Depressa Aurea**', foliage and shoots gold in early summer. C1887. AGM 1984.

'**Hornibrookii**', a contour following creeper with sharply pointed leaves silvery-white beneath. From Ireland. C1923. AGM 1984.

'**Repanda**', a dense, carpeting shrub with leaves which bronze in winter. From Ireland. C1934. AGM 1984.

J. conferta PS

The "Shore Juniper" from Japan's sandy seashores forms large areas of dense, bright apple-green prickly leaves, which contrast well with the dark green varieties of *J. communis* and the grey and blue varieties of *J. horizontalis*. I 1915 by Ernest Wilson. The variety '**Blue Pacific**' has glaucous foliage and is even more prostrate and less prickly.

J. horizontalis PS

The "Creeping Juniper" forms extensive carpets of foliage in varying shades of blue-green often turning purple in winter. A native of the cliffs of N America. C1830. AGM 1984.

The following are good varieties:

'**Bar Harbor**', very prostrate, grey-blue-green tiny leaves. C1930. AGM 1984.

'**Blue Chip**', bright blue leaves. I 1940 from Denmark.

'**Montana**', dense, plumose branchlets with scaly leaves of an intense blue. Highly recommended by Hillier.

'**Plumosa**', dense and compact with grey-green leaves turning purple in winter. C1919. AGM 1984.

'**Wiltonii**' ('Blue Rug'), one of the best carpeters, flat and bright blue. C1914. AGM 1984.

J. x media '**Pfitzeriana Aurea**' SS

A taller, wide spreading sort, the "Golden Pfitzer" is golden-yellow in summer, yellowish-green in winter. I from America in 1923.

INDIGOFERA

This is mostly a scarce genus in cultivation, and is hence little known. It deserves to be popular in mild areas, being highly decorative with profuse pea-like flowers of varying shades of pink or purple, borne in axillary racemes on the current year's growth, giving a long flowering period from mid to late summer. The species are all deciduous with elegant pinnate leaves. The shoots tend to be annual in colder areas, but regenerate generously the following spring: this in any case keeps them bushy, and, if the shoots survive, they are best cut back after flowering. They are not coastal plants in the wild, and so protect from strong winds. They are happiest on dry, light to medium soil in full sun, and appear not to object to chalk. Propagation by cuttings in a slightly heated frame.

I. amblyantha MS − D − O
As like *I. potaninii* as to make no difference. Long racemes of clear shrimp-pink flowers from June to September. China. Introduced by William Purdom in 1908.

I. hebepetala MS − D − O
Wide-spreading with distinctive flowers of rose-pink with deep crimson standards in long racemes in August and September. NW Himalaya. Cultivated at Kew since 1881, but undeservedly neglected.

I. heterantha *(I. gerardiana)* SS to MS − D − O
The most commonly available sort. In mild areas grows up to 10' on a wall, but is usually cut down in winter, and forms thickets of well-clothed luxuriant shoots 2' to 4' high. Racemes of medium length, rosy-purple flowers from July to September. NW Himalaya. C1840. AM 1977. AGM 1984.

I. kirilowii DS to SS − D − O
Long, dense racemes of bright almond-pink flowers on erect stems in June and July. Bright green hairy leaves. N China, Korea, S Japan. I before 1914.

I. pseudotinctoria MS – D – O

Vigorous, similar to *I. amblyantha*, pink flowers in long dense racemes from June to September. I 1897 by Augustine Henry. AM 1965.

LAURUS NOBILIS LS TO st – e – o

The "Sweet Bay" is the laurel of antiquity, cultivated in Britain since at least the 16th century. Sacred to Apollo, it was used for the crowns of conquering heroes and for wreaths for successful poets, hence "poet laureate" It has given its name in more recent times to the academic "bachelor" and "baccalaureate" and the military "knight-bachelor" (Laurel-berry = Latin, *bacca-laureus* = French, *bachelier*). The aromatic leaves have long been used as culinary flavouring, as a remedy for bruises and rheumatism, as an antiseptic, a mild narcotic and as an insect repellent and fumigant. Obviously a useful plant to have around!

"Psalms" has the ungodly "flourishing like a green bay-tree", and, being of Mediterranean origin, this is definitely what it does in a warm seaside garden, where it is remarkably wind resistant as long as it is not exposed to chilling gales. Some leaves will brown if the temperature drops too low, but, left unchecked by nature or shears, it will grow to 40' or more. It is naturally of a dense pyramidal shape with dark, glossy green leaves, small greenish yellow flowers and shiny, black berries. It does not resent being clipped to shape, and makes an excellent hedge. C1562. AGM 1984.

Varieties available are:

L.n. 'Angustifolia' ('Salicifolia'), the "Willow-leaf Bay" has long, narrow, leathery pale green leaves with wavy edges. It is hardier than the type.

L.n. 'Aurea' has gold leaves which are very attractive in spring and winter.

LAVANDULA

Lavenders are the ideal maritime plants, flourishing in dry, sandy soil and full sun. They are native herbs of the Mediterranean region, W Asia, NE Africa and India, and are highly aromatic, making excellent dwarf hedges being tolerant of clipping.

L. angustifolia, "Old English Lavender", was described in the 13th century in the *"Book of the Physicians of Myddvai"*, and it is reasonable to suppose it was introduced by the Romans. It was not at all valued as a decorative plant in those days, being grown for all manner of practical uses. "Lavandula" derives from the Latin *lavandus*, "to be washed", which probably refers to the oil being used to perfume baths. The harvested flower heads were sprinkled among stored clothes and linen, no doubt to disguise obnoxious aromas before the days of dry cleaning and washing machines, and had the additional benefit of being insect repellent (moths, lice and fleas!)

Medicinally it was used for "diseases of the head that come of a cold cause, and comforte the brayne very well": for this it was recommended that the flowers should be "quilted in a cappe and daylye worne". It was prescribed in various forms for "the panting and passion of the hart" and for "them that use to swoune much." And that was only the beginning! Now the world in general knows that in lavender water tinged with pink there's nothing so good for a Pobble's toes.

Although the growing and the distilling of lavender is an industry in the South of France, surprisingly the aromatic oil is more fragrant from plants grown in this country. At one time there were 300 acres of lavender grown near Mitcham in Surrey alone.

L. angustifolia *(L. spica)* SS – E – O
The typical lavender blue flowers in dense spikes on long slender stems. AMT 1962.
Varieties include:

L. 'Alba', much favoured by Queen Henrietta Maria, vigorous, with long, narrow grey green leaves and white flowers in July.

L. 'Folgate', compact, narrow grey-green leaves and lavender-blue flowers in early July. C1933. AMT 1963.

L. 'Hidcote', compact, narrow grey-green leaves and dense spikes of violet flowers in early July. Popular. AM 1950. FCCT 1963. AGM 1984.

L. 'Hidcote Giant', vigorous, strong stems bearing dark lavender-blue flowers in late July. C1950. AGM 1984.

L. 'Loddon Pink', compact, flowers pale pink in early July. C1950. AMT 1963.

L. 'Munstead', raised by Gertrude Jekyll needless to say, compact with brighter blue flowers. C1916. AM 1955. AMT 1963.

L. 'Twickel Purple', compact with comparatively broad leaves and purple flowers in early July. AMT 1961. AGM 1984.

L. 'Vera', the "Dutch Lavender", vigorous with lavender blue flowers in late July. AMT 1962.

All varieties should have flowering stems trimmed off in late summer, and should be clipped to shape in early spring. Propagation is easy by cuttings.

L. stoechas DS − E − O
"French Lavender" is very aromatic with narrow leaves and dark purple flowers on uniquely shaped terminal heads. Definitely a plant for the warmest, driest position. Mediterranean region. Cultivated since the 16th century. AM 1960.
  Varieties include:

L.s. var. leucantha *(albiflora)*, flowers white.

L.s. subsp. pedunculata, flower spikes shorter on long stems. AM 1981.

LAVATERA

This is quite the most perfect genus for a warm seaside garden with all the characteristics you could hope for if you had designed it yourself: wonderfully decorative flowers over a long summer period; handsome foliage; tall quick, vigorous growth on poor sandy soil; resistant to the strongest winds; revels in salty air. The one problem is nomenclature. Here has been adopted the descriptions given by Hillier, which do not necessarily agree with Bean. *"The Plant Finder"* is wisely non-committal. The best and most vigorous of the type with large bright pink flowers was called *L. olbia*, but now is probably bought as *L. thuringiaca* 'Kew Rose'. This might seem pernickety, but, believe you me, it is important if you are seeking strength and flower power: at its best the plant develops into a small tree with a substantial trunk 3' or more in height, from which springs 6' stems carrying axillary flowers for up to 2' of their length from mid-summer or earlier through until autumn – a truly magnificent sight. Once experienced, you will not be satisfied with less.

The genus is deciduous, and is said to be short-lived, flowering and seeding itself to an early demise: this can be ameliorated by cutting back the stems to the trunk after flowering and before seed is set. It undoubtedly performs best on poor soil with sharp drainage in full sun: never feed it.

The leaves are palmate and downy. The flowers are universally mallow-shaped. All varieties are easily propagated by cuttings.

L. maritima (L. bicolor) MS – D – O
Tender and best against a warm wall. Elegant habit with large, pale lilac flowers with purple eyes and veined petals from mid-summer to autumn. SW Europe, N Africa.

L. thuringiaca LS – to ST – D – O
Vigorous and downy overall. Large pink flowers throughout summer. C and S Europe to the W Himalaya. AM 1912.

The following are choice varieties:

L.t. 'Barnsley', flowers almost white with red eyes. Not as vigorous as the type but decorative. AM 1986.

L.t. 'Burgundy Wine', flowers deep purple-pink.

L.t. 'Candy Floss', flowers palest pink.

L.t. 'Ice Cool', white flowers.

L.t. 'Kew Rose', vigorous, many stems dark purple and large bright pink flowers. Previously known as *Lavatera olbia*. AM 1988.

L.t. 'Rosea', pale pink flowers. AM 1920. AGM 1984.

(The true *L. olbia* is a soft-stemmed shrub from the Mediterranean. It has a lax habit, especially if over-fed and watered, and is more at home at the back of an herbaceous border, where its lack of elegance is less obvious).

LEIOPHYLLUM BUXIFOLIUM DS – E – ◗

An attractive little shrub with tiny, dark-green, leathery, box-like leaves and small star-shaped white flowers with prominent stamens in terminal clusters in May and June. The "Sand Myrtle", uncommon in cultivation, is a native of east North America spreading into the mountains of the Carolinas, E Kentucky and Tennessee. It thrives in semi-shade and an acid soil and is hardy. Top-dress regularly with peat. Propagate by seed or cuttings. I 1736. AM 1955.

The variety **'prostratum'** differs in having opposite rather than alternate leaves which are larger, and, although variable, tends to be more spreading. AM 1945.

LEONOTIS LEONURUS (L. OXYMIFOLIA) SS to MS – D – O

The "South African Lion's Tail" is, needless to say, tender, but will survive reasonably well in a mild maritime environment on very sandy, sharply drained soil in full sun. It has unusual square stems, downy lance-shaped leaves and large whorls of downy bright orange flowers from August to October. The protection of a wall or hedge is necessary. Well worth trying for its late flowering and exotic looks. I 1712. AM 1982.

LEPTOSPERMUM

These are the "Tea Trees" or "Manukas" of New Zealand and Australia. They are exceptionally elegant and attractive evergreen shrubs with small leaves and hawthorn-like flowers in a range of colour from white through pink to red, borne profusely in early summer. Unfortunately they are generally tender, and only to be considered in warm gardens in the south and west, where they will also require neutral to acid soil. They are perfectly resistant to wind, but will not tolerate exposure to cold gales. If you can please them with these conditions, and you can give them full sun, and room to develop their wide-spreading root systems, they are really rewarding: truly Antipodean aristocrats!

They will not transplant, and must be grown from small potted specimens. Easily increased by cuttings.

L. humifusum *(L. rupestre, L. scoparium var. prostratum)* PS – E – O
Exceptional in as much as it is extremely hardy. Its red-tinged stems are widely spreading, and the small leaves are bronze-purple in really cold periods; covered in small white flowers in early summer. The spread of one plant can be as much as 10' across, and is a beautiful sight in flower. Useful for a dry wall. Tasmania. I 1930.

L. lanigerum LS to ST – E – O
Erect with slender twigs covered with pale hairs. The longer leaves are pointed and usually silky, occasionally shiny above. White flowers on leafy side growths from June. It will not survive a really hard winter. Tasmania. I 1774. AGM 1984.

The variety **'Silver Sheen'** has silver leaves and reddish stems, flowering later, and is hardier.

L. scoparium MS to LS – E – O

A compact, rounded sort; very twiggy. Leaves small, lance-shaped and pointed. White flowers in spring. It thrives in warm, maritime areas, but will succumb to a hard frost. Australia, New Zealand. I 1772. AM 1972.

There are many forms and garden cultivars. The following is a selection of the choicer sorts:

L.s. 'Chapmanii' MS – E – O

Bronze-coloured foliage and deep rose red flowers.

L.s. 'Keatleyi' MS – E – O

Large soft pink flowers. Immature leaves and shoots silky crimson. AM 1961. AGM 1984.

L.s. 'Kiwi' DS – E – O

Dense habit with profuse deep pink flowers and bronze foliage.

L.s. 'Nanum' DS – E – O

Profuse rose-pink flowers. AM 1952.

L.s. 'Nichollsii Grandiflorum' MS – E – O

Large carmine red flowers and dark bronze purple leaves. A selected form of 'Nichollsii' which received an FCC in 1912 and AM in 1953.

L.s. 'Red Damask' MS – E – O

Double deep red flowers. Raised in California. AM 1955. AGM 1984.

LESPEDEZA THUNBERGII SS to MS – D – O

The "Bush Clover", so named because of its trifoliate leaves, is outstanding, bearing massive and spectacular terminal panicles of rose-purple pea-flowers on semi-woody stems, which are weighed down in graceful arches in September. It is hardy on light sandy soil in a protected position in full sun, and associates well with

Spartium junceum ("Spanish Broom"), which enjoys similar conditions, and is in flower at the same time. It must be cut back hard in early spring. Propagate from small pieces of root stock with roots attached in pots given bottom-peat. N China, Japan. I about 1837 by Siebold. FCC 1871. FCC 1987.

LEYCESTERIA FORMOSA ms – d – o

Named after William Leycester, Chief Justice of Bengal in the early 19th century. He was an avid plantsman who "during a long series of years pursued every branch of horticulture with munificence, zeal and success."

The stems are hollow and as long and straight as canes, covered in a bluish bloom. The leaves are prolific, ovate and pointed, up to 7" long. The drooping flower-spikes are borne on the ends of the shoots from June to September. The flowers themselves are white with prominent claret-coloured bracts, followed by fruits like small, reddish-purple gooseberries.

Its natural habitat is shady forests, but perversely it does much better in this country in full sun where the bracts and berries colour well. Kelway reported that it thrived on her poor, sandy soil in Cornwall. It seeds profusely and spreads itself around generously, and is happy on lime. Cut back hard in spring. Himalaya, W China, E Tibet. I 1824.

LUPINUS ARBOREUS ms – e – o

The Californian "Tree Lupin" is unfairly regarded as a bit on the common side: true, it is profligate with its charms; growing very rapidly from seed, flowering with indecent abandon in the poorest soils in the hottest, most exposed positions, and dying within two or three years from sheer exhaustion, but these are surely not reasons to be niffy. The flowers are typically lupin-like in shades of creamy yellow and are delicately scented, borne in most profusion in June and July. It seeds itself with freedom, and can become naturalised on very sandy soils. Longevity is increased by trimming off seed heads as soon as they appear. There is no better "filler" for a new garden, but it leaves large gaps when it expires. It is perfectly happy in alkaline conditions. C1793. AGM 1984.

The form **'Golden Spire'** has deeper yellow flowers, and **'Snow Queen'** has white flowers. AM 1899.

LYCIUM BARBARUM (L. HALIMIFOLIUM, L. CHINENSE) MS – D – O

The "Chinese Box Thorn" or "Duke of Argyll's Tea Tree"; the latter name referring to the mistaken belief on its introduction in the early 18th century that it was the "Thea" or tea-plant (Miller).

Being exceptionally handsome and obliging, it rapidly became a popular garden plant: it has escaped in many southern maritime areas, and is naturalised, being common on the cliffs, for instance, around Eastbourne and Bournemouth.

The plant is vigorous and rambling with long, occasionally spiny, branches which are arching to prostrate. The leaves are variable in size, shape and colour, from bright green to grey-green. The flowers are purple and funnel shaped, borne from May to July, followed by masses of large scarlet or orange berries in August and September which are truly magnificent.

It is certainly not neat and tidy, but is one of the best and most decorative seaside plants, thriving in full exposure on the driest sand. I about 1700.

MAHONIA AQUIFOLIUM SS – E – O or ●

The popular *M. japonica* finds thin soil too poor to prosper, but its spring flowering relative, *M. aquifolium*, the "Oregon Grape", is perfectly at home on arid sand, in full sun or deep shade, where its handsome, polished pinnate leaves turn a richer red in winter. The flowers are yellow, borne in terminal clusters in spring, followed by very decorative, blue-black berries. W North America. I 1823. AGM 1984.

The variety 'Apollo' is a choice form, more vigorous and spreading, with larger clusters of bright yellow flowers.

MARGYRICARPUS PINNATUS PS – E – O

Although dismissed by Bean as of no great merit, I enjoy my specimen of the "Pearl Berry". It is certainly rare and unusual. Its low spreading branches are densely covered in small pinnate leaves divided into tiny linear leaflets. The flowers are almost invisible, but the small, white, rounded, edible fruits in autumn are quite profuse, and stand out well against the dark green foliage. It is happy in dry soil, cascading over a rockery or wall, in full sun, and is relatively hardy. A native of the Andes and Uruguay and S Brazil. I 1829.

MEDICAGO ARBOREA MS to LS – E – ◗

The "Tree Medick" or "Moon Trefoil", a Mediterranean shrub found in rocky places, would have no place in a seaside plantsman's garden if it were not for its quite remarkable wind tolerance. As underplanting, or on the periphery of groups of taller trees and shrubs, it is a valuable wind-stopper in mild areas.

The profuse trefoil leaves are shiny above, silky beneath, each leaflet being V-shaped in cross-section. The yellow pea-flowers are arranged in short racemes, and appear as the shoots extend from April to autumn continuously, but never in great profusion. The seed pods are shaped like flat rams' horns. The general effect is modest. Remember it is not reliably frost-hardy even by the sea. Easily increased by soft cuttings given bottom heat. I 1596.

METROSIDEROS

Closely related to *Callistemon*, the "Bottlebrushes", this genus is not considered as worthy of a place in Bean, being distinctly tender. However, in the very mildest coastal areas they are remarkably tolerant of salty sea winds. They are spectacularly decorative of leaf and flower, and, if you can tolerate the trauma of losing a totally charming companion to the first fierce frost, then try one of the hardier sorts in the warmest spot you can find. They are substantial shrubs or small trees, and so they are likely to leave a large gap when they inevitably perish. To add to the agony, they are slow to come into flower: only for the truly dedicated and masochistic plantsman! They will put up with lime, but will not thrive on shallow, chalky soil.

M. robusta ST − E − O

This is the "Rata" of New Zealand, a perfectly beautiful tree with a dense habit and round, thick, dark green leaves. The bottlebrush flowers are coppery-scarlet and are borne in late summer. As for its name, it is certainly not robust as regards coolth. AM 1959.

M. umbellata *(M. lucida)* LS to ST − E − O

The "Southern Rata", again from New Zealand, is the hardiest sort, and survives the rigours of Cornwall. It is dense and bushy with small, shiny, dark green leaves like the myrtle and clusters of bright crimson flowers in late summer. It takes literally years to flower, and so much patience is required.

MIMULUS AURANTIACUS MS − E − O

The tender "Shrubby Musk" is bushy and attractive with long, narrow, pointed leaves, dark and shiny above, pale and downy beneath. The flowers are trumpet shaped and variable in colour from yellow to orange, borne throughout the summer. The stems are sticky. It survives well against a warm wall in the south. Tolerates lime. California, Oregon. I late 18th century. AM 1938.

The variety **'puniceus'** has small orange to bright red flowers.

MOLTKIA PETRAEA DS – SE – O

A beautiful small shrub much like a lavender when not in flower. It absolutely requires the driest of well-drained soils in full sun when it produces pendulous clusters of brilliant violet-blue flowers very freely in June and July. It deserves protection from wind and a carefully selected site. Choice and rare. Balkan peninsula. I about 1840. FCC 1871.

There is a hybrid between *M. suffruticosa* and *M. petraea* named **M x. intermedia** which is more readily available.

MYRTUS COMMUNIS LS to ST – E – O

This is the "Myrtle" tree of the Bible and the classical symbol of love and peace sacred to Venus. Wreaths of myrtle were marks of distinction for victors in the Olympic games, and later the Romans used it to garland their poets and playwrights. Today echoes of these ancient associations are found in its traditional place in the bridal bouquet.

Daphne turned herself into a myrtle in the nick of time to escape the lecherous intent of Apollo. This has led to some little botanical confusion as the Greeks now call the myrtle, "Daphne".

It is a profusely leafy shrub, the aromatic leaves being small and elegantly lance-shaped, shiny and dark green. The small flowers are white with a brush of prominent stamens and fragrant, profusely borne in July and August. The fruits are purple-black.

It is only hardy in the mildest areas and even then appreciates the shelter and warmth of a south wall. It succeeds on light soil, and is raised from cuttings given gentle heat. Mediterranean region (probably introduced from Persia or Afghanistan). Known to have been cultivated in England in the 16th century. AM 1972. AGM 1984.

Varieties include:

cv. **'Flore Pleno'** with double flowers.

var. tarentina, the "Tarentum Myrtle" has smaller leaves and profuse flowers which are borne in autumn. The fruits are white. Compact. AM 1977. AGM 1984.

cv. **'Variegata'** has grey-green leaves margined creamy-white.

NOTOSPARTIUM CARMICHAELIAE MS – O

A quite beautiful but tender shrub, the "Pink Broom" is rare even in its native New Zealand habitat. Given a sunny protected site in a warm area, it is apparently easy to please given a light, well-drained soil. It is lime tolerant. The shrub appreciates winter protection when young, but is said to withstand an ordinary winter when a firm woody base has been established.

Only young plants bear tiny sparse leaves: the long, arching, graceful stems are otherwise leafless. The great attraction is in their purplish pink, pea-like flowers borne in terminal racemes in July. Well worth trying. I 1883. FCC 1889.

OLEARIA

This large genus from Australia contains some of the very best evergreen shrubs and trees for the maritime garden, being generally well adapted to drought and wind. However, only a few are totally hardy: the severe winter of 1986 killed the topmost growth of the ubiquitous wind breaks of *O. traversii* in the Channel Islands, but the large majority recovered well, and are now back to their former height.

The olearias are happiest in light, well-drained soil in full sun, and tolerate chalky conditions well.

They are easily propagated by cuttings. Mentioned below is a small selection chosen for their hardiness, decorative value and wind-resistance – not necessarily all found together.

O. avicennifolia MS to LS

A hardy, good hedger with pointed leaves, whitish beneath. The wide corymbs of fragrant white flowers are borne in August and September. The variety **'White Confusion'**, has wavy leaves and profuse flowers.

O. hastii MS

A hardy hedging plant with small leaves and fragrant, off-white flowers in July and August. Not a great beauty, but useful in colder areas for its wind resistance. I 1858. FCC 1873.

O. 'Henry Travers' *(O. semidentata)* MS

Tender, beautiful shrub with grey-green lanceolate leaves, silver beneath, and large, drooping aster-like flowers with purple centres in June. It prefers a moister soil than most. I 1908.

O. ilicifolia MS

A good hardy type with densely borne thick, leathery, toothed leaves, off-white felted beneath and fragrant white flowerheads in June. AM 1972.

O. macrodonta MS to LS

A hardy, strong-growing hedger, the "New Zealand Holly" has sage-green, holly-like leaves, silvery beneath and masses of fragrant white flowers in wide panicles in June. Exceptional in all respects. FCC 1895. AGM 1984.

The variety **'Major'** has larger leaves and flowers. Even better.

O. magalophylla SS

A tender shrub with long, oblong leathery leaves, brown felted beneath, and numerous large heads of white flowers in summer. I 1952. AM 1977.

O. phlogopappa *(O. gunniana, O. stellulata)* MS
The tender Tasmanian "Daisy Bush" bears dense, narrow and toothed, aromatic leaves on erect stems which are smothered in panicles of white flowers in May. I 1848. FCC 1885.

The **"Splendens"** group was introduced by Harold Comber. The flowerheads resemble masses of Michaelmas daisies and there are blue, lavender and rose breaks, named **'Comber's Blue'**, **'Comber's Pink'** and **'Rosea'**. These striking plants need protection from searing winds and salt spray.

O. x scilloniensis MS
This is a fairly tender natural hybrid originating at Tresco in the Scilly Islands. It makes a dense, rounded bush, and is totally enveloped in clear white flowers in May and June. It grows quickly and vigorously, and is hardy by the sea withstanding wind well. Outstanding. AM 1951. AM 1982. AGM 1984.

O. solandri MS
Very unusual for its heath-like appearance with golden, thick and minute leaves and young shoots which are held erect. The small, fragrant white flowers in August are insignificant. Although tender inland, it is remarkably wind and salt tolerant by the sea.

O. traversii ST
Quite outstanding as a windbreak in mild coastal areas: absolutely impervious to salt, and never damaged by the fiercest gale unless the occasional branch is literally torn from the tree, which does not happen often. Added to which it grows reasonably quickly, and thrives in the driest sand. Only succumbs to the coldest conditions.

The leaves are leathery, shiny green above, silvery beneath. Insignificant flowers in summer.

Strikes easily from cuttings. I 1887.

O. 'Zennoriensis' *(O. ilicifolia x O. lacunosa)* MS
A tender elegant shrub resistant to wind with narrow, toothed leaves, dark olive green above, white beneath. Originated at Zennor, Cornwall.

OSMANTHUS

This is a small group of evergreen shrubs and small trees, some resembling the hollies, but are easily identified by their opposite leaves. The flowers are white or yellowish and usually fragrant. The fruits are oval and dark blue or violet. They thrive in any reasonable soil and do not object to chalk.

They strike easily from cuttings given bottom heat.

O. x burkwoodii *(x Osmarea burkwoodii, O. delavayi x O. decorus)*
MS – O
A slow growing, compact shrub with oval, toothed, leathery leaves of a dark shiny green. The white flowers are borne in terminal and axillary clusters in April and May, and are very fragrant. Hardy and tolerant of maritime conditions, making excellent informal hedging. A good foil for grey shrubs. Raised by Burkwood and Skipwith about 1930. AM 1978. AGM 1984.

O. delavayi MS to LS – O to ❱
A particularly beautiful slow growing sort with box-like, small, dark glossy green, toothed leaves and masses of fragrant white flowers like jasmine, borne in terminal and axillary clusters in April. In Cornwall it can grow to 20 feet and more. Protect from direct wind and sea spray. Yunnan and Szechuan, China. I by Abbé Delavay in 1890. AM 1914. FCC 1931. AGM 1984.

O. heterophyllus LS to ST – O
Very holly-like, slow growing shrub or small tree with variable leaves entire or coarsely toothed of a dark glossy green. Flowers white and fragrant in autumn. A good hedger. Japan. I by Thomas Lobb in 1856. FCC 1859.

Varieties include:

'Aureomarginatus', deep yellow margins to leaves.

'Goshiki', leaves yellow mottled, suffused with bronze when young.

'Gulftide', very spiny, twisted leaves.

'**Purpureus**', young leaves deep purple almost black, turning green suffused with purple.

'**Variegatus**', creamy-white borders to leaves. AGM 1984.

OZOTHAMNUS

Australasian shrubs closely related to *Cassinia* and *Helichrysum*, the flower heads resembling the latter.

O. ledifolius *(Helichrysum ledifolium)* SS – E – O
A round, dense shrublet with very small, narrow, leathery, incurved leaves exuding a sweetly scented, yellowish gum beneath. Dense terminal flower heads, the flowers yellow to red with conspicuous white inner bracts. An excellent and unusual sort, which is surprisingly hardy in dry soil and full sun. Tasmania. I 1930.

O. rosmarinifolius *(Helichrysum rosmarinifolium)* MS – E – O
Although its native habitat is wet heath, this almost fastigiate shrub is hardier in this country on sharply drained soil in full sun. The white woolly stems bear dark green, linear, rosemary-like leaves, which are rough above and woolly beneath. The profuse flowers are borne in dense corymbs on main branches: in bud they are tinged crimson red, and open white and scented. Tasmania, SE Australia. I 1827. AM 1968.
The variety '**Silver Jubilee**' has silvery-grey leaves.

PACHYSANDRA TERMINALIS DS – E – ● to ◗

A useful shrublet which spreads, making good ground cover under trees. Diamond-shaped leaves appear on the end of stems. Spikes of green, purple-tinged flowers in February and March. Japan. I 1882. AGM 1984.
The variety '**Variegata**' has white striped and bordered leaves. AGM 1984.

PAEONIA LUTEA VAR. LUDLOWII ms – d – o

Although herbaceous peonies will not tolerate dry, poor soil, this quite magnificent shrubby tree peony from Tibet is perfectly happy on alkaline or acid sand. The large, deeply-cut leaves are outstandingly architectural. Masses of butter-yellow, single flowers are borne on the strong stems in a short flush in May or June. Protect from cold winds. Propagate from seeds. Collected by Kingdon-Ward. AM 1954. AGM 1984.

PARAHEBE

These are mainly natives of New Zealand. They are dwarf plants, intermediate between *Veronica* and *Hebe*, previously classified as the former. Good on any type of soil, and have speedwell-like flowers held above the foliage on erect stems.

P. catarractae *(Veronica catarractae)* ds – d – o
A low, mound-making shrub excellent for ground cover given full sun. Small, oval, serrated leaves and white to rose-purple flowers with crimson central zones in late summer. There are also blue forms. AGM 1984.

Varieties include:

'**Delight**', profuse white flowers veined heliotrope over a long period. AGM 1984.

'**Diffusa**', small leaves, forms thick mats; flowers white with rose-pink veins.

'**Miss Willmott**', white, mauve-veined flowers.

P. lyalli ps – d – o
Prostrate, spreading shrublet with leathery leaves and white, pink veined flowers with blue anthers from July to August. I 1870.

P. 'Mervyn' DS − D − O
Dwarf and spreading, leaves red-edged and flowers lilac-blue in summer.

P. perfoliata DS − D − O
The "Digger's Speedwell" has grey-green leaves and taller upright stems bearing long racemes of violet-blue flowers in late summer. A striking tender plant suited to the hottest, driest position. Australia. I 1834.

PENSTEMON

The penstemons are enjoying a well-deserved revival. Commerical growers are concentrating on the perennial herbaceous plants, but of equal merit are the shrubby species which are mainly natives of California, well adapted to maritime conditions, and are remarkably beautiful. The flowers are tubular and brightly coloured. They thrive in full sun on a light soil, and are easily propagated by cuttings. The taller tender species are rare in cultivation. The hardy sorts described here are dwarf or prostrate, being particularly suited to the rock garden.

P. fruticosus var. **scouleri** DS − D − O
A very pretty shrub with lanceolate leaves and short racemes of pink flowers in May and June. Discovered by David Douglas on the Columbia River and introduced in 1828. AM 1951. AGM 1984.

The variety **'Albus'** has white flowers. AGM 1984.

P. heterophyllus DS − D − O
An erect shrublet with long, lanceolate leaves and flowers shading from lavender blue at the mouth to purplish red at the base borne throughout summer. I by Douglas in 1828.

The variety **'Blue Gem'** has particularly beautiful sky-blue flowers.

P. newberryi DS – E – O
The form in cultivation is '*humilior*', a mat-forming evergreen shrub with small, leathery, rounded leaves and profuse, vivid cerise-crimson flowers in May and June. AGM 1984.

PEROVSKIA ATRIPLICIFOLIA SS – D – O

The "Afghan Sage" is an erect shrub, slow to develop, with long downy stems bearing aromatic, grey-green toothed leaves and terminal panicles of beautiful violet-blue, tiny flowers arranged in whorls, and dusted with white, powdery down. Being spindly, the plants should be planted in groups of six or more to create an impression. Without full sun the stems flop about, and they demand sharply drained limy soil. In spring they should be cut back hard. They do not transplant, but are easily propagated by cuttings. Afghanistan, N Himalaya to Tibet. C1904. AM 1928.

The variety **'Blue Spire'** is of German origin, and is notable for larger flower panicles than the type. AM 1963. AGM 1984.

PHILADELPHUS

The "Mock Oranges" are particularly beautiful deciduous plants, mostly bearing white, fragrant flowers in June and July when most shrubs are past their best. They are especially valuable for their spectacular display on the poorest, chalky soil in sun. Flowering shoots should be pruned back immediately after they are over. They are easily propagated by cuttings given bottom heat.

The following is a selection of the choicer sorts:

P. 'Beauclerk' MS
Large, milk-white, fragrant flowers with basal cerise shading and bright yellow anthers. Raised by the Hon. Lewis Palmer in 1938. AM 1947. FCC 1957. AGM 1984.

P. 'Belle Etoile' MS
Very free-flowering and fragrant, the large flowers being flushed with maroon at the centre. Raised by Lemoine in 1918. AM 1930. AGM 1984.

P. coronarius MS
A vigorous sort with creamy-white flowers which are richly fragrant. Well-suited to the driest soils; probably of wild origin from Italy, Austria and Roumania.

There are two varieties:

'Aureus' with bright yellow young leaves. AM 1983. AGM 1984.

'Variegatus' with cream margined leaves. C1770. AGM 1984.

P. 'Enchantment' SS to MS
Terminal clusters of double white flowers, profuse and sweetly scented. Raised by Lemoine in 1923. AM 1966.

P. 'Erectus' SS
Erect shrub with small leaves and very fragrant flowers in great profusion. Raised by Lemoine in 1890. AGM 1984.

P. 'Manteau d'Hermine' DS
Compact shrub with creamy-white, fragrant, double flowers. Raised by Lemoine in 1899. AM 1956. AGM 1984.

P. 'Sybille' SS
Arching branches bearing saucer-shaped, fragrant flowers with prominent basal staining of purplish rose. Very decorative. Raised by Lemoine in 1913. AM 1954. AGM 1984.

P. 'Virginal' MS
The best double flowered sort. Richly fragrant flowers. Vigorous and erect. FCC 1911. AGM 1984.

PHLOMIS

An excellent genus for hot, dry conditions in full sun protected from winds. The evergreen plants are generally densely woolly with prominent flowers borne in axillary whorls. They are easily propagated by cuttings, and should be trimmed back after flowering.

P. chrysophylla SS
Unusual for its foliage which is dusted golden yellow in late summer. It bears its golden yellow flowers in June, giving of its best when thoroughly roasted. Lebanon. AGM 1984.

P. fruticosa SS
Grey-green, sage-like foliage, weakly scented. The "Jerusalem Sage" has curious, bright yellow flowers which are borne in late summer and autumn, and attract much attention. Mediterranean region. C1596. AM 1925. AGM 1984.
    The variety **'Edward Bowles'** is a larger, more robust version with paler yellow flowers.

P. italica DS
Leaves and stems covered in white hairs. Pale lilac flowers in summer. Tender, needing protection from cold winds. A native of the Balearic Islands, not Italy. C1750.

P. lanata DS
Dense and mound-forming with small, ovate sage-green leaves and golden yellow, hairy flowers in summer. Crete.

P. longifolia var. **bailanica** SS
Woolly white stems, heart-shaped dark green leaves with deep veins. Deep golden yellow flowers in summer. SW Asia.

PHORMIUM

These two evergreen species from New Zealand are totally uncompromising in appearance, and are definitely not compliant companions for any plants other than the equally assertive yuccas. Their appearance is best described as that of giant irises, and are definitely "architectural", their shape being best suited to isolated positions where they are disdainfully impervious to howling gales and the poorest sand. The long sword-shaped leaves grow longer in deeper soil, and may become a mite tatty in a particularly windy winter. Recent hybrids have interesting leaf colour and variegations, but require considerably more in the way of pampering.

They are hardy in all but the coldest areas.

P. cookianum SS to MS
Named after Captain Cook, it occurs naturally on sea-cliffs. The leaves are 2' to 5' high, light green and rather lax. The yellowish flowers are borne on long stems in panicles during summer. I 1848. FCC 1868. AGM 1984.

Varieties are:

'**Cream Delight**' having a cream central band to leaves and narrow stripes of the same colour towards the margins. AGM 1984.

'**Tricolor**', leaves with creamy-yellow edges, margined with narrow red stripes. Discovered by the Maoris in the 1880's. AGM 1984.

P. tenax MS
The "New Zealand Flax" has tough, erect leaves up to 9' long depending on soil conditions. The flowers are dull red, and are borne on majestic stems up to 15' high in summer. It was discovered by Captain Cook on his first voyage (1769–70), but the seeds collected by Sir Joseph Banks did not germinate following their long journey home. Eventually raised at Kew in 1789. Naturalised in the west of Ireland. AGM 1984.

Varieties are:

'**Purpureum**' has purplish leaves up to 6' high. Good as a contrast to low growing grey plants. AGM 1984.

'**Sundowner**' has bronze leaves with deep rose-red margins up to 5' high. AM 1978.

'**Variegatum**' has leaves as tall as the type with a creamy-white margin. C1870, FCC 1864. AGM 1984.

'**Veitchii**' has rich green leaves with stripes of creamy yellow. A much smaller sort. C1866.

There is a wide selection of modern hybrids of varying habits, hues and variegations, mostly small.

PHYGELIUS

These two species of small evergreen sub-shrubs are natives of South Africa, and are remarkable for their relative hardiness in the UK. They resemble the penstemons with similar tubular flowers. Essential requirements are well-drained soil and full sun. I have tried both in these conditions, and have failed to please them. It is suggested that they require soil which is "not too dry": perhaps this is the problem; our sandy loam has certainly been crispy dry over the past few years. In colder areas they die back in winter, and should be treated as herbaceous perennials: in any case some trimming is necessary after flowering. Easily propagated by cuttings.

P. aequalis SS

Flowers buff-pink outside, the mouth yellow with a bright red margin, pendulous, borne in one-sided panicles in late summer and autumn. Appreciates the protection of a warm wall. AM 1936.

The variety '**Yellow Trumpet**' has light green leaves and pale cream-yellow flowers. I by Sir Harold Hillier in 1973. AM 1984. AGM 1984.

P. capensis SS

Hardier: the flowers are scarlet with yellow throats, nodding, and borne in erect terminal panicles during summer and autumn. C1855. AGM 1969. AM 1978.

The variety '**Coccineus**' has bright orange-red flowers. AM 1926. AGM 1984.

P. x rectus SS

Hillier Nurseries have largely been responsible for introducing a number of hybrids between the two species which have flowers in a variety of colours and colour combinations. Consult catalogues.

PIPTANTHUS NEPALENSIS (P. LABURNIFOLIUS)
LS − E − O

The "Evergreen Laburnum" is a vigorous but short-lived shrub with elegant trifoliate leaves and bright yellow pea-flowers in erect racemes in May followed by long seed pods. Deciduous in cold winters. Only hardy in mild areas, and appreciates the protection of a warm wall when it will grow taller. It is well suited to a dry soil and does not object to lime. Propagate by seeds. Himalaya. I 1821. AM 1960.

PITTOSPORUM

Nearly all the species mentioned here are natives of New Zealand, and, although they are only suitable for mild climates, they are particularly valuable for their fondness of maritime conditions. Their foliage is exceptionally decorative and the flowers pleasingly fragrant. Easily propagated by cuttings in gentle heat.

P. crassifolium LS to ST − E − O

The "Karo" is a hardier sort whose long oval leathery leaves, green above and white yellow beneath, are very resistant to salty winds. The dark purple flowers are borne in conspicuous terminal clusters in summer and are followed by round, white felted fruits the size of large marbles.

Being so wind tolerant it is useful as shelter hedging in mild districts. Unfortunately our specimens were killed stone dead by the 1986 winter, having flourished uninjured for twenty five years: they are sorely missed, especially as they have left whopping gaps.

It is scarce in cultivation, but well worth seeking out.

The variety "**Variegatum**" has grey-green leaves margined creamy white. AM 1977.

P. 'Garnettii' *(P. ralphii x P. tenuifolium)* LS – E – O

A conical shrub with grey-green elliptic leaves margined white and tinged pink to red in winter. Raised in a New Zealand nursery before 1957, and named after its discoverer, Mr Arthur Garnett. AGM 1984.

P. ralphii MS to LS – E – O

Very similar to *P. crassifolium*, but with larger leaves and smaller fruits. Flowers dark crimson with yellow anthers. Just as wind-resistant as *P. crassifolium*, but less hardy.

The variety '**Variegatum**' has leaves broadly margined creamy-white. C1957. AM 1979.

P. tenuifolium ST – E – O

A really beautiful columnar tree, very distinctive for its pale green undulant leaves set on strikingly contrasted black twiggy shoots. In mild areas the dark-chocolate, small flowers are borne in great abundance in spring, and are wonderfully and strongly scented especially in the evening. A great favourite with flower arrangers, lasting long in water. A good hedger, but best protected from the coldest winds. New Zealand. AM 1931. AGM 1984.

There are a host of varieties, mostly smaller than the type: consult the catalogues. '**Silver Queen**' only has won awards: its leaves are silver-grey margined narrowly with white. AM 1914. AGM 1984.

P. tobira LS to ST – E – O

A slow-growing sort from Japan and China, but very fine, having bright, glossy-green obovate leaves with a pale mid-rib and conspicuous creamy-white flowers in clusters in summer, which are strongly orange-blossom scented.

It is very drought-resistant, but definitely tender, and only for the open in mild localities. It is widely used as hedging in southern Europe. I 1804. AM 1984. AGM 1984.

POTENTILLA

In "The Plant Finder" there are more than 250 species, varieties and garden hybrids listed belonging to this huge genus. They are mostly very useful in the seaside garden, revelling in light soil and tolerating partial shade, although all but the orange, red and pink sorts (which fade) prefer full sun. They are universally deciduous and hardy, being natives of northern temperate regions, and vary in size from prostrate to medium height. In recent hot summers they have not been particularly happy: I think this is more to do with heat rather than drought.

The flowers resemble small single roses, and are borne in varying quantities from May through to the autumn.

Easily propagated by cuttings, and do not require cutting back.

The nomenclature is chaotic, and I have chosen to follow *"The Hillier Manual of Trees and Shrubs"*. I have only described representative award winning sorts, but there are, of course, many others worth trying.

P. arbuscula DS
Sage-green leaves on shaggy branches and large, rich yellow flowers from midsummer to late autumn. Himalaya. AM 1925. AMT 1965.

The variety **'Beesii'** ('Nana Argentea') has silvery foliage and golden flowers. AMT 1984.

P. davurica 'Abbotswood' DS
Spreading habit. Dark foliage sets off pure white flowers which are abundantly produced throughout summer. AMT 1965.

P. fruticosa var. *grandiflora* MS

A vigorous, erect sort making a dense bush with sage-green foliage and packed clusters of large, canary-yellow flowers. FCCT 1966.

P. parvifolia 'Klondike' DS

Semi-erect with small, neat leaves and bright golden-yellow flowers. C1950. AMT 1965.

GARDEN HYBRIDS

'Daydawn' SS

A sport of 'Tangerine', having unusually coloured flowers of peach-pink suffused with cream. For part-shade and moister soil. AGM 1984.

'Elizabeth' SS to MS

Dome-shaped, bearing larger, rich canary-yellow flowers from late spring to early summer. AMT 1965. AGM 1984.

'Goldfinger' DS

Compact with blue-green leaves and profuse, large, rich golden yellow flowers. AGM 1984.

'Katherine Dykes' MS

Abundant primrose-yellow flowers in summer. C1925. AM 1944. AGM 1984.

'Longacre' DS

Dense, mat-forming sort with large, bright suphur-yellow flowers. C1956. AMT 1965. AGM 1984.

'Primrose Beauty' SS

Arching branches bearing grey-green foliage and profuse primrose-yellow flowers with deeper yellow centres. AMT 1965. AGM 1984.

'Red Ace' DS

Compact, bearing bright green foliage and vivid orange-red flowers. For part-shade and moister soil. C1973. FCC 1975.

'Sunset' SS
Flowers vary between deep orange and brick-red. For part shade and moister soil. AGM 1984.

'Tilford Cream' DS
A dense shrub with rich green foliage and large, creamy-white flowers. AGM 1984.

'Vilmoriniana' MS
A splendid erect sort with very silvery leaves and cream coloured flowers. AMT 1965. AGM 1984.

'William Purdom' SS
Semi-erect shrub with abundant light yellow flowers. FCCT 1966. AGM 1984.

PYRACANTHA

The evergreen "Firethorns" are very similar to the cotoneaster, being related, but they are distinguished by their viciously thorned branches and toothed leaves. They are generally considered to be wall shrubs when they will grow to 15' or more, but they are remarkably successful in the open given reasonable protection from the strongest winds, although they will not be so tall. Provide deep soil, but they do well on limy sand, seeding freely. Good for hedges, making impervious screens. All sorts have profuse, white, hawthorn-like flowers with a musky scent in early summer, but are mainly valued for the highly decorative red, orange or yellow fruits in autumn and winter, which are equally attractive to birds. Many are prone to diseases such as canker, fireblight and scab. All will tolerate light shade.

P. atalantoides LS to ST
Vigorous with large, glossy-green, oval leaves and long-lasting scarlet fruits. China. I by E.H. Wilson in 1907. FCC 1918.
The variety **'Aurea'** has rich yellow fruits. AM 1936.

P. coccinea 'Lalandei' LS

Strong-growing and erect with oval leaves and very profuse dense clusters of orange-red berries. I 1877 as a variety. Origin of type S Europe.

P. 'Mohave' *(P. coccinea* 'Wyatt' *x P. koidzumii)* MS to LS

Dense with large, deep green leaves and very prolific, long-lasting bright orange-red berries. Raised at the US National Arboretum, Washington in 1963. FCC 1984. AGM 1984.

P. 'Orange Glow' (probably *P. coccinea x P. crenato-serrata*) MS to LS

Vigorous and dense with masses of long-lasting, orange-red berries. AGM 1984.

P. rogersiana LS

An excellent and vigorous form with prolific reddish-orange berries. W China. I 1911. AGM 1937. AM 1953. AGM 1984.

The variety **'Flava'** has bright yellow fruits. FCC 1919. AGM 1984.

P. 'Shawnee' MS to LS

Another American cultivar from Washington with particularly spiny, dense branches, very prolific flowers and equally abundant yellow to light orange berries which colour early in late summer. Claimed to be disease resistant. AGM 1984.

P. 'Watereri' *(P. atalantoides x P. rogersiana)* MS to LS

Compact with exceptional abundance of flowers and bright red berries. AM 1955. AGM 1969. AGM 1984.

ROMNEYA

The "Tree Poppies" of California and Mexico are quite the most elegant and spectacular of deciduous shrub. The long, graceful, succulent branches carry deeply lobed glaucous leaves and very large, fragrant, poppy-like, white flowers with prominent golden-yellow stamens, delicate and crinkled when first open, throughout summer.

As befits their origin, the two species, *R. coulteri* and *R. trichocalyx*, appreciate warmth, and are better for the protection of a south or west wall in colder areas. Indeed without warmth the flower buds will not open. In southern counties they are happy in the open in the sunniest position protected from cold winds. They grow well in light but deep soil with adequate nutrition provided, and are happy in alkaline conditions. A hard winter will destroy the stems, but this is of no importance as new ones will spring up rapidly the following season, and flowering will be unaffected. In any case older stems should be cut out every year.

It almost goes without saying that there is a price to pay for all this pulchritude. Although great care has to be taken not to disturb the roots when planting, and the plants may take a year or two to settle, when established they roar away if pleased, spreading rapidly by suckers which can appear up to 40' away from the parents. Somewhat alarming tales are told of suckers penetrating the walls of cellars, and somehow managing to wriggle under walls. At least there is no problem with propagation.

R. coulteri MS

An Irish botanist, Dr. Thomas Coulter, found this plant near Los Angeles in 1833 (the genus is named after his friend, the astronomer, Dr. F. Romney Robinson). I 1875. FCC 1888. AGM 1984.

R. trichocalyx MS

Almost the same, but a little smaller, more slender stems and more deeply divided foliage – also, if possible, more invasive.

R. 'White Cloud' *(R. coulteri x R. trichocalyx)* MS

An American hybrid of great vigour and beauty. It has apparently colonised an area of fifty square yards in the Hillier Arboretum at Ampfield, Hampshire.

ROSA

Seaside conditions do not suit the modern bedding rose no matter which way you look at it. This does not mean to say that the maritime gardener has to forgo the pleasures of this wonderfully diverse and decorative genus. There is a marvellous variety of flower colour and often a great elegance of form in the "wild" roses, which are the distant relatives of the garden hybrids. Some species are totally suited to a dry and windy coastal environment. Many are of very ancient origin, having been introduced to Europe from the Near East at the time of the Crusades. The Romans had valued the rose, and undoubtedly would have cultivated a number of forms in their British gardens. In medieval times their beauty and scent was highly prized, and most of the romantic associations derive from this period.

No doubt the term "wild rose" brings to mind large, straggling bushes with small, insignificant blooms. This is not necessarily true. Some shrub roses are certainly large and occupy a lot of space, but modern hybridists, such as Wilhelm Kordes of Germany, have bred stunning cultivars, which, whilst retaining the vitality and vigour of one parent, have the neatness of form and superlative beauty of flower of the other . Some grow relatively erect, and tolerate clipping, making excellent hedging even in very exposed positions. (Do take into account they are deciduous, and far from attractive in winter despite their summer magnificence).

Only those species and their hybrids which are known to succeed in impoverished, windy conditions are noted below, but there is enormous scope for the adventurous gardener to experiment with other sorts. Reference to such books as *"Classic Roses"* by Peter Beales will give a good indication of roses which tolerate poor soil. Whether or not these would withstand the rigours of the seaside is another matter as no gardeners appear to have recorded their successes and failures, if indeed they have even tried.

No matter how tolerant of poor conditions, any shrub rose will appreciate gentle feeding and a coolish root run. This can be

The large flowers of the 'Hottenot Fig', *Carpobrotus edulis*, appear in May and June on heavy mats of succulent leaves. Only for hot, wide spaces.

The *Lampranthus* family contains succulents ideal for the hot rock garden. All have jewel coloured flowers borne in profusion in high summer.

This is the bountiful *Lavatera thuringiaca* 'Kew Rose', a perfectly adapted large shrub for extreme exposure with summer-long flowers.

The lush-looking 'Valerian', *Centranthus ruber*, is only really happy on dry stone walls where it colonises freely.

A vigorous climber, the 'Blue Passion Flower', *Passiflora caerulea*, must have a sunny, sheltered, warm wall and restricted roots to flower freely.

The flowers of the 'Cape Marguerite', *Osteospermum barberae*, shut when not in the sun and appear well into autumn. The leaves are aromatic.

A nice little arrangement of 'Houseleeks', *Sempervivum*, and the prostrate
Euphorbia myrsinites on a shallow, hot and rocky perch.

The Mexican *Penstemon hartwegii*
likes protection from wind and a
dampish summer.

Fremontodendron 'California Glory'
flowers spectacularly in poor, dry
soil against a warm wall.

provided by heavy mulching before the heat of summer. Remember that large decorative blooms are better if given a modicum of shade at some time during the day. Any tendency to chlorosis (yellowing of the leaves on alkaline soil) can be corrected by an annual dose of sequestrene. Otherwise they do not need pruning, and can safely be left to their own devices, as long as it is recognised that some sorts have an energetic suckering tendency, and will spread indefinitely if unchecked: be warned!

ROSA PIMPINELLIFOLIA

R. pimpinellifolia (*R. spinosissima*, "Burnet Rose", "Scotch Briar") height 3' x spread 3'
Creamy-white single flowers in early summer on characteristic stems densely covered with long prickles. Small, fern-like leaves and round black fruits. Suckers freely. Europe. I before 1600.

R. pimpinellifolia altaica 5' x 3'
Large white single flowers with prominent golden-yellow stamens. Maroon-purple hips. Asia. C1818.

R. pimpinellifolia hispida 6' x 4'
Upright shrub with large soft yellow to white single flowers with prominent stamens. Very hardy. NE Asia, Siberia. C1781.

R. pimpinellifolia lutea 4' x 3'
A less vigorous upright sort with deep yellow single flowers. Asia. Date unknown.

VARIETIES AND HYBRIDS OF **R. PIMPINELLIFOLIA**

'Double Pink', 'Double White', 'Double Yellow', 'Double Marbled Pink' 3' x 3'
These double forms were all introduced in the early 19th century, and their names, along with many others, have been lost

except for the double yellow (*R. x harisonii*) which is the "Yellow Rose of Texas". They have profuse globular flowers borne on neat, leafy bushes, and make rounded specimens or good thick low hedges.

'Andrewsi' 4' x 3'
Deep-purplish red and cream semi-double flowers with yellow stamens on a densely leafy shrub. Occasionally repeats in autumn. Origin unknown. C1806.

'Dunwich Rose' 2' x 4'
A fine prostrate plant with creamy-yellow single flowers profusely borne. Suffolk. Date unknown.

'Falkland' 3' x 3'
Soft lilac-pink to blush white semi-double, cupped flowers on a compact bush. Deep maroon hips. UK. Date unknown.

'Frühlingsanfang' 10' x 6'
Upright shrub with lovely, medium-sized, white single flowers with prominent stamens and a strong scent. Kordes. C1950.

'Frühlingsduft' 10' x 6'
Upright, vigorous shrub with dark green, glossy leaves and large double flowers, soft lemon-yellow, heavily suffused pink and very fragrant. Kordes. C1949.

'Frühlingsgold' 7' x 5'
Large single flowers, rich golden-yellow fading to primrose, profusely borne on a vigorous, upright bush with dark leaves. Kordes. C1937.

'Frühlingsmorgen' 6' x 4'
Large, heavily scented, single flowers, cherry-pink with primrose centres and golden stamens, on an upright dense shrub bearing dark green leaves. Flowers early and occasionally recurrent. Kordes. C1942.

'Glory of Edzell' 5' x 4'

Upright shrub with small but dense foliage and clear pink, single flowers with paler centres and prominent stamens. Date unknown.

'Golden Wings' 5' x 4'

Large, sweetly scented, single flowers, clear golden-yellow with prominent golden-cream stamens, borne in abundance singly or in clusters. Light green foliage. Flowers continuously from June to October. Deservedly popular. Shepherd, USA. C1956.

'Maigold' 12' x 8'

An excellent climber flowering very early and spectacularly. Semi-double flowers, fragrant, rich golden-yellow flushed orange. Rich green, glossy leaves. Kordes. C1953.

'Stanwell Perpetual' 5' x 5'

An arching, graceful plant with an unusually long flowering period. Dense, greyish-green leaves mottled with purple occasionally. Double, quartered flowers, scented, soft blush-pink. Lee, UK. C1838.

ROSA RUGOSA

R. rugosa 7' x 6'

The extremely vigorous type sends up long canes densely covered with prickles and thorns. It suckers freely on light soil in full sun, and its spread is indefinite in these conditions forming impenetrable thickets. It has established itself as a native on the sands at West Wittering, Sussex and parts of the Norfolk coast.

Its formidable presence deters weeds and anything animate except rabbits, which like the security of a good patch of it. It is totally impervious to wind and salt.

The foliage is light to mid-green, crinkled, and the fragrant flowers are single, ranging in colour from clear deep pink to deep cerise red with yellow stamens. Japan, parts of W Asia. I 1796.

R. rugosa alba 7' x 6'
Vigorous with large, fragrant white flowers and large tomato red fruits. Suckers freely. Unknown garden origin. C1870.

R. rugosa rubra 6' x 5'
Larger deep crimson-purple flowers with creamy-yellow stamens. Japan. Date unknown. AM 1955.

Hybrids of R. rugosa
All these sorts are remarkably tough, tolerant and healthy, needing little if no attention and giving great beauty of flower over long periods.

'Agnes' 6' x 5'
Densely bushy with very fragrant, double flowers, amber yellow fading to white, the first flush in June but repeating intermittently. Saunders, Canada. C1922. AM 1951.

'Blanc Double de Coubert' 5' x 4'
One of the most famous roses, known for its highly scented, white, almost double flowers and great vigour. After 20 years our thicket, fully exposed to ferocious gales, is 30' deep and more than 150' long, having been started from a few suckers from a friend's garden. Her plant had come with her when she moved from Scotland to Alderney. Cochet-Cochet, France. C1892. AM 1895. AGM 1984.

'Conrad Ferdinand Meyer' 10' x 8'
Exceptionally robust with very fragrant, large, silver-pink double flowers. Prone to rust. F. Müller, Germany. C1899.

'Fimbriata' ('Phoebe's Frilled Pink', 'Dianthiflora') 4' x 4'
Atypical small double flowers with frilled petals, like a dianthus, white, shaded pink in clusters. An upright, compact sort. Morlet, France. C1891.

'F.J. Grootendorst' 4' x 3'
Small, crimson double flowers with frilled petals in clusters throughout summer. Vigorous and bushy. De Goey, Holland. C1918.

'Frau Dagmar Hartopp' ('Fru. Dagmar Hastrup') 3' x 4'
Bushy plant with excellent, fragrant, clear silver-pink flowers good in autumn. Tomato-like fruit. Hastrup, Germany. C1914. AM 1958. AGM 1984.

'Hansa' 4' x 3'
Vigorous plant with highly fragrant, reddish-purple, double flowers. Good red hips Schaum and Van Tol, Holland. C1905.

'Lady Curzon' 3' x 6'
Vigorous, arching, procumbent plant with beautiful, fragrant, large, pale rose-pink, single flowers. Turner, UK. C1901.

'Max Graf' 2' x 8'
A trailing, spreading sort for ground cover. Long shoots densely covered with large, dark green leaves. Flowers deep silvery-pink and single. Bowditch, USA. C1919. AM 1964.

'Mrs Anthony Waterer' 4' x 5'
Vigorous bush with fragrant, rich deep crimson, semi-double flowers in profusion. Waterer, UK. C1892.

'Pink Grootendorst' 4' x 3'
Like 'F.J. Grootendorst' but flowers soft pink. Tends to revert when both colours can appear at the same time. Grootendorst, Holland. C1923.

'Robusta' 5' x 4'
A really tough, vigorous plant suitable for hedging with fragrant large, rich scarlet single flowers. Kordes, Germany. C1979.

'Roseraie de l'Hay' 6' x 5'
Another justifiably famous rose. Vigorous, densely bushy with a continuous show of superb, strongly fragrant, large, rich crimson-purple, double flowers with cream stamens. Excellent for hedges. Cochet-Cochet, France. C1901. AGM 1984.

'Sarah van Fleet' 4' x 3'
Bushy, upright plant with profuse, silky-pink semi-double flowers. Inclined to rust. Van Fleet, USA. C1926.

'Scabrosa' 6' x 4'

Dense, upright shrub with profuse very fragrant, large, rich silvery-cerise single flowers with prominent stamens. Equally abundant, large tomato-like hips. Excellent for hedges. Harkness, UK. I 1960. AM 1964. AGM 1984.

'Schneezwerg' ('Snow Dwarf') 5' x 4'

Pure white, semi-double flowers with prominent yellow stamens. Rich red fruit appearing with flowers later in the season. P. Lambert, Germany. C1912.

ROSA VIRGINIANA

R. virginiana 5' x 3'

Upright, bushy plant, very attractive with dense, light glossy green foliage, which colours progressively through purple to orange-red; crimson and yellow in autumn. The flowers are single, fragrant, rich clear pink with yellow stamens from June to August. The small fruits are round, bright red and shiny. Excellent for seaside sand. E North America. I before 1807. AM 1953. AGM 1984.

"Rose d'Amour" ("St. Mark's Rose") 7' x 5'

Vigorous and free-flowering. Taller than the type with almost thornless stems and fragrant, deep pink double flowers with paler outer petals from mid to late summer. Garden origin before 1820. FCC 1980.

N.B. American gardeners apparently clip the bushes over after fruiting. This may be in the interests of conformity, or the fact that the plants tend to hang on to dead leaves.

ROSES FOR TALL SEASIDE HEDGES

All the following are varieties of *R. rugosa*, and are described in detail above. They should be planted 3' to 4' apart when the plants will quickly join together to provide a tough, well foliated, wind and salt proof barrier of great beauty in the summer. The ground should be carefully prepared, dug deeply and provided with a generous supply of peat mixed with bone meal. No further care is needed, but annual spring mulching, and the removal of old stems keeps them in prime form. Suckering should be carefully controlled.

R. *rugosa alba*	'Robusta'
'Blanc Double de Coubert'	'Roseraie de l'Hay'
'Frau Dagmar Hartopp'	'Scabrosa'

ROSMARINUS

A native of the Mediterranean, rosemary is well adapted to hot, dry conditions, and has been cultivated since ancient times, playing an important part in religious ceremonies. *Ros* is the Latin for dew, hence the interpretation of the generic name as "Sea-dew".

R. *officinalis* MS

An evergreen shrub which spreads as wide as it grows high. The leaves are densely borne and lavender-like, dark green above, white-felted beneath, aromatic when crushed. Axillary clusters of pale violet-blue flowers are borne on previous year's growth in May. It withstands wind well, and makes good informal hedging, but becomes sprawling and gnarled when old – not necessarily unattractive, and can be clipped and shaped immediately after flowering. Readily increased by cuttings.

Its cultivation in Britain could be romantically associated with the Romans, but it is definitely known to have been grown for at least 400 years.

Apothecaries attributed to it the property of stimulating the memory, hence its old name, the "herb of memory", and Ophelia's "There's rosemary, that's for remembrance". This also gave rise to its association with the dead: Bean quotes the old chanson:

A l'entour de sa tombe, romarin l'on planta,
Sur la plus haute branche, le rossignol chanta.

The volatile oil distilled from the plant is an ingredient of *Eau de Cologne*. It is well-liked by bees, and gives a good flavour to honey. AGM 1984.

Varieties include:

'**Benenden Blue**', vivid blue flowers. A smaller, semi-erect sort introduced from Corsica and tender. AM 1933.

Other tender Corsican clones with excellent flower colour are '**Corsican Blue**' *(R. corsicus)* and '**Corsicus Prostratus**'. My plant of the latter is superb in a dry, sunny spot tumbling down steps, and has so far survived some hard snaps.

'**Majorca Pink**', moderately hardy and erect with very early lilac-pink flowers.

'**Miss Jessup's Upright**', hardy, erect and robust with broader, sea-green leaves. Excellent for hedges. AGM 1984.

'**Severn Sea**', dwarf with arching branches bearing brilliant blue flowers. Raised by Norman Hadden in his garden at West Porlock, Somerset. AGM 1984. AM 1989.

'**Sissinghurst Blue**', upright with profuse rich blue flowers. Raised at Sissinghurst Castle about 1958. AM 1983.

'**Tuscan Blue**', erect and only hardy in mild areas. Light green leaves and clear ceanothus blue, large flowers often starting in winter. A hedger in Tuscany. W. Arnold Foster, who introduced it, recommended that it can be induced to flower more freely by topping the long flowering spikes.

RUTA GRAVEOLENS ss – e – o

Shakespeare's "Herb of Grace" is a small aromatic shrub with glaucous, fern-like foliage and terminal corymbs of small, mustard-yellow flowers from June to August. Cultivated in England since at least 1652 for its antseptic properties. It can cause in susceptible persons quite a severe contact dermatitis. S Europe.

The variety 'Jackman's Blue' is a much superior garden form of bushy, compact habit and vivid, glaucous-blue leaves. AGM 1984.

SALVIA

Only the "Common Sage", *S. officinalis*, in this huge genus is a European native and truly hardy. The remainder are tender to a varying degree, coming from such hot places as Mexico, Texas and S America, but are of such beauty of flower that they repay cossetting in the hottest, driest spot you can find for them – only in the mildest areas. These delicate gems are borderline shrubs, and should be treated as herbaceous perennials in most instances.

Almost all the sorts are more or less hairy in all their parts, and are aromatic. On no account should they be grown in fertile soil, or fed: they will develop more foliage than flower if they are given too much nitrogen. They are easily propagated by softwood cuttings in summer.

S. fulgens SS – D
The "Mexican Red Sage" or "Cardinal Sage" has large, hairy, heart-shaped leaves and bright crimson-scarlet flowers in long, showy racemes in late summer and autumn. Only hardy in the mildest areas in sheltered spots. Mexico. I 1829. AM 1937.

S. gregii SS – D
A slender plant with small, narrow leaves and small clusters of small rose-scarlet flowers borne continuously from June onwards. Best against a south wall – definitely tender. Texas, Mexico. C1885. AM 1914.

S. guaranitica SS – D
A really spectacular plant with downy, heart-shaped leaves and long racemes of very bright royal blue flowers profusely borne

during summer and autumn. Needs support. S America. I 1925. AM 1926.

There are two varieties, **'Black and Blue'** *(S. caerulea)* with deep blue flowers with black calyces, AM 1989, and **'Blue Enigma'** *(S. ambigens)* which is shorter with smaller, paler blue flowers with green calyces.

S. involucrata ss to ms – D
Smooth, long, pointed, rich green leaves and spikes of rose-magenta flowers from late summer to autumn. Tender. Mexico. I 1824. The form **'Bethellii'** *(S. bethellii)* is justifiably popular for its large heart-shaped leaves and substantial racemes of brilliant magenta-crimson flowers from mid-summer to autumn. Garden origin. FCC 1880.

S. microphylla ss to ms – D
Very small, dull green leaves and small, bright magenta-crimson flowers fading to bluish-red over a very long period, from early summer to late autumn. Mexico. I 1829.

The sort ***S.m.* var.** *neurepia* has larger, paler green leaves and wonderful rosy-red flowers in late summer and autumn. Mexico. Both need the warmth of a south wall in mild districts.

S. officinalis DS – SE
The "Common Sage" is found wild in Spain and Yugoslavia. Elsewhere in S Europe it has become naturalised, having been cultivated from time immemorial for sage-beer and infusions, as well as for culinary purposes. It was introduced to Britain by the Romans, and much valued by medieval apothecaries as the source of a general tonic. Before the invention of toothpaste the rough sage leaves were used to clean the teeth and strengthen the gums. The leaves are grey-green and strongly aromatic: the flowers relatively inconspicuous, bluish-purple during summer.

Varieties include:

'Albiflora', flowers white, the best culinary sort.

'Aurea', compact with yellow leaves.

'**Icterina**', leaves variegated gold and light green, low and spreading. AGM 1984.

'**Purpurascens**', striking purple stems and young leaves. AGM 1984.

'**Tricolor**', relatively tender, compact with grey-green leaves, suffused with purple and pink and splashed with creamy-white.

SANTOLINA

These low growing, charming shrubs are natives of the Mediterranean, at their happiest in poor, dry soil and full sun. They are strongly aromatic when crushed. Sadly they do not grow old gracefully, and should be discarded as soon as they become unattractively attenuated and straggly. However, they are very easily propagated by cuttings in mid-summer when they will root within a few days.

S. chamaecyparrisus DS – E
A very white bush forming a dense mound, the "Lavender Cotton" has crowded, narrow, felted leaves on semi-woody, upright stems, which persist throughout winter. The profuse small, button-shaped flowers are bright lemon yellow, borne at the end of long stalks in July. Very beautiful when grown well, and a splendid contrast plant. It has been cultivated in Britain since the mid-16th century, being valued then as a cure for intestinal worms and as a border for knot gardens. S France, Pyrenees. AGM 1984.

The variety '**Nana**' is smaller and more compact, well-suited to the rock garden. AGM 1984.

S. pinnata DS – E
This is grown as *Subsp. neapolitana* with longer cylindrical leaves and a laxer habit than *S. chamaecyparrisus*, it is also differs in being greener. Flowers are bright lemon-yellow and very profuse in July. To retain its neat form and white felt, poor, hot conditions are essential. NW and C Italy. AGM 1984.

Varieties are '**Edward Bowles**' with grey-green leaves and creamy white flowers, and **'Sulphurea'**, grey-green leaves and pale primrose flowers.

S. rosmarinifolia *(S. viridis, S. virens)* DS
Very similar in form to its relatives, but leaves and stems a rich deep green. Flowers are bright lemon-yellow. SW Europe. C1727.
The variety **'Primrose Gem'** has pale primrose-yellow flowers.

SENECIO see *BRACHYGLOTTIS*
SOLANUM CRISPUM – see under CLIMBERS

SPARTIUM JUNCEUM LS – D

The "Spanish Broom" is the ideal seaside shrub, vigorous and totally adapted to hot, poor, alkaline soil and wind. It is spectacular in flower, the fragrant blooms being large, pea-like and a rich yellow, borne in long, loose terminal racemes on slender, rushy stems from June to September. The leaves are tiny and sparse.

It can become gaunt and unattractive if too protected from wind, and certainly benefits from underplanting to disguise its unprepossessing bottom end. It sets profuse seeds if allowed, and will die from exhaustion at a young age if not clipped over as soon as it has finished flowering. It should be raised from seed and planted very young, disliking root disturbance.

The plant comes from the maquis around the Mediterranean, where it has many uses: the flowers yield a yellow dye, baskets are made from the stems, which also provide fibres for weaving and rope. An alkaloid can be extracted which is purgative, emetic and diuretic. I about 1548. AM 1968. FCC 1977. AGM 1984.

TAMARIX

The "Tamarisks" are the archetypal shelter shrubs for seaside conditions, indeed their tolerance of dry sand is due to their absorption of salt, which helps to prevent damaging excessive transpiration, along with the tiny, scale-like leaves on long, whippy branches. The whole effect is one of light featheriness. The flowers are very small in shades of pink, and borne in racemes forming large plumose inflorescences at the ends of branches. The choicer species and varieties can be spectacular, especially when massed. The plants tend to be naturally shapeless and straggly and benefit from pruning. This should be done in late February and March for those which flower on the current year's growth, and immediately after flowering for those which flower on the previous year's growth.

Propagation is gratifyingly easy: cuttings about a foot long are taken of the previous summer's wood, and planted in open ground in early winter where you wish. Two thirds of the length of the cuttings should be buried.

All species make excellent hedging.

T. gallica *(T. anglica)* LS to ST – D
Dark, purple-brown branches and sea-green foliage. Flowers light pink during summer on current year's growth. Workmanlike. Naturalised on some parts of the English coast. SW Europe.

T. parviflora *(T. tetrandra* var. *purpurea)* LS to ST – D
Brown or purple branches and bright green foliage. Profuse flowers deep pink in May on previous year's growth. Elegant and beautiful. SE Europe, W Asia. C1853.

T. ramosissima *(T. pentandra, T. odessana)* LS to ST – D
Red-brown branches and light pink flowers during summer on current year's growth. Widely distributed from S Russia to China. I about 1885. AM 1903. AGM 1984.

There are three varieties:

'**Rosea**' with a terrific display of rose-pink flowers on current year's growth in late summer and early autumn. Truly ornamental, but must be cut back almost to old wood to get best effect. C1883. AM 1933.

'**Rubra**', has darker pink flowers. AGM 1984.

'**Pink Cascade**', vigorous with richer pink flowers.

***T. tetrandra** (T. caspica)* LS – D
An open shrub with black branches and light pink flowers in May on previous year's growth. Decorative. E Balkans, Asia Minor and S Russia. I 1821. AGM 1984.

TEUCRIUM FRUTICANS MS – E – O

The "Shrubby Germander" is a rapid grower ideally suited for a warm, seaside sand, standing wind well. It is undoubtedly tender coming from Portugal, the W Mediterranean and the Adriatic: the Latinised name derives from the Greek equivalent, *teukrion*. In its native lands it is often used as hedging, and is happy to be clipped. It is easily propagated by cuttings.

The small aromatic leaves on long, white felted square stems are shiny, bright green above and white beneath, giving a pretty effect. The summer flowers are pale lavender and are borne in racemes. I 1714. AM 1982 (for foliage). AGM 1984.

The variety '**Azureum**' is well worth growing for its deep blue flowers contrasting nicely with the foliage, but is more tender and probably will need a warm wall even in mild areas. AM 1936.

THYMUS

An Old World genus much appreciated wherever it grows for its wonderful fragrance and medicinal and culinary uses. Having been popular for so many centuries and having so many local species and varieties, complicated by the hybridising zeal of gardeners, there are innumerable sorts, and no little confusion with nomenclature.

The evergreen plants, small in all their parts, are generally hardy, and thrive on poor, alkaline, sandy soil in sun. They are not long-lived, but are easily propagated by cuttings. The mat-forming sorts can be increased by division.

They have many garden uses, according to habit. I like dotting them around generously between low-growing herbaceous plants and shrubs, and over areas where I am nurturing bulbs which like the same conditions. They make weeding a positive pleasure. Being expendable and easily increased, I am not stricken with guilt if they get squeezed to death, as often happens. The following is a selection based on nothing more than personal preference:

T. x citriodorus *(T. pulegioides x T. vulgaris)*

An ancient garden plant described by Parkinson as "the wilde Tyme that smelleth like unto a Pomecitron or Lemon", the "Lemon Thyme" is a spreading little bush a foot high. The flowers are pale lilac from May to July.

Varieties are:

'Aureus', much lower and spreading with rich gold foliage.

'E.B. Anderson', slow growing and lower with bright gold leaves.

T. doerfleri

Discovered by J. D. Doerfler on the border between erstwhile Yugoslavia and Albania in 1916. It has dark grey, woolly leaves and lavender flowers in summer and early autumn. Very low mat former.

T. drucei *(T. praecox arcticus)*

The wild thyme of Britain's chalk downs "that smells like dawn in Paradise" (Kipling). Shakespeare knew "a bank whereon the wild thyme blows . . . there sleeps Titania some time of the night, lull'd in these flowers with dances and delight" The amateur botanist George Claridge Druce distinguished between this species and *T. serpyllum* in 1924: a person on a galloping horse would not be able to. From this grows some confusion, especially as regards varieties. For you and I both species are carpeters a few inches high with deep green leaves and small rosy purple flowers on erect stems in summer and early autumn.

T. serpyllum

Rare in Britain, common in Europe: very similar to *T. drucei*. Many varieties are ascribed to it, among which are:

'**Albus**', with white flowers; '**Annie Hall**', soft pink flowers; '**Bressingham**', clear pink flowers; '**Coccineus**', profuse, bright crimson purple flowers and '**Coccineus Major**', larger in all its parts.

T. vulgaris

The "Common Thyme" of the kitchen garden is a Mediterranean garigue plant, a small compact bush a foot high and highly aromatic. Neat, dark green foliage and pale purple flowers from May to July. Introduced by the Romans, and known by Gerard to be "good against windes in the belly" and "profitable for such as are fearfull melancholicke and troubled in minde."

Varieties include:

'**Golden King**', lemon-scented with gold variegated new leaves in spring.

'**Spring Queen**', sharply variegated white and grey-green leaves.

ULEX

The "Furze", "Gorse" or "Whin" is a coloniser of dry heath, and despite its magnificence of bloom is much taken for granted. Anyone who has tried establishing one of the three native species will have a very different attitude: they can be most remarkably pernickety, demanding firm, undug soil of the very poorest sort and preferably acid. They will not succeed on shallow, chalky soils and must be pot grown. Given too rich a soil, a protected site or lack of sun, they will grow gaunt, leggy and ugly: not plants for a formal garden! They are useful however, where almost nothing else will grow. Propagation of *U. europaeus*, the "Common Gorse", is probably best by seed planted *in situ*. None will transplant.

As the plants grow outwards they leave behind dead branches: this makes them very inflammable, and care should be taken when siting them, especially as regards buildings.

U. *europaeus* SS to MS

The "Common Gorse" is densely spiny, dark green with chrome-yellow, pea-like flowers from February to May and intermittently thereafter. Much superior is the form **'Flore Pleno'**, the "Double-flowered Gorse", which is slower growing and more compact with a magnificent display of flowers in April and May. It can only be propagated by cuttings, as no seed is set: this can be easily achieved by taking new wood in August. C1828. AM 1967. AGM 1984.

U. *gallii* PS to DS

A much smaller shrub with deep golden flowers from August to October.

U. *minor* *(U. nanus)* PS to DS

Similar to *U. gallii*, very dense and compact, but in a garden will develop slender, upright branches. Golden-yellow flowers in autumn. It deteriorates badly if not on poorest soil.

VIBURNUM TINUS MS to LS – E – O to ◗

Sadly the "Laurustinus" is the only one of the beautiful viburnums that puts up with drought. Grown in partial shade and sand our plant is now 10' tall after 15 years, and has been undamaged by the severest gales, although, I grant you, it is partially protected by much taller growths of evergreens. It does not, however, appreciate severe cold. It is quite beautiful at some time during the winter, depending on the weather, when the cymes of delicately fragrant, white flowers are generously borne, contrasting well with the dense, glossy green leaves which cover the plant to the ground. It is a good hedger, and can be propagated by cuttings taken in late summer, and given bottom heat.

In its native southern Europe, it is an inhabitant of the richer maquis and woodland. Cultivated in Britain since the 16th century.

I cannot find anybody who has tried the varieties by the sea: they may not be as tolerant of dry conditions, but here is a selection:

'Eve Price', compact with smaller leaves and carmine buds opening to light pink flowers. AM 1961. AGM 1984.

'French White', vigorous with large cymes of white flowers.

'Gwenllian', compact with small leaves and deep pink buds opening to white flowers suffused pink. AGM 1984.

'Lucidum', vigorous with larger, glossy green leaves and larger, white flowers in March and April. AM 1972.

'Pink Prelude', unusual in that flowers open white then gradually turn deep pink. C1966.

'Purpureum', dark green leaves which are suffused purple when young.

'Variegatum', more tender, leaves strongly variegated with creamy-yellow.

YUCCA

This apparent epitome of a sub-tropical shrub was grown by the barber-surgeon John Gerard in his garden off Fetter Lane, Holborn in 1596: he had been given the plant by his colleague Thomas Edwards of Exeter. He was nurturing *Y. gloriosa*, although he thought it was the yuca, or cassava, of the Caribbean. This incorrect name stuck.

Nobody knows when it was introduced, but it must have been one of the first plants to come from that part of the New World, Mexico and Florida, so recently opened up by Cortez, and it is tempting to speculate that some Devonian privateer purloined some specimens from a returning Spanish galleon. Why else should it have been called "Spanish Bayonet"? However it happened, the yucca proved astonishingly hardy, and rapidly became a popular garden plant in the south of England, being easily propagated by rooting the tops of flowering stems in sand.

They are really spectacular in flower, very long stems rising rapidly from the centre of rosettes of stiff, pointed leaves to burst into huge panicles of white, bell shaped blooms.

Although perfectly hardy and mostly wind-proof, they are happier and flower more freely in hot sandy conditions in full sun. *Y. gloriosa*, the largest of the type, is reputed to flower only occasionally. Our specimens are either very pleased with their position, or have responded to a succession of dry, warm seasons: since 1986 they have not let us down. Unlike the agave, which they resemble, they do not suffer the ultimate penalty of death for flowering so majestically.

Y. filamentosa DS – E

Typical rosettes of long, pointed leaves whose margins are decorated with white threads. No trunk develops. It flowers reliably on stems up to 5' tall: the blooms are drooping and yellowish white in July and August. Ideal for the smaller garden. Spreads by suckering. SE United States. C1675. AGM 1984.

The two most available varieties are:

'**Bright Edge**', with a narrow golden yellow margin to leaves.

'**Variegata**', with leaves margined white. AGM 1984.

Y. flaccida DS – E

Another beautiful yucca for the small garden, the leaves like *Y. filamentosa*, but recurved outwards, being, as the name suggests, lax (and therefore prone to wind damage). Very free flowering, the blooms being the same as *Y. filamentosa*. Also spreads by suckering. SE United States. I 1816.

There are two varieties easily available:

'**Golden Sword**', leaves with a central stripe of creamy-yellow.

'Ivory', exceptionally free flowering, having horizontally held blooms. AM 1966. FCC 1968. AGM 1984.

Y. gloriosa MS – E

The giant of the family – in all ways. Very substantial, stiff, wickedly pointed leaves (hence 'Spanish Bayonet') and stupendous flower spikes over 6' high when happy from July to September. It grows on a slowly developing trunk. SE United States on sand-dunes. I about 1550. AM 1975.

The variety **'Variegata'** has leaves margined and striped creamy-yellow. FCC 1883. AGM 1984.

Y. recurvifolia SS – E

Similar to Y. *gloriosa* in all its parts except smaller and the outer leaves are recurved. Young leaves are glaucous. Better on damp soils. SE United States. I 1794. AGM 1984.

The variety **'Variegata'** has leaves with a pale green central stripe.

Y. whipplei SS – E

The most magnificent of all yuccas, but, coming from southern California, it must have warmth in late summer and autumn to develop flower spikes. Although hardy, plants are lost to damp. Only for the optimistic! I 1854. AM 1945.

12

Wall Plants

Below is a list of plants noted in the catalogue of shrubs which appreciate the protection of a warm wall. Those marked (N) will do well on difficult shaded and dry North walls. (Refer to the individual entries for cultivation requirements.) Most of the shrubs will put up with the driest conditions, but remember that the foot of a wall is excessively parched and permeated with builders' débris. It is worthwhile digging down at least two spits, and removing the junk before planting. If you come across the foundations, move your hole away until you are clear of them. Bear in mind that the plants are intended to live in their quarters for as long as their natural lives: there is no worse job than attempting to dig up the remains of a deceased resident, especially as much of them will probably be under paving stones or other plants. Give each plant, therefore, every consideration, and include in the generous planting hole plenty of peat and bone meal (not manure) or a proprietary planting compost. Thereafter water well during the first growing season, and mulch thickly every spring.

There are notable exceptions to this rule, one being Fremontodendron: it takes positive exception to feeding and watering. Indeed, water it at any time, and it will die with alarming alacrity. How it sustains its magnificence I do not know.

Abutilon vitifolium
Acacia
Aloysia triphylla
Azara
Buddleia auriculata
Calceolaria integrifolia
Callistemon
Carpenteria californica
Cassia corymbosa
Ceanothus
Choisya ternata
Clianthus puniceus
Cotoneaster horizontalis (N)
Cytisus battandieri
x fatshedera lizei (N)
Fatsia japonica (N)

Fremontodendron
  'California Glory'
Garrya elliptica (N)
Grevillea
Hibiscus
Indigofera
Leonotis leonurus
Mimulus aurantiacus
Myrtus communis
Notospartium carmichaeliae
Phygelius piptanthus nepalensis
Pyracantha (N)
Romneya
Rosa 'Maigold'
Salvia (tender species)
Teucrium fruticans 'Azureum'

13

Climbers

Sadly there are very few climbers that will put up with the dry soil and windy conditions of a seaside garden, despite the compensating warmth: I know only too well as I have tried many of the more likely ones, and have failed miserably more often than not. Substantial wall plants, as mentioned above, are much more satisfactory, responding magnificently to the radiated heat from warmed up South or West facing brick work, stone or concrete, an effect which continues long after the sun has disappeared below the horizon.

Lack of success is not hard to explain: the effort that a climber makes to send up and sustain enormously long stems, which are then expected to produce abundant foliage, and furthermore flower and fruit generously, is nothing short of astonishing. In order to power this herculean task, readily available water and food is usually required in quantity, neither of which is an obvious natural attribute of light, sandy soil. Of course, you can make valiant attempts to provide both, but it is an unremitting task, and not to be undertaken if your objective is to enjoy your garden rather than to slave in it. Inevitably wind and drought is likely to defeat both you and the plant.

There are, however, a few select climbers which somehow have achieved over the millenia the seemingly impossible feat of adapting themselves to straitened circumstances. These are of immense value in a walled garden where some protection is provided against unremitting and malevolent gales. The wisteria clad cottage is not a realistic aspiration when the view of the sea is uninterrupted – so is the exposure!

In our walled garden near the sea many of the climbers mentioned below have succeeded beyond all expectations: this has mostly been a matter of trial and error.

Some I attempted only because friends had succeeded with them in similar positions; others I tried because they came from native habitats which could offer no better surroundings than I could. The list is not long, but all have proved their worth. A few are irremediably tender, thus demonstrating the beneficient "oven effect" of warm walls.

As regards cultivation the same rules apply as to any other wall plant: dig a deep hole in autumn, discard rubbish, avoid foundations, fill the hole plentifully with enriched humus (not manure!), water the plant in, and mulch thickly every year. Needless to say there are exceptions: one is the "Passion Flower" (Passiflora). This species requires a severely restricted root run to survive, and so you must fill the bottom of the hole with rubble – almost anything will do. Having done everything else to please it, thereafter make sure that the root run remains shaded and relatively cool using paving or other plants: indeed this is probably the most important prerequisite for the success of any climber as it helps to conserve moisture. Above all avoid the temptation to water your climbers other than in the first growing season: apart from the fact that it is probably illegal in these days of restriction, your plants should not need it when established; after all they have spent a very long time getting used to long, dry summers. But **never** plant in spring; the lack of rainfall during the first growing season will spell disaster to any infant plant struggling to perform its pre-programmed effort on an inadequately developed root system.

CLEMATIS

The luscious hybrids so beloved by inland gardeners working on fertile, moist soil simply will not do. The water requirement of these plants is astonishing. Christopher Lloyd (*"Clematis"*, 1989) calculates that a growing plant needs 4.5 gallons per square yard in each ten day period, the equivalent of an inch of rain. This is not a likely happenstance in spring and early summer by the sea. If, by some unlikely monsoon-like manifestation, this sort of copious rain did fall, it is more than likely that the free draining sand would ensure that the water would run off, and the wind would soon disperse through evaporation any remaining vestiges. I have tried a number of varieties, obeying all the rules as regards planting and positioning: none have actually died, but their performance has been pathetic. Even vigorous species such as *C. montana*, *C. alpina* and *C. tangutica* have found the aridity a total turn-off. Only two species have been successful; *C. flammula* and *C. cirrhosa*: both these are natives of the Mediterranean maquis, which explains their tolerance of conditions totally unsuitable for all others.

C. cirrhosa E – O

Not a great beauty by any means, but useful for its winter flowering and the small but profuse evergreen leaves. The flowers are diminutive, creamy-white, bell-shaped and nodding. The "Virgin's Bower" was discovered in Andalucia in the late 16th century, and was introduced into England by 1596.

The variety **'balearica'**, the "Fern-leaved Clematis", is more attractive with deeply divided leaves and pale yellow flowers spotted with purple. My specimen has behaved impeccably, but has dropped its leaves in a bad winter: these have always regenerated vigorously in early spring – so far. Majorca, Minorca, Corsica. I 1783. AM 1974.

C. flammula D – O

Vigorous with dark green shiny, bi-pinnate leaves and abundant, very fragrant, delicate, tiny, cruciform, white flowers borne in panicles in late summer. It can safely be grown through such shrubs as escallonia and olearia, which suits it as its lower parts are relatively naked. S Europe. Cultivated in England since the 16th century. AM 1984. AGM 1984.

C. x jouinana *(C. heracleifolia* var. *davidiana x C. vitalba)* D – O
The reasons why this non-clinging clematis survives in our arid
garden is rather a puzzle: *C. heracleifolia*, the non-clinging parent,
comes from Eastern China; *C. vitalba* is our native "Traveller's
Joy" or "Old Man's Beard": it is probably because *C. vitalba* is so
inherently rampant and that our plant is grown in light shade. It is
entirely herbaceous, the stems dying to the ground in winter, and
starts into growth again in very early spring, when you will have to
decide whether or not to train it upwards, or let it wander its way
at ground level. The leaves are attractive, comparatively large,
composed of three or five coarsely toothed leaflets and are a light
green. The flowers are small and pale lilac, borne towards the end
of the stems in large, loose panicles from August to October.

E. Jouin was apparently the manager of the Simon-Louis
nurseries at Metz in the late 19th century.

There are two varieties: **'Côte d'Azur'** with azure-blue
flowers and **'Praecox'** with earlier, pale blue flowers.

CLIANTHUS PUNICEUS E – O

The New Zealand "Parrot's Bill" or "Glory Pea" is a fabulous,
vigorous subject for a warm wall on open, sandy soil in the milder
parts of Britain. Its beauty of flower and leaf is so good that it is
worth taking a risk, especially as it is so easily raised from seed. The
pinnate leaves are luxuriant and graceful: the flowers are of a complex pea form, brilliant red, borne in pendulous racemes in early
summer. It grows up to 20' and 10' in width.

The generic name is derived from the Greek; *kleos* = glory,
anthos = flower. *Puniceus* is Latin for reddish-purple. I 1831.

ECCREMOCARPUS SCABER E – O

This semi-hardy, vigorous climber comes from Chile, and is usually treated as an annual. Given a mild winter it can survive against

a warm, sheltered wall, and, if it does, it will form a woody base. If it is damaged by cold, more often than not in a mild area it will regenerate from ground level the following spring.

It has the climbing habit of a clematis, the tendrils towards the end of the 8'-10' stems clinging to anything within reach. As it is rather bare at the bottom end, it looks better behind foreground planting, or it can be grown through medium-sized shrubs.

The leaves are bi-pinnate and glabrous; the flowers, bright orange-red and tubular, borne in racemes from June throughout summer. It seeds freely: the seeds can be sown in February, and planted out in May. Alternatively seeds sown in August can be overwintered under glass to give larger plants. Plants require generous watering during the first growing season and during particularly dry summer spells thereafter. They prefer a well-drained soil. I 1824. AGM 1984.

HEDERA

I suspect I am not alone in secretly and slightly guiltily disliking ivy: I am sure this is due to a childhood association with its acrid smell in dry, dusty, dirty, dim corners of unfamiliar gardens – the bits where you hid rather fearfully in games of "hide and seek". This is a pity because some of the sorts can be gloriously bright and cheerful. They are certainly willing and accommodating creatures, mostly putting up with any conditions without reservation, although they have a preference for limy soil. The variegated forms, of course, must have adequate sunlight to develop their markings properly.

Other commonly held objections to ivy are equally unwarranted. The aerial roots, which enable it to climb so effectively, do not damage the fabric of buildings; indeed the evergreen foliage keeps walls dry and warm. It is not poisonous; animals so inclined chomp at it voraciously without coming to any apparent harm. It will not strangle trees.

If you have to find fault with ivy it may be in the vigour of some of the climbing sorts. Unchecked these can achieve 100'. Plant one in a small garden, and you will risk creating a deluge of foliage which you will be hard pressed to stem. This truly amazing energy, however, can be put to good use in covering tree stumps, otherwise unproductive humps, arid banks, unsightly sheds, the shady bits under trees, man-hole covers and any other eye-sore you can think of.

H. *canariensis* 'Gloire de Marengo'

This is the tender "Canary Island Ivy" variety which is ubiquitous in the gardens of S Europe as a screen grown up chain-link fencing. Excellent when protected and warm, but it will not put up with cold winds. Better known in Britain as an indestructible house plant. The large leaves are dark green shading to silvery-grey and heavily margined with white. FCC 1880. AMT 1979. AGM 1984.

H. *colchica*

The vigorous and exotic "Persian Ivy" or "Elephant's Ear Ivy" has very large, dark green, thick and leathery leaves, and is perfectly hardy. C1850. AGM 1984. Outstanding varieties are:

'Dentata Variegata' with large leaves, bright-green margined creamy-yellow. An excellent hardy and very decorative alternative to "Gloire de Marengo". AM 1907. FCCT 1979. AGM 1984.

'Sulphur Heart' ('Paddy's Pride') with leaves irregularly splashed with yellow. Very cheerful. AMT 1979. AGM 1984.

H. *helix*

The "Common Ivy" might be the work horse of the genus, but it contains some remarkably beautiful varieties. Among the following sorts you will find the truly rampaging ivies, which are so accommodating in scrambling over large eye-sores, and covering bare patches of dusty soil under trees where even grass is unwilling to grow.

Although I have only described a few of the worthiest and most useful varieties below, there are an astonishing 300 sorts available through the one specialist nursery in Britain, Whitehouse Ivies of Maldon in Essex. If you should become addicted to the remarkably diverse genus, this is obviously your nirvana.

'Adam', smaller leaves, green and grey-green centrally with creamy-white margins. C1968. AGM 1984.

'Angularis Aurea', a high grower with bright yellow juvenile leaves which make a startling contrast with the mature dark green foliage.

'Atropurpurea', dark green leaves suffused with purple which deepen during winter, making the plant a brilliant backdrop to silver or yellow leaved shrubs or early flowers. C1884. AMT 1979.

'Buttercup', a slow growing sort with superb rich yellow leaves which mature to light green. C1925. AGM 1984.

'Glacier', silvery-grey leaves with narrow white margins. C1950. AMT 1979. AGM 1984.

'Goldheart', compact growth with leaves heavily splashed centrally with yellow. AM 1970. AGM 1984.

'Ivalace', an excellent neat ground cover with curly, bright green leaves. C1955. FCCT 1979. AGM 1984.

'Sagittifolia Variegata', compact growth with a prominent traingular central lobe to leaves which are grey-green margined creamy-white. C1965. AGM 1984.

H. hibernica

The "Irish Ivy" has larger leaves than *H. helix*, dark green, and are scaly and five-lobed. Very vigorous and good for ground cover. AMT 1979. AGM 1984.

HUMULUS LUPULUS 'AUREUS' d – o

This golden form of the beer "Hop" does well in our dry garden
with its roots shaded and its head growing through a large bay tree
into full sun, which it likes. The contrast with the rather funereal
dark green bay leaves is excellent. The leaves are attractively palmate, and elegant for a basically industrial plant. As could be expected, it is enormously vigorous if given ideal conditions (which
are not necessarily found by the sea). The whole plant is herbaceous, dying back in winter to ground level when chilled: being a
native of S Europe, it enjoys warm conditions.

The female flowers are yellowish-green, borne in clusters at the
end of summer. The fruit is the vital constituent of proper beer,
containing phenolic lupulin.

The ancient name "Willow Wolf" refers to its habit of growing
through willows (*Lupulus* is Latin for a small wolf).

JASMINUM OFFICINALE se – o or ◗

Nobody knows when our best beloved jasmine was introduced; it
was certainly a very long time ago. It is a native of the Caucasus, N
Persia, Afghanistan, the Himalaya and China, and so prefers the
warmth of S England, although it is happy on a sunny wall in the
north.

Its growth is not exactly neat, and it responds well to careful
training when it will reach 40'. It can power up to 6' of growth in a
season when established on its favourite light soil. It requires tying
in when young, but, if pruned well in spring, is self-supporting
thereafter.

All this trouble is eminently worthwhile for the clusters of small
white flowers which have the most delicious of scents; they are
borne from June to October. The attractive pinnate leaves do not
fall in a warm winter. It needs protection from vicious cold winds
AGM 1984.

LATHYRUS LATIFOLIUS D – O

The rough and ready "Everlasting Pea" is the perennial near-relation of the "Sweet Pea", and is suitable for the informal cottage garden: it is certainly not aristocratic, but when established is willing and hardy. The typical flowers are carmine-red, borne from July to autumn.

The varieties **'Albus'** and **'Snow Queen'** have white flowers; **'Roseus'**, bright rose-pink.

LONICERA

The "Honeysuckles" are essentially woodland plants, and most are not, most definitely not, suitable for dry sandy conditions. However, there are two worth trying which are described below.

L. etrusca D or SE – O
An enormously vigorous and spectacular species from the Mediterranean seabord, unusual for its love of dry conditions and full sun. The leaves are oval, glaucous and downy, and are retained in a warm winter. The flowers are scented, opening cream suffused with red, maturing to yellow, and are borne in June and July. I mid-18th century.

The two varieties are worth seeking out:

'Donald Waterer' has red new shoots and flowers which are red outside and white inside, maturing to orange-yellow. Donald Waterer found it in the French Pyrenees in 1973. AM 1985.

'Michael Rosse' has pale yellow flowers darkening when mature. Found in the garden at Nymans, West Sussex. AM 1982.

H. japonica 'Halliana' SE to E – ◗ to ●
In a small, shady London back garden I shared a wall with next door neighbours who grew this prodigious climber to the

exclusion of almost everything else. I spent many happy hours hacking at its intruding shoots, which threatened to envelop totally my precious wall plants. I seriously considered a night-time paraquat raid!

For a dark, cold, inhospitable place it cannot be bettered, but once happy, and given a free rein, its rampagous nature threatens any gardener with pretentions to sophistication with hysterics.

Having got this off my chest, I confess to having planted one in a position which has defeated every other tough nut. This is a windy, shaded, north-facing, tall stretch of plastic netting which closes off the nether end of our otherwise protected courtyard. It is now in its second season, and has managed 3' of growth, although I am aware that its roots have spread much further: only time will tell if it lives up to its much vaunted capabilities. Americans consider it to be a weed to be taken extremely seriously.

The white flowers offer compensation in that they are very fragrant, and are borne continuously throughout summer. Japan, Korea, Manchuria, China. I 1806. AGM 1984.

Varieties worth considering are:

'Aureoreticulata' has bright green leaves mottled gold. I by Robert Fortune before 1862. AGM 1984.

'Hall's Profilic' developed in Holland; flowers more abundantly in its youth.

PASSIFLORA CAERULEA E to SE – O

There is only one of this most exotic South American genus which can pretend to be a useful asset in the average mild British garden; *P. caerulea*, the "Blue Passion Flower". In common with any other sort you may wish to try, it demands a sunny, sheltered, warm wall to perform to anything approaching its potential. In addition the roots must be strictly confined to ensure flowering: when planting

Romneya coulteri is a 'Tree Poppy' from Los Angeles. The huge flowers develop on long, graceful, succulent branches throughout summer given protection from cold winds.

The Canary Islands biennial *Echium wildpretii* is tolerant of the rough and tumble of a seaside site sending up tall spires of red flowers.

The most hostile desiccated position is perfect for the dwarf 'Candytuft' *Iberis sempervirens* where it is indestructible, long-lived, neat and decorative.

The ravishing 'Madonna Lily' is the only lily which enjoys hot, dry conditions.

The well-adapted wooly stems of *Ballota pseudodictamnus* thrive happily in full sun.

Suitable ornamental grasses provide graceful contrasts of form and colour in mixed plantings despite their lack of flower power.

Captain Cook's 'New Zealand Flax', *Phormium tenax*, makes bold architectural statements in exposed positions with tough, erect leaves and majestic flower stems.

The only 'Arum Lily' tolerant of dry conditions is *Zantedeschia aethiopica* 'Crowborough', which buries itself to an astonishing depth before flowering.

Cordyline australis, the 'Cabbage Palm', can make a good isolated specimen in exposure. Here it is underplanted with *Euphorbia characias wulfenii* in full flower.

the bottom of the hole should be packed with rubble. After the first season no watering is required, although the roots appreciate the shade of other plants or paving. It should not be fed.

Having set about torturing your tender friend, it will respond by producing an abundance of shoots which cling with wire-like tendrils, prolific lobed leaves which only drop in severe winters (in the Channel Islands), and a continuous, but never super-abundant, display of the peculiarly attractive flowers during summer, followed by large, egg-shaped fruits. After two or three years it will have achieved a 20' to 30' growth, and will show no signs of flagging. I have a friend who dug his up, bagged the root bowl, and replanted it successfully, suitably arranged, on the wall of the new house extension.

The formation of the flowers gives rise to the common name. Jesuit priests in South America interpreted the arrangement as follows: the three stigmas, the three nails of Christ's crucifixion; the five anthers, the five wounds; the corona, the crown of thorns or the halo; the ten petals (or tepals), the the trustworthy apostles; the lobed leaves and tendrils, the hands and whips of the persecutors.

The petals are white; the filaments of the corona are blue at the tip and shade from white to purple towards the centre; the whole flower measuring about 3" in diameter. The fruit of this variety is not edible. S Brazil, Argentina. I 1609. AGM 1984.

It is worth trying the other more tender sorts for fun. My *O. mollissima* has survived its first season (without flowering).

PELARGONIUM PELTATUM D to SE – O

The "Ivy-leaved Geranium", which we all grow as a magnificent tender trailing plant in our annual summer containers, is apparently a first rate perennial climber in warm areas against a South wall. Christine Kelway pointed this out, and had seen for herself whole cottage sides on the Somerset coast covered in what she identified as 'Madame Crousse'. Having been enthused, I am trying myself:

so far, having cut out side shoots ruthlessly, the caned leaders are doing quite well. If it works, the results should be quite spectacular.

POLYGONUM BALDSCHUANICUM (FALLOPIA BALDSCHUANICA) D – O

The "Russian Vine" is the "Mile-a-minute Plant" of evil repute. A friend's daily help leant her bicycle against his specimen over an early summer weekend, and had problems disentangling the spokes on Monday. It is a good forty footer and as much across. Being so totally superabundant, it does well in conditions which would daunt anything less willing. Good for obliterating any relatively immobile large object you do not like looking at. The leaves are ovate and pale green; the tiny flowers are white tinged with pink borne in profuse panicles throughout summer and autumn. SE Russia. C1883. AM 1899.

ROSA

There are very few climbing roses adapted to arid, windy conditions. In fact there are two only which I think are worth trying. Wilhelm Kordes of Germany introduced **'Maigold'** in 1953 (see section on "Rosa"): this hybrid of R. *pimpinellifolia* produces luxuriant foliage and good, fragrant, rich golden-yellow semi-double flowers in dry soil, achieving 12' when established.

Quite another proposition is **R. filipes 'Kiftsgate'**. This is the intercontinental ballistic missile of the rose family. Nothing exceeds its vigour: it is known to climb to 40' and to spread 60'. Its origin is not known, but it was introduced from a nursery in 1938 to the garden at Kiftsgate Court in Gloucestershire, where it can still be seen. The species, R. *filipes*, was discovered by E.H. Wilson in NW Szechwan in 1908.

It takes three or four years to establish itself, after which, given good sunlight, it throws out its enormously long stems, handsomely clothed with deep green leaves, armed with sparse but vicious thorns, and bearing a magnificent display of huge clusters of small pure white single flowers of an intense fragrance in June and July.

Obviously this is not an ideal subject for a modest sized garden. Needless to say I have planted one in my courtyard. This I did through a combination of wanton devilment and frustration. No other climbing rose had survived the deprivations of the dry and windswept West wall, and my local nursery in London happened to have a particularly nice specimen in stock one day four years ago. It is fed once a year, watered never, and is behaving with reasonable circumspection. I have cut out the occasional errant stem; the remaining five are now 15' long and increase by 3' or 4' a year, producing the promised blooms on cue. So far I have not regretted my aberration, apart from the occasional torn shirt. In another four years I may not feel as sanguine.

SOLANUM

This is a huge genus, but there are only two satisfactory sorts for mild British gardens. Both require poor soil and full sun to flower freely, and are definitely tender. Should they be cut back by a hard winter, this is of no consequence as they will invariably spring up again from ground level.

S. crispum SE – O
The "Chilean Potato Plant" is not a self-supporting climber: it requires tying in. Once established, however, it appreciates the company of other wall plants, and will scramble successfully through these without much attention. It enjoys chalky soils. It is certainly vigorous, and will send up stems up to 20' long. The leaves are ovate, pale green and slightly downy: the flowers are small with purple-blue petals and yellow anthers borne in generous corymbs from July to September.

It takes a year or two to establish itself, but is very attractive when it has achieved some stature. I about 1830. AM 1989.

The variety **'Glasnevin'** has a longer season of flower. AM 1955. AGM 1984.

S. jasminoides SE – O

Unlike *S. crispum* this sort is twining and self-supporting. However, it is more tender, and is likely to behave in colder areas in an entirely herbaceous manner, dying to the ground in winter. This is of no great importance as it regenerates vigorously from ground level in spring, making up to 20' of growth in a season given a good summer. The leaves are shiny and delicate: the flowers very similar to *S. crispum* but with pale blue petals, borne from mid-summer to autumn. Definitely benefits from the warmest position. Brazil. I 1838.

The variety **'Album'** has white flowers with yellow stamens.

SOLLYA

The members of this evergreen genus from Australia are modest sized twiners of great and delicate beauty for the warmest wall in the mildest localities in the driest soil.

S. heterophylla E – O

The "Bluebell Creeper" has ovate leaves on slim 7' stems and prolific clusters of sky-blue, bell-shaped flowers throughout the summer and autumn. It appreciates the support of other wall plants. I 1830.

S. parviflora E – O

Even slighter than *S. heterophylla*, scarce in cultivation, with dark blue flowers borne singly or in pairs during the same period. I 1838. AM 1922.

TRACHELOSPERMUM

The two twining species worth considering in warm areas bear jasmine-like flowers with a strong fragrance in July and August and evergreen foliage. They prefer light acid soils, and so copious peat should be added to the planting holes especially on alkaline sand. The tough, leathery leaves withstand salt and wind well. Easily propagated by cuttings taken in July or August, and so common in cultivation.

T. asiaticum E – O

A well-branched climber up to 15' with small, oval, shiny, dark green leaves and very hairy new shoots. The flowers are yellow-white, and borne in small terminal cymes. It is hardier than *T. jasminoides*, and has a neater habit. Japan, Korea. All plants derive from a single specimen originally grown in Kew.

T. jasminoides E – O

A slow-growing species eventually achieving 12' or more. The flowers are white maturing cream, very fragrant. It was introduced by Robert Fortune in 1844, and was a favourite Victorian greenhouse plant because of its intense scent. In recent times its relative hardiness has been recognised, and it is now a valued plant for warm walls outside. It is certainly quite hardy in these conditions once established. C and S China. AM 1934. AGM 1984.

There are three varieties:

'Japonicum', a very much more vigorous sort with larger leaves turning bronze in winter.

'Variegatum', with leaves splashed creamy white.

'W. 776' ('Wilsonii') was collected by Ernest Wilson in Hupeh, China in 1907. Its foliage is particularly attractive, the leaves being heavily veined in light green with a bronze tint in winter.

14

Perennial Plants

One glance at any dictionary of perennial plants is guaranteed to reduce the innocent gardener to an indecisive jelly. The range of choice is truly phenomenal. In many ways the gardener who has a seaside or a hot and dry site to cultivate is in luck; the huge majority of species will not thrive. Once you have recognised that the traditional herbaceous border is simply not an option, the battle is won. Your choice is immediately limited to sturdy, self-sufficient plants which positively thrive in conditions which would spell instant disaster to most familiar favourites.

You simply must focus your attention on the natural habitat and characteristics of a chosen plant, and relate these to the environment you have to offer. It should be perfectly obvious that tall hybrid lupins and delphiniums will be mown flat by the first gale, and that moisture loving hostas and astilbes will be rapidly reduced to shrivelled skeletons. On the other hand some appropriate plants which are impossibly "difficult" in inland gardens will find your hot and probably windswept plot a perfect haven of harmony.

The following table of perennial plants contains only those sorts which have proved to be successful in dry, rugged conditions, and will not need staking or watering once established. It is well to remember, however, that herbaceous plants are not usually long-lived, and that the more tender species will succumb to the first really cold winter. They must mostly be considered entirely ex-pendable luxuries to be used as colourful and obliging transients within the tough and permanent framework of wind and drought resistant shrubs and trees.

The same planting rules apply as those used for shrubs: large holes filled generously with a peat-based compost, "puddling in" with copious water, a thick mulch to conserve moisture, wind protection when young and appropriate local pest control. Always plant in autumn.

NAME	FOLIAGE	FLOWERS	HT × SPRD	FLOWER-ING TIME	ORIGIN	COMMENTS
ACANTHUS						
spinosus	Long, arching deep green and spiny leaves	Long spikes of soft mauve flowers like fox-gloves	5' × 3'	7–10	S Europe	Bold and architectural. Needs full sun to flower freely. Origin of the Corinthian capital.
AETHIONEMA						
grandiflorum	Blue grey leaves on wiry stems	Deep pink, cress-like flowers	12" × 9"	5–7	Armenia	For walls and crevices in full sun.
AGAVE						
americana	Rosette of grey-green, sword-shaped, tough, succulent leaves, viciously pointed	Spectacular spike of pale cream flowers on 25' stem	3–5' × 6–10'	5–7	Mexico	Surprisingly hardy desert species. Flowers phenomenally after 5–10 years then dies. Offsets freely. Tolerates part shade in very sandy soil.
'Marginata'	Yellow margins to leaves	– ditto –	6' × 6'	5–7	Mexico	Decorative. Much used in S Europe as an urn specimen where it will tolerate total neglect on

ALLIUM

moly	Grey, lanceolate leaves	Upturned, star-shaped, bright yellow flowers in clusters	12" × 4"	6–7	S Europe	Good for naturalising on alkaline sand. Seeds itself freely but not a terrible nuisance.
neapolitanum	Narrow, strap-shaped, mid-green leaves	Umbels of star-shaped white flowers	12" × 4"	3–5	Mediter-ranean	Only hardy in mild areas. Spreads vigorously by seeds.
rosenbachianum	Linear, lanceolate, mid-green leaves	Large umbels of star-shaped rich purple flowers on stout stems	24" × 9"	5–6	Bokhara	Good border plant.

ALYSSUM

argenteum	Grey-green, oblong leaves	Profuse heads 2–3" across of cross-shaped, bright yellow flowers	18" × 12"	6–8	SE Europe	Good for rock gardens and dry walls in full sun.
saxatile	Evergreen, lanceolate, grey-green leaves	Profuse corymbs 4–6" long of bright golden-yellow flowers	12" × 18"	4–6	E Europe, Balkans, Russia	Many gardeners prefer the more subdued varieties: 'Citrinum', lemon-yellow; 'Dudley Neville', fawn-yellow. Excellent in driest conditions, especially draped over walls.

NAME	FOLIAGE	FLOWERS	HT × SPRD	FLOWER-ING TIME	ORIGIN	COMMENTS
AMARYLLIS						
belladonna	Strap-shaped mid-green leaves disappear before flowering	Heads of pale pink, fragrant, trumpet flowers on naked, purple stems	30" × 12"	8–10	S Africa	Plant 6" deep in good, light soil. Water in July to encourage flowering. Requires hottest position and a south-facing wall in colder areas. Takes time to settle in and flower. Select good forms; *purpurea*, 'Spectabilis', or 'Rosea'.
ANEMONE						
blanda	Lobed, mid to deep green leaves	Blue, 1" across	6" × 4"	2–4	Greece	Grow in firm, good quality, alkaline, well drained soil in part shade or sun. There are mauve, pink and white forms. Plant 2" deep.

coronaria	– ditto –	White or shades of blue and red, poppy-like flowers up to 2" across	6" × 4"	3–4	E Mediterranean	Grow in same soil but in full sun. Short-lived, but is cheap and so plant generously 2" deep every 2 years. Withstands wind well.
'de Caen'	– ditto –	Similar flowers to type, but more profuse over a longer period	6–12" × 6"	Early summer	garden	Good varieties: 'Hollandia', scarlet; 'Mr Fokker', blue; 'Sylphide', magenta; 'The Bride', white. Also mixed strains.
'St. Brigid'	– ditto –	Double or semi-double with same colour range but less profuse	6–12" × 6"	Early summer	garden	Good varieties: 'Lord Lieutenant', blue; 'The Admiral', magenta; 'The Governor', scarlet.
x fulgens	– ditto –	Scarlet, 2" across	12" × 6"	3–5	garden	Longer lived than strains of *A. coronaria*
ANTHEMIS						
cupaniana	Pretty, finely, divided, aromatic, grey-green leaves in mats	Prolific, white, daisy-like with yellow centres, 2" across	6–12" × 24"	6–8	Italy	Easy on sandy soil in wind. Good hanging over a wall or for carpeting.

NAME	FOLIAGE	FLOWERS	HT × SPRD	FLOWER-ING TIME	ORIGIN	COMMENTS
ARABIS						
caucasica	Obovate, grey-green hoary leaves in mats	White, ½" across	9" × 24"	2–6	Caucasus	Vigorous and invasive but good value for dry borders with aubretia and alyssums. Partial shade required. Less invasive varieties are: 'Coccinea', crimson and 'Flore Pleno', double white.
ferdinandii–coburgii	Mats of rosettes of lanceolate leaves	White, ½" across	3" × 12"	Spring	Greece	Part shade required.
ARMERIA						
maritima	Hummocks of mid to grey-green, grass-like leaves	Pink flower heads 1" across on long stems	6–12" × 6–12"	5–7	Europe	In the wild makes spectacular displays. Short-lived subjects for the rock garden, but happy in exposed sand. Varieties: 'Alba', white and 'Vindictive', rose-red.

ARNEBIA

echioides	Tufts of green, hoary, lanceolate leaves	Clusters of tubular, bright primrose yellow flowers on branching stems	9–12" × 9"	4–6	NE Turkey	Good in ordinary well drained soil in sun. Decorative but scarce.

ARTEMISIA

absinthium ("Wormwood" or "Absinth")	Deeply dissected, silvery grey leaves	Masses of mimosa-like yellow flowers	3' × 3'	Summer	E Mediterranean	Excellent foliage plant. Even better varieties: 'Lambrook Silver', whiter leaves; 'Powys Castle', non-flowering with dense silver leaves. For dry, hot, sunny positions like most artemisias.
arborescens	Very finely divided, silvery-white leaves	Panicles of globose yellow flowers	4' × 4'	6–7	S Europe	Magnificent foliage plant, semi-evergreen and much taller in a warm, protected site. Requires crispy dry, hot conditions being an inhabitant of rocky seaside areas.
canescens	Narrow spires of very finely divided, curling leaves	Insignificant and yellow	18" × 18"	8–9	garden	The miniature equivalent of *A. arborescens*

NAME	FOLIAGE	FLOWERS	HT × SPRD	FLOWER- ING TIME	ORIGIN	COMMENTS
ludoviciana ("White Sage")	Willow-shaped, silvery-white leaves on long stems	Insignificant and yellow	4' × 2'	Summer	Nebraska to the Rockies	Invasive and only useful for ground cover in rough areas.
stelleriana ("Dusty Miller")	Deeply lobed, ovate almost white, felty leaves on lax stems	Panicles 4–6" long of yellow flowers	24" × 15"	8–9	Japan and Korea (sand dunes)	A good carpeter. Naturalised in SW English coastal areas.
ASPHODELUS						
albus	Clusters of long, narrow leaves	Spires of star-shaped, white flowers veined brown centrally	3' × 3'	Summer	S Europe	Good for driest position. Very elegant.
AUBRETIA						
deltoidea	Small, obovate, hoary leaves in mats	Profuse short spikes of cross-shaped flowers in shades of purple to rose-lilac	4" × 24"	3–6	Sicily to Asia Minor	Excellent for dry walls or banks in sun. Numerous named varieties with larger, colourful flowers. Trim lightly after flowering. Requires alkaline soil.

BERGENIA

cordifolia	Evergreen, large rounded leaves with crinkled edges	Large, drooping heads of bell-shaped, lilac flowers on thick stalks	12" × 12"	3–4	Siberia	Happy in dry soil in sun or part shade, making good ground cover under shrubs and trees. The form 'Purpurea' has pink-purple flowers and purple-tinged leaves.
crassifolia	Upright rosettes of smaller ovate leaves, rich carmine beneath	Panicles of pale pink, bell-shaped flowers on stalks	12" × 12"	1–4	Siberia	Excellent ground cover in dry, partial shade.

CAMPANULA

garganica	Kidney-shaped mid-green leaves on prostrate stems	Profuse 6" long panicles of pale blue, star-shaped flowers	5" × 12"	5–9	Greece, Italy	Non-invasive dwarf. Good in sun or part shade. Varieties are 'Hirsuta' with grey hairy leaves and 'W.H. Paine' with rich blue flowers with white eyes.
isophylla	Heart-shaped, toothed mid-green leaves on tangled stems	Profuse star-shaped blue flowers 1" across	6" × 18"	8–9	N Italy	Tender but usually safe in warm areas in UK. 'Alba' has white flowers; 'Mayii' has variegated foliage.

NAME	FOLIAGE	FLOWERS	HT × SPRD	FLOWER-ING TIME	ORIGIN	COMMENTS
portenschlagiana	Dense, heart-shaped, toothed leaves	Masses of bell-shaped, deep purple-blue flowers	6" × 24"	6–11	S Europe	Best in light shade. Invasive but useful in difficult spots.
poscharskyana	Rounded, sharply toothed, mid-green leaves	Long sprays of star-shaped, lavender-blue flowers	12" × 36"	6–11	Dalmatia	Rampant. Good in part shade.
CARPOBROTUS						
edulis ("Hottentot Fig", "Kaffir Fig")	Evergreen, succulent, tapering, mid-green leaves 5" long, triangular in cross-section, on heavy thick stems forming dense mats	Large daisy flowers up to 5" across in yellow, purple or pink	6" × indefinite	5–6 and intermittently throughout summer	S Africa	A truly remarkable plant of uncompromising vigour which is outstanding for its use on large expanses of sandy soil where even maram grass has problems. Impervious to wild weather and rabbits but half-hardy. Parts of our colonies were killed in the exceptionally hard winter of 1986. Our largest patch is about 60 yards long and is a magnificent sight in full flower. Much better looking at all seasons than a tatty attempt at a lawn.

	Leaves	Flowers	Size	Flowering	Origin	Notes
CATANANCHE						
caerulea	Strap-shaped, hairy, grey-green leaves	Blue, cornflower-like flowers on thin, wiry stems, 1½" across	18" × 18"	Summer	W Mediterranean (garigue)	Easily propagated by shallowly planting long lengths of stem wherever you need it. Spreads quickly. The fruits are edible but not a gastronomic delight.
CENTAUREA						
dealbata	Deeply dissected, pinnate leaves, grey-green above, silver beneath	Rose-pink cornflowers 3" across on branched stems	24" × 24"	6–7/9	Caucasus, Persia	Requires drought and protection from strong winds. Cut back stems after flowering. 'Major' is more robust with larger flowers. This may need staking but is free flowering. Varieties are 'John Coutts', bright rose-pink flowers with pale yellow centres; 'Steenbergii', deep pink flowers. All centaureas like light, alkaline soil in full sun.

NAME	FOLIAGE	FLOWERS	HT × SPRD	FLOWER-ING TIME	ORIGIN	COMMENTS
pulcherrima ("Caucasian Cornflower")	Finely cut, silvery pinnate leaves	Bright pink cornflowers 2½" across on slender, branching stems	24" × 12"	6–7	Caucasus	A choice plant for admiring at close quarters.
pulchra 'Major'	Smooth, grey, pinnate leaves, silvery beneath	Cyclamen pink cornflowers 2" across on stiff stems	3'+ × 3'	6–7	garden	Architectural clump forming when mature. Not entirely hardy in cold areas. Give some wind protection.
CENTRANTHUS						
ruber ("Valerian")	Ovate fleshy green leaves	Large panicles of deep pink or red, tiny star-shaped flowers	3' × 1'	6–9	Europe (Mediterranean and Atlantic coasts on rock)	Unusually lush-looking plant with a liking for the roughest chalky soil. Seeds freely. Colonies old dry stone walls. 'Coccineus' has bright crimson flowers; 'Albus', white.

CERASTIUM

tomentosum ("Snow-in-Summer")	Small, silvery grey, lanceolate leaves forming a dense mat	Profuse white cup shaped flowers ¾" across	6" × 24"++	5–6	S and E Europe	An extremely wide-spreading, invasive plant but excellent for dry banks and walls. The variety "Columnae" is less invasive.

CHEIRANTHUS

x 'Bowles' Mauve'	Dark green lanceolate leaves making a rounded bush	Rich mauve flowers on lengthening stems	2½" × 2½"	Summer	garden	A wallflower with a non-stop display. Trim back flowering stems in July to encourage more flowers in autumn. Shelter from cold winds as it is not entirely hardy. Long-lived and choice, enjoying the seaside and sunny, dry, alkaline conditions.
cheiri 'Harpur Crewe'	– ditto – but becomes lank with age	Small, golden yellow double flowers	12" × 12"	4–6	garden	'Harpur Crewe' is sterile and is propagated by cutting in June or July. It is long-lived, unlike most other wallflowers which seed themselves to death. All enjoy the dry seaside conditions and alkaline soil inhibited by their Greek ancestors.

NAME	FOLIAGE	FLOWERS	HT × SPRD	FLOWER- ING TIME	ORIGIN	COMMENTS
CHIONODOXA ("Glory of the Snow")						
luciliae	Bright green strap-shaped leaves	Loose racemes of bright blue star shaped flowers ¾" across with white centres on 6" stems	6" × 4"	3–4	Turkey	Vigorous and spreading in full sun in well drained soil, but not for grass. Plant bulbs 3" deep and leave undisturbed. Hardy.
sardensis	– ditto –	Deeper blue flowers with small white centres	7" × 4"	3–5	Turkey	All are excellent for rockeries, one bulb producing several flower stems.
CHRYSANTHEMUM						
frutescens ("French Marguerite")	Pale green, neatly divided leaves	Profuse white daisies with yellow centres, 2" across	3' × 3'	Summer	Canary Islands	A magnificent, tender, shrubby plant which survives most winters by the sea in mild areas. White, yellow and pink forms and many named varieties.

	Leaves	Flowers	Size	Season	Origin	Notes
hosmariense	Silver, narrow, divided, stiff leaves	White daisies with yellow centres, 1½" across	8" × 12"+	11–3	Asia Minor	Unusual winter flowering alpine plant.
maximum ("Shasta Daisy")	Lanceolate, toothed, dark green leaves	White daisies with gold centres, 3" across	3' × 18"	Summer	Pyrenees	Only the original single flowered type is stout and reliably self-supporting, which is a pity because the coloured hybrids are very decorative.
rubellum	Mid-green leaves on a bushy plant	Fragrant, pink, single flowers 2" across	2' × 2'	8–10	garden	Plant in groups for mutual support. None of the varieties are better than the type. Propagate by cuttings in spring.

COLCHICUM
("Naked Ladies")

The autumn crocuses are good tuberous plants for a sandy garden, the more vigorous sorts increasing rapidly and naturalising in grass happily. The large crocus-like flowers in shades of lilac or white appear with late summer rain on bare stems. Their disadvantage is in the large coarse leaves which develop in spring and cannot be cut down until they die in July as doing so jeopardises future flowering; a heavy price to pay for the short-lived beauty of the previous year. The only appropriate positions are in grass which will help to obscure the leaves, or perhaps beneath shrubs where they are tolerant of partial shade. Plant 3–5" deep in early September. Disappointingly the heavy, vaguely obscene flowers overburden their slender stems and fall over with unreasonable alacrity soon after they open.

Recommended species and hybrids are:
C. *autumnale* and its double varieties; C. *byzantinum*, large and free-flowering, a pale rosy-lilac; C. *cilicicum*, similar to the previous but darker colour; C. *speciosum*, reputedly the best with an excellent variety 'Album', white, and hybrids 'Atrorubens', rich purple-crimson; 'Disraeli', deep violet-mauve; 'Huxley', deep rosy-lilac; 'The Giant', a strong growing sort with rosy-lilac flowers having a marked white throat; 'Water Lily', the double rosy-lilac flowers are huge but fall over as soon as they open.

NAME	FOLIAGE	FLOWERS	HT × SPRD	FLOWER-ING TIME	ORIGIN	COMMENTS
CONVOLVULUS						
mauritanicus (*sabatius*)	Ovate, mid-green leaves forming mats	Soft, periwinkle blue, convolvulus flowers 1" across	3" × 24"	6–9	N Africa	A lovely trailing plant in sandy soil in the warmest spot. Tender, and so take cuttings in late summer, and overwinter in a frame.
CRAMBE						
cordifolia	Huge leathery leaves, deep green, lobed and wavy, 3' long	Masses of small white flowers on many branched stems, strongly scented	6' × 4'	Summer	Caucasus	A massive, sub-tropical looking, architectural specimen which resembles a giant gypsophila. Flowers need wind protection. Propagate by seeds.
CREPIS						
incana	Rosettes of grey-green, ovate, jagged leaves	Soft pink dandelion flowers on thin, stiff branches	18" × 12"	7–8	Greece	Excellent in poor sandy soils in full sun.

CROCOSMIA

x crocosmiiflora ("Montbretia")	Upright, long arching, sword-shaped, mid-green leaves	Trumpet-shaped flowers ranging from yellow to deep red, 1½" long on long stems	2' × 4"	7–9	S Africa	The hardiest of this type, and is invasive but easily controlled. Naturalised in rough ground in warmer areas. Bulbous. Many good named varieties. Happy in sun or part-shade.
masonorum	– ditto – but broader	Larger upturned flowers in shades of orange and scarlet packed on arching stems	2½' × 6"	7–8	S Africa	Strong-growing with vivid colouring. An excellent selection is 'Firebird' from Bressingham which is bright orange-red outside with a large yellow circle inside.

CROCUS

Coming from the Mediterranean seaboard the crocuses are the ideal plants for a hot, dry, sandy garden where they will thrive if left undisturbed in sunny positions. All appreciate autumn and spring rains, but will not tolerate anything but sharp drainage. The species spread rapidly by seeds. The larger flowered hybrids are sterile and spread by division of the corms. If you are clever in choosing what you plant, the flowering season can be continuous from late August to March. The choice is enormous and the colour range truly incredible. All prefer alkaline soil and should be planted 2–3" deep. Having retractile roots they will adjust themselves appropriately. Mentioned below is a selection of the most beautiful and vigorous sorts.

Late August through November:

C. *speciosus* varies in colour from deep mauve-blue to white, the form 'Oxonian' is the bluest sort; C. *banaticus*, rich bluish-purple; C. *kotschyanus kotschyanus*, exotic but vigorous, deep rose-lilac with orange spots and yellow throat; C. *niveus*, large, white with bright yellow throat; C. *nudiflorus*, large, deep purple, imported by the Knights of St. John of Jerusalem; C. *serotinus dusii salzmannii*, large, lilac with deep yellow throat, vigorous, from N Africa but hardy.

December to mid-February:

C. *chrysanthus*, varies in colour from deep yellow to bright orange, named varieties include 'Blue Pearl', pale blue with orange stigmata; 'Blue Peter', violet blue with white edges; 'Cream Beauty', pale cream-yellow; 'Gipsy Girl', butter-yellow marked with chocolate; 'Lady Killer', white marked with deep mauve; 'Moonlight', large, pale sulphur yellow; 'Snow Bunting', white, outside feathered with dark lilac; 'Zwanenburg Bronze', large, deep orange inside, outside suffused deep purple-brown. C. *imperati*, large and exotic, an amalgam of yellow, purple and bright lilac-mauve. C. *tomasinianus*, "Tommies" are ultra-vigorous and very variable, shades of bright mauve, occasionally white, named varieties include 'Barr's Purple', rich purple-lilac inside, pale mauve-grey outside and 'Whitewell Purple', pale silver-mauve inside, purple-mauve outside.

Mid-February to March:

C. *corsicus*, inside lilac-mauve, outside pale lilac beautifully feathered with deep purple. C. *dalmaticus*, large, pale-lilac. C. *sieberi*, perhaps the most beautiful and vigorous, deep mauve with distinguishing orange-yellow throat, varieties include 'Bowles's White', pure white with deep yellow base; 'Hubert Edelsten', large, banded mauve-purple and white with gold throat; 'Tricolor', large, banded mauve, white and lilac; 'Violet Queen', smaller but deep violet.

Garden Varieties:

The "Dutch Crocuses" are exceptionally vigorous and only suitable for naturalising in grass. There is a wonderful choice of pure colour in white, deep purple and golden yellow and a variety of striped sorts. Flowering will suffer if the leaves are not allowed to die back before they are cut along with the grass. Among the best are 'Snowstorm', 'Vanguard', 'Negro Boy', 'Purpureus Grandiflorus', 'The Bishop' and 'Dutch Yellow'.

CYCLAMEN

A wonderfully rich genus with almost as long a flowering period as Crocus. The often lusciously coloured and elegant flowers and decorative leaves belong to corms which spread freely by seed, and are happiest in part shade in well drained soil planted no more than 2" deep.

The species are hardy, and demand no more than a light dressing of leaf mould and bonemeal as nurture. They are perfectly happy in alkaline conditions. Patches can be increased by transplanting seedlings. When planting a corm make sure it is the right way up: there is a small indentation which distinguishes the top.

cilicium	Round with silver markings, slightly toothed	Fragrant, pale pink with basal red spot to each petal, 1" long	4" × 6"	10–11	Asia Minor	Almost hardy.
coum	Round with silver markings occasionally, dark red beneath	Flowers variable in colour from pink through to white, 3/4" long	3" × 6"	12–3	SE Europe to Caucasus	Hardy. Varieties include C. coum album, white; C.c.c. 'Pewter Leaf and 'Silver Leaf, decorative silvery foliage.
europaeum (purpurascens)	Rounded leaves mid-green with silvery markings	Deep carmine flowers with a strong fragrance, 3/4" long	4" × 6"	7–9	Hungary to Italy	One of the hardiest. There is a rare white variety, 'Album'.
hederifolium (neapolitanum)	Rounded leaves deep green above with silver markings, red beneath	Mauve to pale pink 1" long	4" × 6"	8–11	Italy, Greece	Hardy. Floriferous and vigorous when pleased. The variety 'Album' has white flowers.

NAME	FOLIAGE	FLOWERS	HT × SPRD	FLOWER–ING TIME	ORIGIN	COMMENTS
persicum	Very variable leaves deep green to yellow-green	White, pale pink or carmine-pink, fragrant, 1–1½" long on 6"+ stems	9" × 9"	3–4	E Mediterranean	Half-hardy. The most beautiful, but only happy in warm areas in protected positions. The parent of the florists' cyclamen. There are numerous spectacularly coloured even less hardy named varieties which are worth trying in favoured areas.
pseudibericum	Cordate, toothed leaves marked yellow-green above, deep crimson beneath	Deep crimson-carmine to purplish flowers marked pale pink or white, 1" long on 6" stems. Fragrant	6" × 6"	1–3	Cyprus, Crete, Rhodes, Lebanon, N Africa	Beautiful but tender. Worth trying in a warmer area.
repandum ("Ivy-leaved Cyclamen")	Variable leaves, toothed and wavy with silver markings above	Pink, crimson or white flowers 1" long. Fragrant	6" × 6"	3–5	S Europe, Aegean Islands	Although half-hardy is vigorous enough to naturalise in part shade in warm areas.

CYNARA

carduncularis ("Cardoon")	Huge, 3–4' long, silver-grey, pointed, deeply divided, recurved leaves	Huge purple thistle-like flowers on leaved, stout stems	6' × 3'	Summer	Mediter-ranean (garigue)	A fantastical architectural specimen for the larger garden. Needs dry sand and full sun, but hardy once established.

DIANTHUS

A genus which finds seaside conditions totally to its liking. All species, varieties and hybrids must be tried, but every one will require gritty, light, alkaline soil but not pure sand. Bone meal is the only feeding they require, and all dislike over-watering once established. Do not add peat to the planting hole, and never apply organic mulches, they can cause stem rot. They are generally short-lived, but are easily propagated by taking non-flowering side shoots in June or July.

For the truly dedicated seaside gardener the family *Dianthus* offers the opportunity of capitalising on ideal conditions, an unique occurrence where the choice of material is so prolific and attractive.

In "*The Plant Finder*" approximately 725 species, varieties and hybrids are listed as available from a number of specialist nurseries: surely enough to keep most enthusiasts fully occupied for several lifetimes!

There is no up to date specialist reference work available other than "*The International Dianthus Register*": this suggests that there is a good case for starting with long familiar species, the wild pinks, and extending your knowledge through the old-fashioned single pinks to the numerous modern hybrids. All will provide a thoroughly vivid display of flower colour and often a seductive fragrance. Unfortunately the more sophisticated your tastes become, the more diseases are invited: a price you have to pay for the privilege.

NAME	FOLIAGE	FLOWERS	HT × SPRD	FLOWER-ING TIME	ORIGIN	COMMENTS
DICTAMNUS						
albus ("Dittany")	Deeply divided, fragrant leaves on erect stems	Upright spikes of handsome white flowers	3' × 2'	5–7	Europe, Asia	An ancient and long-lived plant known as the "Burning Bush" as the volatile oil exuded on a hot, windless day from ripening seed pods can be ignited with a match.
purpureus	– ditto –	Soft mauve-purple, delicately veined	3' × 2'	5–7	– ditto –	
DIERAMA						
pulcherrimum ("Wand Flower")	Long, thin, erect, evergreen leaves	Drooping calyces of bell-shaped flowers of varying shades of pink on tall, wiry stems	5' × 1'	7–9	S Africa	The "Venus' Fishing Rod" is a most graceful and unusual plant. "Black Bird" has violet-mauve flowers and there is a dwarf form.

DIGITALIS

purpurea ("English Foxglove")	Rosette of deep green leaves	Long, spikes of bell-shaped flowers on long stems, purple, red or maroon, spotted	3–5' × 1"	6–7	W Europe	Naturalised on cliffs. Usually biennial but perennial if pleased. The many varieties need more moisture and some shade.

ECHINOPS

ritro	Spineless, deep grey-green, jagged leaves, downy beneath	Deep steel-blue globular florets 2" across	4' × 2'	7–8	S Europe, Balkans	A typical but spineless thistle. Compact and vigorous. 'Veitch's Blue' has deeper coloured flowers.

ECHIUM

fastuosum	Rosettes of long, lanceolate, rough leaves. Evergreen	Multiple spires of bright blue flowers	6' × 10'	4–6	Unknown	Excellent bushy, evergreen architectural plant for the poorest, driest conditions. Tolerates part shade even under pines. Trim off dead flower heads.

NAME	FOLIAGE	FLOWERS	HT × SPRD	FLOWERING TIME	ORIGIN	COMMENTS
wildpretii	Rosettes of very long (1') lanceolate rough leaves, mid-green with silvery hairs. Evergreen	Very tall erect spires of funnel shaped red flowers, densely packed	8' × 2'	4–7	Canary Islands	An almost hardy biennial of spectacular stature. Wonderful specimen plant in poor dry soil given some wind protection.
ERIGERON						
glaucus	Evergreen, dense clumps of spathulate, grey-green leaves on short stems	Profuse, pale mauve, stout daisies with large yellow centres, 1½" across	8–12" × 2+	6–10	W North America	Naturalised on cliffs in S of England. A vigorous, long-lived, long-flowering carpeter, perfectly happy in inhospitable hot, dry, windy conditions. Exceptionally useful and decorative. 'Elstead Pink' has clear lilac-pink flowers.

ERIOPHYLLUM

lanatum ("Oregon Sunshine")	Grey–white, hairy leaves on long stems	Profuse yellow daisies, 1" across	1' × 1'	Summer	North America	Long-flowering but common-looking plant for hot, dry positions. Useful.

ERODIUM

carifolium	Feathery, silver leaves	Saucer-shaped rich magenta–purple flowers with a maroon blotch	18" × 2'	6–9	Spain	Excellent for hot, dry, alkaline positions
chrysanthemum	Basal clumps of distinguished, finely divided silvery leaves	Sprays of bright yellow saucer-shaped flowers, ¾" across	6" × 15"	6–9	Greece	The "Heron's Bills" have highly decorative foliage and flowers, well-suited to dry, alkaline, rough places. Long-flowering.

ERYNGIUM

The "Sea Hollies" are quite magnificent plants for dry, sandy gardens, and are tough enough to withstand strong summer winds. They are happy on rough, alkaline soils in blazing sun when they produce a succession of highly decorative flower heads in mid-summer.

There are two distinctive groups of species: one from Europe, the other from S America. Hybridisation has been free between the European species, grown in England from the 16th century, and the more recently introduced American sorts. The resultant confusion is difficult to resolve, but generally the Americans have evergreen, narrow leaves, and the Europeans deciduous, rounded or lobed leaves.

NAME	FOLIAGE	FLOWERS	HT × SPRD	FLOWER-ING TIME	ORIGIN	COMMENTS
agavifolium	Rosette of 2' long, green, sword-shaped, serrated leaves	Green, thimble-shaped flower heads on long stems	5' × 2'	7–8	Argentina	Evergreen and exotic although of no great elegance. Tender and requires shelter from cold winds.
alpinum	Dark green-blue rosettes of heart shaped leaves. The stem leaves are deeply cut	Steel-blue, cone-like flowers, 1" long, surrounded by spiny, prominent bracts on tough blue stems	2' × 18"	7–9	Europe	A really excellent, low-growing sort.
bourgatii	Deeply cut, curly basal foliage, grey-green with white veins	Elongated blue-green thistle-like flowers, 1½" long on branching, wiry stems	2' × 1'	7–8	Pyrenees	Compact and beautiful. "Oxford Blue" has deeper blue flowers.
bromeliifolium	Rosettes of mid-green, toothed, strap-shaped leaves	Green, thistle-like flower heads 1" long on long arching stems	3' × 2'	7	Mexico	An elegant, hardy and evergreen plant.
eburneum	Long (1–2'), arching, profusely spiny, sword-like basal leaves	Green flowers with white stamens, ½" long on leaved, arching, branched, pale green stems	5' × 2'	7–9	Colombia, Argentina	Elegant, hardy and evergreen.

giganteum ("Miss Willmott's Ghost")	Blue, cream-shaded, round toothed, heart-shaped basal leaves	Silver-blue flower heads 2" long on blue stems	4' × 2½"	8–9	Caucasus, Iran	A biennial, but seeds freely. A legendary plant which must be grown if you have room.
maritimum ("Sea Holly")	Silver green, rounded basal leaves; deeply cut, spiny stem leaves	Steel-blue flower heads 1" long on much branched stems	12" × 18"	7–9	Europe	It must have the hottest, driest, poorest conditions.
x oliverianum	Deeply cut, round, blue-green basal leaves	Deep blue flower heads 1" long on vivid steel-blue stems	4' × 2'	7–9	garden	A truly aristocratic hybrid with the best blue flowers.
planum	Dark green, heart-shaped leaves	Deep blue, globular flowerheads ½" across	2' × 18"	7–8	E Europe, Asia	Not as good as *E. tripartitum* but has an excellent dwarf form 'Blauer Zwerg' ('Blue Dwarf').
tripartitum	Spineless, dark green basal rosettes	Blue flowers ½" long on many, widespreading, blue, wiry stems	2½' × 2'	7–9	Mediterranean	Excellent, but flops about without support.
x zabelii	White, marbled leaves	Blue flowerheads 1½–2' long	2½' × 2'	7–9	garden	The best large flowered blue. 'Violetta' has deep violet flowers on violet-blue stems.

NAME	FOLIAGE	FLOWERS	HT × SPRD	FLOWER–ING TIME	ORIGIN	COMMENTS
EUPHORBIA						
characias wulfenii	Long stems fully clothed with long, lance-shaped, grey-green leaves	Large, columnar panicles of bright green-yellow florets	3–4' × 3'	3–4	Mediter-ranean	Flowering stems are biennial, forming one year, flowering the next. A stately, evergreen plant thriving in sun or part shade. Architectural. 'Lambrook Gold' has gold flower heads.
myrsinites	Glaucous grey, succulent leaves closely packed on trailing stems	Heads of bright green-yellow florets	6" × 1'	4–5	S Europe	A strange and wonderful spreading plant for trailing over hot, dry banks and walls. Evergreen with biennial flowering stems.
polychroma (*epithimoides*)	Low rounded dome of clustered rosettes of bright green ovate leaves	Profuse, flat heads of bright yellow florets 3" across on 12" stems	18" × 2'	4–5	E Europe	The bright flower heads rival any other spring plant with their intense colour. Good autumn foliage.

robbiae	Rosettes of dark green leaves on 9" stems	Heads of flat, lime-green flowers 1" across	2' × 2'	6–10	Asia Minor	Excellent evergreen, spreading ground cover under trees and shrubs where the soil is dry, starved and shaded. Introduced by Miss Robb via her hat box.
segueirana niciciana	Narrow, glaucous leaves on slender stems	Profuse heads of lime yellow flowers	18" × 18"	5–9	Turkey, SE Europe	A long-flowering clump former appreciating full sun and dry conditions. Non-invasive.
FASCICULARIA						
bicolor	Rosettes of narrow, prickly leaves, bases of leaves bright pink	Stemless clusters of small, pale blue flowers in centres of rosettes	18" × 2'	7–10	Chile	Only hardy in warm coastal areas where it thrives in the poorest soil in sun or shade. Evergreen.
pitcairniifolia	Brilliant red centre to rosettes	– ditto –	18" × 5'	7–10	– ditto –	As above. Evergreen.

NAME	FOLIAGE	FLOWERS	HT × SPRD	FLOWER- ING TIME	ORIGIN	COMMENTS
FELICIA						
amelloides ("Blue Marguerite")	Ovate, mid-green leaves on a bushy plant	Sky-blue daisy flowers 1½" across on long stems	18" × 18"	6–8	S Africa	Perennial, but usually grown as an annual except in mild areas where they may survive. Also known as *Agathaea coelestis*.
pappei	Linear, pale green, thick leaves on a bushy plant	Sky-blue daisy flowers 1" across on long stems	15" × 15"	6–10	Africa	Quite the prettiest little half-hardy sub-shrub. Evergreen, and flowers well over a long period in a hot, dry position. Also known as *Aster pappei*.
FERULA						
communis	Finely lacy, green leaves forming a mound 2' high, 4' across	Multiple heads 1' across of yellow cow-parsley flowers on a tall, stout stem	7' × 4'	Summer	N Africa, Mediter- ranean	The plant takes several years to establish itself in deep, light soil in full sun: it will then flower spec- tacularly. The "medicinal fennel". Plant small; does not transplant.

FOENICULUM

	Foliage	Flowers	Size	Season	Origin	Notes
vulgare ("Fennel")	Fine and delicate, aromatic, green leaves	Heads of yellow-green cow-parsley flowers on smooth, branching stems	6' × 2'	Summer	Europe, Mediterranean	The culinary fennel is a thoroughly decorative garden plant as well as being excellent in salads. Naturalised in coastal areas. Seeds freely. *F. purpureum* has magnificent bronze leaves

GERANIUM

The "Cranesbills" are not the "geraniums" used for summer bedding, but excellent perennial ground cover plants for sun or part shade on dry soil. The flowers are small and decorative, never profuse, and are borne over a long period. The foliage is always attractive.

There are many species and hybrids to try, the majority hardy. The taller sorts need more moisture than usually available by the sea: in any case they require staking. The low growing sorts are good for underplanting the old roses that like maritime conditions. Consult catalogues.

GLADIOLUS

	Foliage	Flowers	Size	Season	Origin	Notes
byzantinus	Green, strap-like leaves	Elegant purple-red flowers on long stems	3' × 1'	6	S Europe, Mediterranean	Not at all like the large flowered hybrids. Graceful, and does not need staking. Increases vigorously on light soil. Only for warmer areas.

NAME	FOLIAGE	FLOWERS	HT × SPRD	FLOWER- ING TIME	ORIGIN	COMMENTS
GYPSOPHILA						
paniculata	Insignificant grass-like leaves	Large airy mound of tiny, star-shaped white flowers	4' × 4'	6–8	E Europe, Siberia	Thrives on poor, but alkaline soil. Good for covering gaps left by spring flowering bulbs and *Papaver orientalis*. 'Bristol Fairy', double white flowers; 'Flamingo', 'Compacta Plena', double pale pink flowers.
repens	Mats of linear, grey-green leaves	Cloud of tiny white to deep pink flowers on wiry stems	6" × 2'	6–8	Europe	Good draping over walls.
'Rosy Veil' ('Rosenschleier')	– ditto –	Clear pink flowers	1' × 18'	6–8	garden	A hybrid of good form.

There are a number of other varieties of G. *paniculata* and G. *repens*.

HELLEBORUS

Name	Leaves	Flowers	Size	Flowering	Origin	Notes
corsicus	Decorative, tripartite, pale green leaves with spiny edges on stout stems	Large panicles of yellow-green flowers on stout stems	2–3' × 3'	3–4	Corsica, Sardinia, Balearic Islands	Evergreen. A most handsome shrub-like plant for the driest positions in sun or shade. The huge panicles of flowers fall over eventually: otherwise faultless. Protect from cold winds.

HIERACUM

Name	Leaves	Flowers	Size	Flowering	Origin	Notes
villosum	Mat of woolly grey leaves	Bright yellow dandelion flowers on long stems	1' × 1'	6–7	Central Europe	Only hardy in warm areas, but seeds itself generously. Not distinguished, but useful for impossible places in sun.

IRIS

Name	Leaves	Flowers	Size	Flowering	Origin	Notes
histrioides 'Major'	Strap-like leaves 1" long at flowering time, extend to 18"	Royal blue, 3½" across	4" × 2½	12–1	Asia Minor, Turkey, NW Persia	One of the first to flower for the driest soils, but fertilise after flowering.

NAME	FOLIAGE	FLOWERS	HT × SPRD	FLOWER-ING TIME	ORIGIN	COMMENTS
pumila	– ditto –	Shades of purple, white and yellow, 3" across stemless	4" × 2"	4	SE Europe	A species from mountainous regions, needing stony, dry conditions. Divide every second year. A good range of hybrids with a wide variety of colours.
reticulata	Leaves extend above the flowers	Deep blue–purple, 3" across	6" × 4"	2–3	Russia, Caucasus, N Persia	Prefers light, dry alkaline soil. Feed after flowering. A good range of hybrids.
KNIPHOFIA						
uvaria ("Red Hot Poker")	Long strap-like leaves, evergreen lax and untidy	Long spikes of scarlet and yellow tubular flowers on stout stems	5' × 2'	7–9	S Africa	Almost hardy on light soil, giving a good display in late summer, but spoiled by being distinctly untidy. Unfortunately the refined hybrids require more moisture when coming into flower than is usually available in hot dry sandy soil.

LAMPRANTHUS

Brilliant hardy perennial plants of the Mesembryanthemum group. They are all dwarf and shrubby, much branched with thick, tapering succulent leaves and masses of vividly coloured daisy flowers from June to October. All species grow quickly. Never fade. They will only thrive in the very poorest, driest soil in the hottest position. In warm areas they mostly survive a mild winter. They are easily propagated by taking stem cuttings 2" long and rooting them in pure sand in late summer. Overwinter under glass.

amoenus	Bright green turning red in hot sun	Brilliant purple flowers 3" across	9" × 12"	Summer	S Africa
aurantiacus	Glaucous green leaves	Bright orange flowers 1½" across	16" × 12"	Summer	S Africa
brownii	Grey-green leaves	Tangerine-orange maturing to deep red	12" × 12"	Summer	S Africa
coccineus	Grey-green leaves	Brilliant carmine flowers 1½" across	15" × 12"	Summer	S Africa
conspicuus	Bright green with red tips	Purple red flowers 2" across	18" × 12"	Summer	S Africa
elegans	Grey-green leaves	Rose-red flowers 1½" across	15" × 12"	Summer	S Africa
roseus	Bright green leaves	Cerise-pink flowers 1½" across	15" × 12"	Summer	S Africa
spectabilis	Bright green leaves	Vivid purple flowers 3" across	12" × 12"	Summer	S Africa
'Zeyheri'	Bright green leaves	Purple violet flowers 3" across	15" × 12"	Summer	S Africa

N.B. In the Channel Islands in a good summer the spread of the more prostrate species can be considerably more than that quoted above, and can look particularly good cascading down stone walls

NAME	FOLIAGE	FLOWERS	HT × SPRD	FLOWER-ING TIME	ORIGIN	COMMENTS
LIMONIUM						
latifolium ("Sea Lavender" "Statice")	Rosettes of eliptic, downy mid-green leaves. Evergreen	Generous sprays of small lavender-blue flowers 9" long	2' × 18"	7–9	Bulgaria, S Russia	Thrives in a sunny, open position. Seek out the really good varieties: 'Blue Cloud', light lavender blue; 'Violetta', violet
LINARIA ("Toadflax")						
alpina	Blue-green linear leaves	Sprays of violet snap-dragon flowers each ½" long	6" × 9"	6–8	European alps	Hardy and compact. Full sun.
dalmatica	Glaucous blue lanceolate leaves	Clear yellow snap-dragon flowers 1½" long with an orange stripe to lower lip	3' × 2'	6–9	SE Europe	Needs full sun and poor, well-drained soil.
purpurea	Mid-green linear leaves	Slender spikes of tiny, purple blue snap-dragon flowers	3' × 18"	7–9	S Europe	Full sun and poor soil. Seeds freely. Varieties are 'Alba', white; 'Carron Went', light pink; 'Yuppie Surprise', light

triornithophora	Grey-green lanceolate leaves	Deep lilac snap-dragon flowers with yellow markings on the tip ¾" long on many branched stems	2' × 18"	6–9	Portugal, Spain	A tender plant for hottest, driest position. There are pink, mauve and purple strains available.
LINUM ("Flax")						
arboreum	Mid-green, narrow triangular leaves	Profuse terminal clusters of golden yellow open funnel-shaped flowers 2" across	12" × 12"	5–6	Crete	Tender and like all the flax family is short-lived and requires a hot, dry, poor soil.
flavum	Glaucous green leaves	Golden yellow typical flowers 1" across	18" × 9"	6–8	Mid-Europe	Hardy. The variety 'Compactum' is neater.
narbonense	Grey-green, narrow, lanceolate leaves	Profuse panicles of rich blue typical flowers 1" across	2' × 12"	5–9	S Europe	Hardy. Evergreen in mild areas. Long flowering season.
perenne	Grey-green, narrow lanceolate leaves	Profuse clusters of sky-blue typical flowers 1" across	18" × 12"	6–8	Europe	Hardy, but only lives for two or three years. Easily raised from seed. There is a white variety.

NAME	FOLIAGE	FLOWERS	HT × SPRD	FLOWER-ING TIME	ORIGIN	COMMENTS
LIRIOPE						
muscari	Compact clump of decorative, deep green, glossy, grass-like leaves	3" spikes of small mauve-like flowers resembling the grape hyacinths	18" × 15"	8–11	Japan, China	Excellent for ground-cover in dry soil with a low lime content. Flowers more freely in sun, but tolerates partial shade.
LITHOSPERMUM						
diffusum	Small, dark green, ovate leaves on spreading stems	Five lobed deep blue flowers ½" across in profusion	4" × 2'	6–10	S Europe	A beautiful sub-shrub for poor sandy soil, but is totally intolerant of lime. Add plenty of peat when planting. Excellent forms are 'Grace Ward' and 'Heavenly Blue'.
LYCHNIS						
coronaria ("Dusty Miller")	Rosettes of woolly, grey-green leaves	Round, pink-like plum-red flowers 1½" across	3' × 18"	7–9	S Europe	Short-lived but ideal plant for dry, poor, hot soil.

flos-jovis ("Flower of Jove")	Thick, woolly, silver lanceolate leaves in dense tufts	Profuse heads of reddish purple flowers ½" across on short branching stems	2' × 12"	6–8	Europe	A smaller sort from alpine areas in gritty soil.
MARRUBIUM						
incanum	Silky grey, nettle-like evergreen leaves	Terminal spikes of small white flowers in grey woolly calyces	3' × 3'	Summer	S Europe, Asia Minor	One of the loveliest silvery plants on dry, alkaline soil.
MELISSA						
officinalis ("Lemon Balm")	Hairy with strong lemon scent when crushed	Insignificant	2' × 18"	Summer	E Europe	A very ancient herb sacred to Diana. Paracelsus believed it was the elixir of life, and for thousands of years it was used to "renew youth, strengthen the brain and relieve languishing nature". It seeds freely and is happiest in partial shade. The form 'Allgold' is excellent for gold leaves.

NAME	FOLIAGE	FLOWERS	HT × SPRD	FLOWER- ING TIME	ORIGIN	COMMENTS
NARCISSUS Attempting to grow the more exotic garden hybrid narcissi on an exposed maritime site is not appropriate, if only because the choice blooms can be damaged by spring gales. Their wild robust relatives, however, are quite magnificent in light, dry soil in warm areas when they can be left undisturbed: they will naturalise happily and will flower for years. Among the wild species of daffodils and narcissi there is a wide range of form from miniatures to really quite substantial plants.						They are mostly natives of S. Europe and W. Africa, and are well attuned to arid, poverty stricken conditions. There is a good list in the Reader's Digest "Encyclopedia of Garden Plants and Flowers"'. They are quite the most cheery harbingers of spring. Never cut off leaves after flowering: if you are worried by the untidiness in small gardens, tie them up in neat bundles with garden string. Plant three times the depth of the bulb.
NEPETA ("Catmint")						
x faassenii	Grey-green, small ovate, aromatic leaves	Lavender-blue spikes of small flowers 6" long	18" × 12"	5–9	garden	An indispensable plant for dry, sunny positions. Its good looks are so often ruined by cats who like nothing better than a good roll in it. The variety 'Six Hills Giant' is larger in all its parts.
sibirica	– ditto –	Spikes of blue flowers on erect stems	3' × 18"	5–9	Far East	Spreads vigorously on light soil.

'Souvenir d'André Chaudron'	– ditto –	Similar	18" × 18"	5–9	garden	A smaller version of *N. sibirica*.
NERINE						
boudenii	Mid-green, narrow strap-like leaves after flowering	Umbels of pale pink lily-like flowers with frilled petals and long stamens on stout stems	2' × 9"	9–11	Cape Province	An elegant plant for mild areas on dry, sunny soil. Plant shallowly with the nose of the bulb above ground. Two forms worth seeking out for their vigour and beauty are 'Mark Fenwick' and 'Pink Triumph'.
ODONTOS-PERMUM						
maritimum	Mid-green, downy leaves	Bright yellow compact daisies, 1" across	12" × 12"	5–9	S Africa	A very decorative small plant for sunny, dry positions. Particularly useful for late flowering.

NAME	FOLIAGE	FLOWERS	HT × SPRD	FLOWER– ING TIME	ORIGIN	COMMENTS
OENOTHERA ("Evening Primrose")						
acaulis	Rosettes of toothed, mid-green leaves like dandelions	Prostrate branches bear 3" flowers initially white turning rose, opening in the evening	6" × 12"	5–10	Chile	Deep-rooting and only reliably perennial on light, hot soil.
missouriensis	Lanceolate, mid-green leaves	Prostrate branches bear yellow flowers 3" across opening in the evening	6" × 18"	6–8	S Central USA	Deep-rooting and requires light sandy soil. The flowers last several days.
ONOSMA						
tauricum	Hairy, grey-green narrow leaves. Evergreen	Hanging racemes of ¾" long deep yellow flowers	8" × 12"	4–8	SE Europe	Not particularly spectacular but useful for long flowering period and evergreen leaves in dry walls and stony places. Scarce in cultivation.

ORIGANUM

amanum	Mat of profuse light green ovate leaves on slender stems	Tubular deep rose flowers 1½" long	3" × 6"	7–9	Turkey	Half-hardy and dislikes winter wet. Only for hot, dry positions in warm districts.
hybridum	Woolly, dark grey, ovate leaves on a plant of neat form	Round clusters of pink flowers 1½" long on slender stems	10" × 18"	6–8	Levant	A worthwhile tender plant for hot dry spots.
rotundifolium	Blue-green, smooth round leaves on a wide spreading plant	Clusters of minute pink flowers hidden in pale but bright green bracts on lax stems	8" × 12"	8–9	NE Turkey	A highly decorative plant for hot, dry places.
vulgare ("Marjoram")	Mid-green ovate aromatic leaves in alternate pairs	Minute rose purple flowers in terminal clusters 4" long	18" × 12"	7–8	Europe	A hardy perennial herb for food flavouring. The variety 'Aureum' is an attractive gold but needs protection from the hottest sun to prevent scorching.
ORNITHOGALUM ("Star of Bethlehem")					
balansae	Mid-green, long linear basal leaves	Small umbels of white flowers, star-shaped with green stripes on short stems	6" × 4"	3–4	Asia Minor	Hardy bulbous plant for a sunny dry position. Leave undisturbed.

NAME	FOLIAGE	FLOWERS	HT × SPRD	FLOWER‑ING TIME	ORIGIN	COMMENTS
nutans	– ditto –	Spikes of a dozen bell-shaped pale jade green flowers on long stems	18" × 6"	4–5	S Europe	Hardy and grows well in part shade. Good cut flower. Increases freely – beware!
umbellatum	– ditto –	Profuse, star-shaped, white flowers in larger umbels	12" × 8"	4–5	Europe, N Africa, Asia Minor	Hardy and decorative but spreads rapidly in light sandy soil. Happy in part shade. Plant all species in October 2–3" deep. Dead head unless you need seeds.
OSTEOSPERMUM (Dimorphotheca)						
barberae ("Cape Marguerite")	Mid-green, downy, lanceolate, aromatic leaves	Lilac pink daisies, dull purple beneath, 2½" across	18" × 12"	5–9	S Africa	Excellent tender plant for warm maritime conditions. Survives most winters. Cut back in October. Flowers of all species shut when not in sun.

barberae 'Compactum'	– ditto –	Deep pink daisies, otherwise as above	8" × 24"+	5–9	S Africa	A spreading mat former ideal for exposed positions. Trim over in very early spring to keep neat. Surprisingly hardy.
'Buttermilk'	– ditto –	Daisies yellow shading to white, bronze stripe beneath	18" × 18"	5–9	garden	There are an increasing number of garden hybrids of brighter flower colour. The only one I do not particularly like is 'Whirligig' which has peculiar propeller-like flowers.
ecklonis	– ditto –	Daisy flowers with white petals and deep blue central disc, blue purple beneath	24" × 24"	4–11	S Africa	A remarkable tender sub-shrub forming a quite substantial bush, the flowers held on long stems. Long flowering season. Dead-head regularly. The mat forming 'Prostrata' is hardier.
OTHONNA (*Othonnopsis*)						
cheirifolia	Spreading clump of blue-grey, fleshy leaves of paddle shape	Rich yellow daisies	10" × 12"+	4–5	S Africa	A good foliage plant for extra dry hot places.

NAME	FOLIAGE	FLOWERS	HT × SPRD	FLOWER-ING TIME	ORIGIN	COMMENTS
PAPAVER						
orientale ("Oriental Poppy")	Mid-green, hairy, deeply cut leaves, becoming unsightly and coarse after flowering	Brilliant scarlet flowers 4" across	2' × 2'	5–6	America	A truly spectacular flowering plant for a very few weeks after which it should be cut down to the ground and other plants allowed to fill the gap. Unfortunately the host of gorgeous garden hybrids need staking.

PENSTEMON
These American evergreen plants are definitely fashionable, and new garden hybrids abound. They are without exception only for warm, well-drained sites apart from the alpine species which are hardy. They also dislike wind, and do best on reasonably fertile soil in the protection of a wall: really only for the most wind-sheltered spot.

There is a wide choice of species and varieties. Being relatively new to the UK many varieties are untested in maritime conditions, but all must be worth trying as even the most tender sorts could well survive an average winter by the sea protected from wind. Having such a long and colourful flowering season, it is not surprising they are becoming increasingly popular.

NAME	FOLIAGE	FLOWERS	HT × SPRD	FLOWER-ING TIME	ORIGIN	COMMENTS
hartwegii	Mid-green lanceolate leaves	Racemes of wine-red snap-dragon flowers 2" long	2' × 18"	6–7	Mexico	This is a scarce species which survives in our wind-sheltered garden in arid conditions. It could be worth trying some of the many hybrid progeny in similar positions.

PHLOX

Another highly decorative American genus, and it would be nice to be able to tell you that it is reliable. I have attempted to grow all appropriate alpine species in sheltered sunny positions, and have failed abysmally. Although they like well-drained soil, I suspect that the hot, dry, sandy conditions combined with a degree of alkalinity are not appreciated. If you can please them, they are magnificent.

PTEROCEPHALUS

perennis	Mats of soft, grey, velvety, oblong leaves	Scabious-like heads of tiny mauve-pink flowers 1½" across on short stalks	3" × 12"	6–8	Mediterranean, Greece, Asia	An ideal edger for dry, hot conditions. Very pretty.

PULSATILLA

vulgaris ("Pasque Flower")	Finely divided, fern-like, mid-green foliage	The hairy buds open into wide, cup-shaped, rich purple flowers up to 3" across	10" × 12"	4–5	Europe	A wild plant found in dry, sunny, alkaline meadows. Happy in sand. There is a white form 'Alba' and a red form 'Rubra'.

NAME	FOLIAGE	FLOWERS	HT × SPRD	FLOWER-ING TIME	ORIGIN	COMMENTS
SAPONARIA						
ocymoides ("Bouncing Bet", "Rock Soapwort")	Mid-green oblong leaves on spreading stems	Bright rose-pink campion-like small flowers in profuse sprays	3" × 12"+	7–9	S Europe	Ideal vigorous plant for walls and dry places in full sun. Good on chalk. The sprays of flowers do bounce up and down in a breeze. In the Channel Islands flowers much earlier.
SAXIFRAGA						
x urbium ("London Pride")	Rosettes of mid-green, thick, spoon-shaped leaves, coarsely toothed. Evergreen.	Panicles of small star-shaped flowers, the white petals spotted red on long upright stems	12" × 18"	5	garden	A vigorous saxifrage, but only happy in shade. Useful for edging. Almost all others of this genus do not like the hot, dry conditions on offer.

SCILLA

peruviana ("Cuban Lily")	Strap-shaped, mid-green leaves	Large head 6" across of many dozens of lilac-blue, star-shaped flowers on sturdy 9" stems	12" × 8"	5–6	Central Mediterranean	Absolutely nothing to do with Cuba or Peru, but arrived in Bristol in a ship called "*Peru*". Needs a sunny, warm position.
sibirica 'Spring Beauty'	– ditto –	Vivid prussian-blue bell-shaped flowers ½" long 2 to 5 in number on 3 to 4 8" stems per bulb	8" × 4"	Early spring	Central to S Russia	Hardy bulbs. Like all Scillas should be planted 3" deep. The two sorts described here do not mind dry, sandy conditions, and are vigorous, S.s. 'Spring Beauty' being suitable for naturalising in grass.

SEDUM

Although this genus of succulent plants has a reputation for drought resistance, the taller species need plenty of humus in the soil which must however remain free draining. Some of the small "Stonecrops" are highly invasive, but are useful for their tolerance of extremes of heat, drought and poverty: in any case they are easily controlled by pulling them out. There is great variety of leaf form and colour. The small star-shaped flowers are borne in panicles, and come in shades of yellow and pink and white. Only a selection of the more readily available species are noted below.

NAME	FOLIAGE	FLOWERS	HT × SPRD	FLOWER-ING TIME	ORIGIN	COMMENTS
acre ("Biting Stonecrop")	Mats of egg-shaped, bright green leaves on slender stems. Evergreen	Yellow flowers on heads ½" across	2" × 12"+	6–7	Europe, N Africa, W Asia	Invasive if let loose in sunny, dry places. The variety 'Aureum' has bright yellow shoot tips in spring.
aizoon	Mid-green, lanceolate, coarsely toothed leaves	Flat heads of yellow flowers 3" across	18" × 18"	7	Far East	Compact. The form, 'Aurantiacum', (syn. 'Euphorbioides') has brighter flowers, darker leaves and reddish stems.
alboroseum	Grey-green leaves on sprawling stems	Flat heads of white flowers with pink eyes, 3" across	12" × 24"	8–9	Far East	Clump-forming. The variety 'Medio-variegatum' has leaves distinctly marked with cream-yellow.
album	Mats similar to *S. acre* but leaves cylindrical. Evergreen	Clusters of white flowers, 3" across	4" × 15"+	7	Europe, N Africa, W Asia	Invasive when suited.
'Autumn Joy'	Pale grey-green toothed, obovate leaves	Pink flower heads maturing to orange-red about 6" across	24" × 24"	9–10	garden	Better than both parents, *S. spectabile* and *S. telephium*. Divide occasionally in spring. Requires humus in soil. Not boggy in sand

	Leaves	Flowers	Size	Zone	Origin	Notes
cauticola	Tufts of grey-green ovate leaves on spreading stems. Deciduous	Crimson flowers in heads 4" across	6" × 12"+	8	Japan	Good on a dry wall for late flowering.
kamtschaticum floriferum 'Weihen-stephaner Gold'	Tufts of glossy deep green leaves on spreading, twiggy stems	Bright green-yellow flowers in lax terminal clusters. Profuse	4" × 12"+	7–9	E Siberia to N China	Requires semi-shade where it is vigorous. The variety 'Variegatum' has leaves margined white.
sieboldii	Round flat leaves on long stems, grey edged with purple	Flat clusters of pink flowers 2" across	3" × 15"	10	Japan	A really elegant plant but only half hardy. Survives on my warm wall in hanging pots totally unnurtured. The variety 'Medio-variegatum' has a white stripe on leaves.
spathulifolium	Mat of evergreen rosettes of fleshy spathulate leaves, grey-green tinged purple	Flat heads of bright yellow flowers 2" across	4" × 9"+	5–6	W USA	The variety 'Cape Blanco' has white flowers. 'Purpureum' has deep purple leaves.
spurium	Mat of evergreen obovate, toothed, mid-green leaves on red stems	Flat heads of rich pink flowers 2" across	4" × 12"+	7–8	Caucasus, N Iran	The variety 'Album' has white flowers. 'Schorbusser Blut' has deep red leaves and is an excellent contrast plant.

NAME	FOLIAGE	FLOWERS	HT × SPRD	FLOWER-ING TIME	ORIGIN	COMMENTS
x 'Vera Jameson'	Bronze-purple leaves on lax stems	Flat heads of smokey pink flowers 2" across on long stems	10" × 15"	9–10	garden	A beautiful hybrid which I have admired but not yet tried to grow. It might not like really extreme conditions of heat and aridity.

SEMPERVIVUM
("Houseleek")
All species and varieties of this succulent genus, which are numerous, have evergreen fleshy ovate leaves arranged in tight rosettes producing abundant off-sets. The flowers are generally insignificant, star-shaped and carried in sprays on long stems. The rosettes are 1–2" × 2–4". The leaves vary in colour from grey to jade green often with red tips.

Collect as many sorts as you can for the shallowest dry soil in full sun where they will be at their happiest, and where nothing else apart from small sedums will grow. They are easily propagated by detaching offsets which have rooted. Grow on in pots of sandy soil or transfer immediately to their permanent homes.

SENECIO

NAME	FOLIAGE	FLOWERS	HT × SPRD	FLOWER-ING TIME	ORIGIN	COMMENTS
cineraria maritima ("Sea Ragwort")	Rosettes of deeply cut silvery grey leaves	Unremarkable yellow flowers 1" across	24" × 12"+	7–9	Mediter-ranean	One of the finest silvery leaved plants with several varieties all worth a place in the driest soil in full sun. Usually treated as an annual but survives winters in warm areas.

	Foliage	Flowers	Size	Month	Origin	Notes
SILENE						
acaulis ("Moss Campion")	Narrow leaves in tight pale green mats	Masses of bright pink flowers ½" across	2" × 18"	5–6	N Hemisphere	All campions are easy going plants which tolerate part shade.
maritima 'Flore Pleno' (Double "Sea Campion")	Ovate grey-green leaves on long prostrate stems	Profuse double white flowers like pinks 1" across	4" × 18"+	6–7	garden	Excellent spreading over a dry wall but does require adequate soil around roots.
schafta	Lanceolate mid-green leaves in mats	Magenta-pink flowers in sprays ¾" across	6" × 12"	7–10	Caucasus	Good in rockeries.
STACHYS						
olympica (lanata) ("Lamb's Ears")	Ovate mid-green leaves covered with white wool	Purple flowers ¼" across in spikes of no great value	12" × 12"	7	Caucasus	Half-hardy but survives most winters as long as not too damp. Excellent ground cover in crispy dry sunny spots, or as contrast at front of borders. 'Silver Carpet' is a non-flowering variety. Cut down in November.

NAME	FOLIAGE	FLOWERS	HT × SPRD	FLOWER- ING TIME	ORIGIN	COMMENTS

TULIPA

Exposed windy sites are not suitable for the multitude of tall varieties so much used for early flowering bedding. The low stout wild species are ideal, however, where protection can be given from lashing spring gales. Only a very few will naturalise happily: most slowly fade away and require replacing regularly. They enjoy well-drained sandy soil on the alkaline side where they should be planted 6–8" deep in a position that provides plenty of hot sun in the summer to give the baking they require to prosper.

Experiment with them all: they are really magnificent. I have a permanent planting of *T. kaufmanniana* which shows no sign of disappearing despite the recommendation that the bulbs should be lifted annually and dried off. This species and its hybrids and varieties are described below.

Kaufmanniana hybrids and varieties (Division 12)

'Alfred Cortot', deep scarlet with black base, leaves mottled.

'César Franck', carmine-red edged with yellow outside, deep yellow inside.

'Fair Lady', cream with red stripes outside, cream with yellow base, flushed red inside.

'Fritz Kreisler', mauve with yellow edge outside, deep pink with deep yellow base and carmine-red markings inside. Tall.

'Glück', sulphur yellow striped with carmine-red outside, sulphur yellow with deep yellow base inside.

'Goudstuk', carmine-red and gold large flowers.

'Heart's Delight', carmine-red with paler edge outside, white flushed rose with yellow base inside. Tall.

'Shakespeare', salmon pink, flushed with scarlet with a yellow base inside.

'Stresa', deep golden yellow with single orange-red stripe outside, deep yellow with red base inside.

'The First', ivory-white flushed red outside, ivory-white with yellow base inside. Early flowering.

VERONICA

cinerea	Mats of grey narrow leaves	Masses of light blue saucer shaped small flowers on racemes 2" long	4" × 15"+	6–8	Asia Minor	Excellent bulb covering in dry sunny places. Quick growing.
filiformis	Mid-green rounded leaves in spreading mats	Profuse bright blue flowers ⅓" across	1" × 4+	4–7	Asia Minor	Rampagingly invasive but great ground cover in sun.
prostrata	Mats of mid-green, toothed, ovate leaves	Deep blue flowers in racemes 3" long	6" × 18"	5–7	Europe, N Asia	Many varieties including 'Rosea' with deep pink flowers, 'Spode Blue' with china-blue flowers and 'Trehane' with brilliant gold foliage which needs protection from full sun.

NAME	FOLIAGE	FLOWERS	HT × SPRD	FLOWER-ING TIME	ORIGIN	COMMENTS
ZANTEDESCHIA						
aethiopica 'Crowborough' (''Arum Lily'')	Mid-green glossy, spear-shaped, broad leaves	White spathes 5–9" long with deep yellow spadices	2–3' × 2'	5–7	South Africa	Although the ordinary ''Arum Lily'' demands moisture at its roots, the variety 'Crowborough' thrives in dry conditions. Plant rhizomes 4" deep and they will eventually bury themselves to an amazing depth.
ZAUSCHNERIA						
california (syn. *Epilobium canum*) ('Californian Fuchsia')	Grey-green, narrow, lanceolate leaves on a bushy plant	Generous sprays of bright scarlet tubular flowers with expanded mouths	18" × 18"	8–10	California, Mexico	Quite spectacular in dry, hot conditions: especially valuable for autumn colour. Associates well with blue flowered *Ceratostigma willmottianum*, which blooms in the summer time. The variety 'Dublin' has extra bright flowers.

15

Appendices

DEFINITIONS IN APPENDICES

All plants are deciduous and hardy unless otherwise noted.

E   = EVERGREEN

SE = SEMI-EVERGREEN

T   = TENDER: that is damaged by a hard frost, although the plant may regenerate. A mild, maritime climate obviously helps enormously.

HH = HALF-HARDY: applied to trees and shrubs means that they will survive all but the hardest winter in a mild area, especially in a protected position against a wall or behind tough windbreaks.

GC = GROUND COVER: densely growing, spreading plants which suppress weeds.

APPENDIX I
CLASSIFIED SHRUBS AND TREES

LARGE SHRUBS AND SMALL TREES

Abutilon vitifolium (T)
Acacia (T)
Arbutus (E) (HH)
Azara microphylla (E) (HH)

Baccharis halimifolia, patagonica (E)
Brachyglottis rependa (E) (T)
Buddleia alternifolia

Ceanothus arboreus 'Trewithen Blue' (E) (HH), *thyrsiflorus* (E) (HH)
Clerodendrum trichotum (T)
Colutea arborescens, buhsei
Cordyline australis (E) (HH)
Corokia macrocarpa (E) (HH)
Cotinus
Cotoneaster bullatus, 'Cornubia' (SE), 'Exburiensis', *salicifolius* (E)
Cytisus battandieri (HH), 'Porlock' (SE) (HH)

Dendromecon rigida (E) (T)

Elaeagnus angustifolia, x ebbingei, macrophylla, pungens, umbellata (all E)
Escallonia rubra var. 'Macrantha' (E) (HH), 'Iveyi' (E) (HH)
Eucalyptus (ST to LT but not in windy areas) (HH)
Euonymus japonicus (E)

Fremontodendron 'California Glory' (E) (HH)
Fuchsia 'Riccartonii' (HH)

Garrya elliptica (E)
Genista aetnensis, tenera 'Golden Shower'
Griselinia littoralis (E) (HH)

Hoheria (D, SE, E)

Laurus nobilis (E)
Lavatera thuriangiaca
Leptospermum lanigerum (E) (T)

Metrosideros robusta (E) (T), *umbellata* (E) (T)
Myrtus communis (E) (HH)

Osmanthus heterophyllus (E)

Piptanthus nepalensis (E) (HH)
Pittosporum crassifolium (E) (HH), 'Garnettii' (E) (HH), *tenuifolium*
    (E) (HH), *tobira* (E) (T)
Pyracantha atalantoides (E), *coccinea* 'Lalandei' (E), *rogersiana* (E)

Spartium junceum

Tamarix

MEDIUM SIZED SHRUBS

Abelia (SE) (T)
Aloysia triphylla (HH)
Atriplex halimus (SE)
Aucuba japonica (E)
Azara dentata (E) (T)

Berberis darwinii (E), *x stenophylla* (E)
Beschorneria yuccoides (E) (T)
Brachyglottis elaeagnifolius (E) (HH), *reinoldii* (E) (HH), *viravira* (E)
    (T)
Buddleia auriculata (HH), *davidii, globosa* (SE), 'Lochinch'
Bupleurum fruticosum (E)

Callistemon citrinus 'Splendens' (E) (T), *sieberi* (E) (HH)
Carpenteria californica (E) (HH)
Cassia corymbosa (T)

Ceanothus 'Autumnal Blue' (E) (HH), 'Delight' (E) (HH) 'Gloire de Versailles', 'Henri Desfosse', *impressus* (E) (HH), *impressus* 'Puget Blue' (E) (HH), 'Indigo' (T)
Choisya ternata (E) (HH)
Cistus x cyprius (E) (HH), 'Elma' (E) (HH), *ladanifer* (E) (HH), 'Peggy Sammons' (E) (HH)
Clianthus puniceus (SE) (T)
Colletia hystrix (E)
Colutea x media, multiflora, orientalis
Corokia buddleiodes (E) (HH), *x virgata* (E) (HH)
Coronilla emerus, valentina subsp. glauca (E) (HH)
Cotoneaster lacteus (E), *pannosus* (E), *simonsii* (SE)
Cytisus 'Burkwoodii', 'Hollandia', 'Johnson's Crimson', 'Luna', *scoparius*

Desfontainea spinosa (E) (T)

Elaeagnus commutata
Escallonia 'C.F. Ball' (E) (HH), all "Donard" varieties (E) (HH to H), 'Langleyensis' (E), *rubra* 'Crimson Spire' (E)
Eupatorium ligustrinum (E) (HH)
Euphorbia mellifera (E) (T)

Fabiana imbricata (B) (T)
x fatshedera lizei (E)
Fatsia japonica (E)

Genista cinerea, tinctoria var. 'Virgata'

Halimodendron halodendron
Hebe x andersonii 'Variegata' (E) (HH), *salicifolia* (E) (HH)
Hibiscus sinosyriacus, syriacus
Hippophaë rhamnoides
Hydrangea macrophylla
Hypericum 'Hidcote' (SE), 'Rowallane' (SE) (HH)

Indigofera amblyantha (HH), *hebepetala* (HH), *pseudotinctoria* (HH)

Lavatera maritima (T)

234

Leptospermum scoparium (E) (HH)
Leycesteria formosa
Lupinus arboreus
Lycium barbarum

Medicago arborea (E) (HH)
Mimulus aurantiacus (E) (T)

Notospartium carmichaeliae (T)

Olearia avicennifolia (E), *hastii* (E), 'Henry Travers' (E) (T), *ilicifolia* (E), *macrodonta* (E), *phlogopappa* (E) (T), *scilloniensis* (E) (HH), *solandri* (E) (HH)
Osmanthus x burkwoodii (E), *delavayi* (E)
Ozothamnus rosmarinifolius (E) (HH)

Paeonia lutea var. ludlowii
Philadelphus 'Beauclerk', 'Belle Etoile', *coronarius*, 'Virginal'
Phormium tenax (HH)
Potontilla fruticosa var. 'Grandiflora', 'Katherine Dykes', 'Vilmoriniana'
Pyracantha 'Mohave' (E), 'Orange Glow' (E), 'Shawnee' (E), 'Watereri' (E)

Romneya (HH)
Rosa (many mentioned in text)
Rosmarinus officinalis (E)

Teucrium fruticans (E) (T)

Viburnum tinus (E)

Yucca gloriosa (E)

SMALL SHRUBS

Berberis thunbergii
Brachyglottis compactus (E), *monroi* (E), 'Sunshine' (E)

Calceolaria integrifolia (T)

Caryopteris x clandonensis
Cassinia fulvida (E)
Ceratostigma willmottianum (HH)
Cistus x aguilari 'Maculatus' (E) (HH), 'Anne Palmer' (E) (HH), *x
corbariensis* (E) (HH), *palhinhae* (E) (HH), 'Pat' (E), *populifolius*
var. *lasiocalyx* (E), *x purpureus* (E) (HH)
Colletia paradoxa (E)
Convolvulus cneorum (E) (HH)
Cotoneaster rotundifolius (E)
Cytisus x praecox, purpureus

Escallonia 'Apple Blossom' (E) (HH), 'Peach Blossom' (E) (HH),
'Red Elf' (E) (HH), *rubra* 'Woodside' (E) (HH)
Euphorbia characias (E)

Genista hispanica (E), *tinctoria* 'Royal Gold'
Grindelia chiloensis (E) (T)

Halimium alyssoides (E) (T), *lasianthum* (E) (T)
Hebe 'Alicia Amherst' (E) (T), 'Autumn Glory' (E), 'Carnea' (E),
cupressoides (E) *x franciscana* 'Blue Gem' (E) (HH), 'Great Orme'
(E) (HH), *hulkeana* (E), 'La Seduisante' (E), 'Midsummer
Beauty' (E), 'Mrs. Windsor' (E), 'Purple Queen' (E) (T), *recurva*
(E), 'Simon Delaux' (E), 'Spender's Seedling' (E)
Helichrysum splendidum (E) (HH)
Hypericum forrestii, kouytchense (SE)

Juniperus x media (E)

Indigofera heterantha (HH)

Lavandula angustifolia (E)
Leonotis leonurus (T)
Lespedeza thunbergii (E) (HH)

Mahonia aquifolius (E)

Olearia megalophylla (E) (T)
Ozothamnus ledifolius (E) (HH)

Perovskia atriplicifolia
Philadelphus 'Erectus', 'Sybille'
Phlomis chrysophylla (E) (T), *fruticosa* (E) (T)
Phormium cookianum (E) and some varieties of *P. tenax*
Phygelius (E)
Potentilla 'Daydawn', 'Elizabeth', 'Primrose Beauty', 'Sunset', 'William Purdom'

Rosmarinus officinalis 'Benenden Blue' (E) (T)
Ruta graveolens (E)

Salvia fulgens (T), *greyii* (T), *guaranitica* (T), *involucrata* (T), *microphylla* (T)

Ulex europaeus (E)

Yucca recurvifolia (E), *whipplei* (E)

PROSTRATE AND DWARF SHRUBS

Ballota pseudodictamnus (SE)

Calluna (E)
Ceanothus thyrsiflorus 'Repens'' (E)
Cistus x danseureaui 'Decumbens' (E) (HH), *x pulverulentus* (E) (HH)
Cotoneaster conspicuus 'Decorus' (E), *horizontalis*
Cytisus ardoinii, x beanii, x kewensis, scoparius subsp. maritimus

Erica (E)

Fuchsia procumbens

Genista lydia, pilosa, tinctoria 'Golden Plate', 'Plena'
Grevillea alpina (E) (T)

x halimiocistus (E) (T)
Halimium commutatum (E) (T), *ocymoides* (E) (T)

Hebe albicans (E), *armstrongii* (E), *buchananii* (E), 'Emerald Green' (E), 'Hagley Park' (E), *macrantha* (E) (T), *ochracea* (E), 'Pewter Dome' (E), *pinguifolia* 'Pagei' (E), *rakaiensis* (E), 'Youngii' (E)
Helianthemum (HH)
Helichrysum italicum (E) (HH), *subsp. serotinum* (E) (HH), *petiolare* (E) (T), *plicatum* (E) (T)
Hypericum calycinum (E), *empetrifolium* (E), *x moserianum, olympicum*
Hyssopus officinalis (SE)

Iberis (E)

Juniperus (E) (all mentioned in text except J. *x media*)

Indigofera kirilowii (HH)

Lavandula stoechas (E) (T)
Leiophyllum buxifolium (E)
Leptospermum humifusum (E), *scoparium* 'Kiwi' (E), *nanum* (E)

Margyricarpus pinnatus (E) (HH)
Moltkia petraea (SE) (HH)

Pachysandra terminalis (E)
Parahebe
Penstemon
Philadelphus 'Manteau d'Hermine'
Phlomis italica (E), *lanata* (E)
Potentilla arbuscula, davurica, parvifolia, 'Goldfinger', 'Longacre', 'Red Ace', 'Tilford Cream'

Rosmarinus officinalis 'Corsicus Prostratus' (E) (T), 'Severn Sea' (E)

Salvia officianalis (SE)
Santolina (E)

Thymus (E)

Yucca filamentosa (E), *flaccida* (E)

EVERGREEN SHRUBS AND SMALL TREES

Abelia (SE) (T)
Arbutus (T)
Atriplex halimus (SE)
Aucuba
Azara (T)

Ballota pseudodictamnus (SE)
Berberis darwinii, x stenophylla
Beschorneria yuccoides (T)
Brachyglottis (Senecio)
Buddleia globosa (SE)
Bupleurum fruticosum

Callistemon (T)
Calluna
Carpenteria californica (HH)
Cassinia fulvida
Ceanothus arboreus 'Trewithen Blue', 'Autumnal Blue', 'Delight',
    impressus, impressus 'Puget Blue', *thyrsiflorus*
Choisya ternata
Cistus (HH)
Clianthus puniceus (SE) (T)
Colletia
Convolvulus cneorum (T)
Cordyline australis (ha)
Corokia (HH)
Coronilla valentina subsp. glauca (T)
Cotoneaster conspicuus 'Decorus' (GC), 'Cornubia' (SE), *lacteus, sali-
    cifolius, pannosus, rotundifolius, simonsii* (SE)

Dendromecon rigida (T)
Desfontainea spinosa (T)

Elaeagnus x ebbingei, macrophylla, pungens
Erica
Escallonia (HH)

Eucalyptus (all hardy except *globulus*)
Euonymus japonicus
Eupatorium ligustrinum (T)
Euphorbia chariacas, mellifera (T)

Fabiana imbricata (T)
Fatsia japonica
Fremontodendron 'California Glory' (T)

Garrya elliptica
Genista hispanica
Grevillea (T)
Grindelia hailoensis (T)
Griselinia littoralis (T)

x halimiocistus (T)
Halimium (T)
Halimodendron halodendron
Hebe (some T)
Helichrysum (HH-T)
Helianthemum (HH)
Hoheria angustifolia, 'Glory of Amlwch' (SE), *populnea, sexstylosa*
Hypericum calycinum, empetrifolium, 'Hidcote' (SE), *kouytchense* (SE),
    'Rowallane' (SE)
Hyssopus officinalis (SE)

Iberis

Juniperus

Laurus nobilis
Lavandula (some T)
Leiophyllum buxifolium
Leptospermum (T)
Lupinus arboreus

Mahonia aquifolium
Margyricarpus pinnatus (HH)
Medicago arborea (T)

Metrosideros (T)
Mimulus aurantiacus (T)
Moltkia petraea (SE) (HH)
Myrtus communis (HH)

Notospartium carmichaeliae (T) (no leaves)

Olearia (some T)
Osmanthus
Ozothamnus (HH)

Pachysandra terminalis
Phlomis (T)
Phormium
Phygelius (HH)
Piptanthus nepalensis (HH)
Pittosporum (HH) (T)
Pyracantha

Rosmarinus (some T)
Ruta graveolens

Salvia officinalis (SE)
Santolina

Teucrium fruticans (T)
Thymus

Ulex

Yucca

ARCHITECTURAL SHRUBS AND THOSE WITH BOLDLY
COLOURED FOLIAGE

Beschorneria yuccoides (E) (T) (arch)

Choisya ternata 'Sundance' (E) (HH) (yellow, good shape)
Cordyline australis (E) (HH) (arch)
Cotinus coggyria hybrids and *obovatus* (red)

Cotoneaster salicifolius (E) (arch)

Elaeagnus commutata (silver), *x ebbingei* varieties (var gold), *pungens* varieties (var yellow) (all E)
Eucalyptus (E) (T to hardy) (blue)
Euonymus japonicus varieties (E) (var gold, white, yellow)
Eupatorium ligustrinum (E) (HH) (pale bright green, good shape)
Euphorbia characias and varieties (E) (arch, blue-green)

Fatsia japonica (E) (arch, ornamental foliage)

Grevillea (E) (difficult) (grey-green to deep green needle foliage, good shape)
Griselinia littoralis and varieties (E) (bright yellow-green or var)

Hebe x andersonii 'Variegata', 'Emerald green', *x franciscana* 'Variegata', 'Mrs Windsor', *ochracea* (all E) (bright green, var)
Hydrangea macrophylla var. *normalis* (arch)
Hypericum 'Rowallane' (SE) (HH) (difficult) (arch)

Juniperus communis subsp. depressa varieties, *horizontalis* varieties, *x media* 'Pfitzeriana Aurea' (all E) (blue)

Laurus nobilis and varieties (E) (arch, var gold)
Leptospermum (E) (T) (bronze foliage, good shape)

Olearia 'Zennoriensis' (E) (T) (arch)
Osmanthus heterophyllus varieties (E) (var)

Paeonia lutea var. *ludlowii,* (arch)
Philadelphus coronarius varieties (bright yellow, var)
Phormium and varieties (E) (arch, var bronze, purple)
Pittosporum and varieties (E) (HH) (arch, var yellow)

Romneya (HH) (arch, glaucous)

Salvia officinalis varieties (SE) (gold, var)

Thymus varieties (E) (arch, var)

Yucca (E) (arch, var)

APPENDIX II
GROUND COVER

SHRUBS AND PERENNIAL PLANTS
FOR LOW GROUND COVER

SHRUBS

Ballota pseudodictamnus (SE)
Calluna (E) (for acid soils)
Ceanothus thyrsiflorus 'Repens' (E)
Cistus x corbariensis (E) (HH), *palinhae* (E) (HH)
Convolvulus cneorum (E) (T)
Cotoneaster conspicuus 'Decorus' (E), *horizontalis* (E) (good in shade)

Erica (E) (for acid soils)

Halimium alyssoides (E) (HH), *lasianthum* (E)
Hebe pinguifolia 'Pagei' (E), *rakaiensis* (E)
Hedera helix (E) (good in shade)
Helianthemum (E)
Hypericum calycinum (E) (good in shade)

Iberis sempervirens (E)

Juniperus (E) (prostrate sorts detailed in text)

Pachysandra terminalis (E) (good in shade)
Parahebe catarractae

Rosmarinus officinalis 'Corsicus Prostratus', (E) (HH)

Thymus x citriodorus (E), *vulgaris* (E)

PERENNIALS

Anthemis cupaniana

Arabis caucasica (for part shade)
Aubretia deltoidea
Bergenia cordifolia (E) (good in shade)

Campanula portenschlagiana, poscharskyana
Carpobrotus edulis (E) (T)
Cerastium tomentosum

Erigeron glaucus (E)
Euphorbia robbiae (E) (good in shade)

Geranium

Osteospermum barberae 'Compactum' (E) (HH)
Othonna cheirifolia (HH)

Saponaria ocymoides
Saxifraga x urbium (for shade)
Sedum acre (E), *album* (E), *kamtschaticum floriferum* (for part shade)
Stachys olympica

Veronica cinerea, filiformis

SHRUBS FOR LOW EVERGREEN GROUND COVER ON DRY
SOIL IN SUN

Calluna (acid soil)
Cistus x dansereaui 'Decumbens' (HH)
Cistus x pulverulentus (HH)
Convolvulus cneorum (HH)
Cotoneaster conspicuus "Decorus"
Cotoneaster horizontalis

Erica (acid soil)

Hebe albicans
Hebe pinguifolia 'Pagei'
Hebe rakaiensis

Juniperus (all prostrate forms mentioned in the text)

Rosmarinus officinalis 'Corsicus Prostratus' (HH)

Thymus (almost all)

SHRUBS FOR LOW EVERGREEN GROUND-COVER IN SHADE

Hypericum calcyinum
Pachysandra terminalis

All the above plants are fully described in the text

APPENDIX III
CLASSIFIED PERENNIAL PLANTS

PERENNIAL PLANTS WITH SILVER, GREY, OR GREY–BLUE
FOLIAGE

Agave americana
Artemisia

Centaurea
Cerastium tomentosum

Dianthus

Echinops glaucus
Elymus arenarius
Erianthus ravennae (grass)
Eriophyllus lanatum
Erodium carrifolium
Eryngium maritimum
Euphorbia characias wulfenii, myrsinites

Festuca glauca (grass)

Gypsophila repens, 'Rosy Veil'

Helictotrichon sempervirens (grass)
Hieracum villosum

Linaria triomithophora
Linum narbonense, perenne
Lychnis

Marrubium incanum

Nepeta

Onosma tauricum (E)
Origanum hybridum

Pennisetum alopecuroides, orientale (grass)

Pterocephalus perennis

Sedum alboroseum (E), 'Autumn Joy', *cauticola, spathulifolium* (E)
Sempervivum (E) – silvery grey sorts
Silene maritima
Senecio cineraria maritima
Stachys olympica
Stipa calamagrostis, gigantea (semi-E) (grass)

Veronica cinerea

Zauschneria californica

PERENNIAL PLANTS WITH PINK FLOWERS

Aethionema grandiflorum
Amaryllis belladonna
Anemone blanda – pink form
Armeria maritima
Aubretia – pink forms

Bergenia cordifolia

Centaura
Centranthus ruber
Chrysanthemum rubellum
Crepis incana

Dianthus – pink sorts
Dierama pulcherrimum

Gypsophila 'Rosy Veil'

Lampranthus roseus

Nerine bowdenii

Origanum
Osteospermum barberae

Pterocephalus perennis

Saponaria ocymoides
Sedum 'Autumn Joy', *spurium, x* 'Vera Jameson'
Silene acaulis, schafta

Tulipa kaufmanniana 'Shakespeare'

Veronica prostrata 'Rosea'

PERENNIAL PLANTS WITH RED, CARMINE, CRIMSON, SCARLET OR ORANGE FLOWERS

Anemone coronaria, 'de Caen', 'St. Brigid' – red and scarlet forms
Anemone fulgens

Centranthus ruber 'Coccineus'
Crocosmia masonorum

Kniphofia uvaria

Lampranthus aurantiacus, brownii, coccineus, elegans
Lychnis coronaria

Papaver orientale
Penstemon hartwegii

Sedum cauticola

Tulipa kaufmanniana 'Alfred Cortot', 'César Franck', 'Goudstuck', 'Heart's Delight'

Zauschneria californica

PERENNIAL PLANTS WITH PURPLE, VIOLET, MAUVE OR LILAC FLOWERS

Acanthus spinosus
Allium rosenbechianum
Aubretia deltoidea

Bergenia cordifolia

Cheiranthus x 'Bowles' Mauve'
Cynara cardunculus

Dictamnus purpureus
Digitalis purpurea

Erigeron glaucus
Erodium carrifolium

Gladiolus byzantinus

Iris reticulata

Lampranthus amoenus, conspicuus, spectabilis, zeyheri
Linaria alpina, purpurea
Liriope muscari
Lychnis flos-jovis

Origanum vulgare

Pterocephalus perennis
Pulsatilla vulgaris

Stachys olympica

Tulipa kaufmanniana 'Fritz Kreisler'

PERENNIAL PLANTS WITH BLUE OR LAVENDER–BLUE
FLOWERS

Anemone – blue forms

Campanula
Catananche caerulea
Convolvulus mauritanicus

Echinops ritro
Eryngium – blue species

Fascicularia bicolor
Felicia

Iris histrioides 'Major'

Limonium latifolium
Linum narbonense, perenne
Lithospermum diffusum

Nepeta

Veronica

PERENNIAL PLANTS WITH YELLOW FLOWERS

Allium moly
Alyssum argenteum, saxatile
Arnebia echioides
Artemisia

Cheiranthus cheiri 'Harpur Crewe'
Crocosmia – yellow forms

Eriophyllus lanatum
Erodium chrysanthemum
Euphorbia polychroma, segueirana

Ferula communis

Hieracum villosum

Linaria dalmatica
Linum arboreum, flavum

Narcissus – yellow sorts

Oenothera
Onosma tauricum
Odontospermum maritimum
Othonna cheirifolia

Sedum acre, aizoon, spathulifolium
Senecio (unremarkable)

Tulipa kaufmanniana 'Gluck', 'Stresa'

PERENNIAL PLANTS WITH WHITE FLOWERS

Allium neapolitanum
Anemone blanda – white form
Anemone 'de Caen', 'The Bride'
Anthemis cupaniana
Asphodelus albus

Cerastium tomentosum
Chrysanthemum frutescens, hosmariense, maximum
Crambe cordifolia

Dianthus – white sorts
Dictamnus albus

Gypsophila paniculata, repens

Marrubium incanum

Narcissus – white sorts

Oenothera acaulis
Ornithogalum balansae, umbellatum
Osteospermum ecklonis

Saxifraga x urbium
Sedum alboroseum, album

Tulipa kaufmanniana 'The First', 'Fair Lady'

Zantedeschia aethiopica 'Crowborough'

PERENNIAL PLANTS WITH GREEN FLOWERS

Eryngium agavifolium, bromeliifolium, eburneum
Euphorbia characias wulfenii, myrsinites, robbiae

Foeniculum vulgare

Helleborus corsicus

251

Ornithogalum nutans

Sedum kamtschaticum floriferum 'Weihenstephaner Gold'

EVERGREEN PERENNIAL PLANTS

Agave
Alyssum saxatile
Artemisia (Semi-E)
Aubretia deltoidea

Bergenia

Dierama pulcherrimum

Erigeron glaucus
Euphorbia characias wulfenii, myrsinites, robbiae

Fascicularis bicolor, pitcairnifolia
Felicia (HH)

Helleborus corsicus

Lampranthus (HH)
Limonium latifolium

Onosma tauricum
Osteospermum (HH)

Saxifraga x urbium
Sedum acre, album
Sempervivum

PROSTRATE, MAT OR MOUND FORMING PERENNIAL PLANTS

Anthemis cupaniana
Arabis caucasica, ferdinandii-coburgii
Armeria maritima
Aubretia deltoidea (E)

Bergenia (E)

Campanula - all sorts (some invasive)
Carpobrotus edulis
Cerastium tomentosum (invasive)
Convolvulus mauritanicus

Erigeron glaucus (E)
Euphorbia robbiae (E)

Geranium - low-growing sorts
Gypsophila repens, 'Rosy Veil'

Lampranthus (E) (HH) low-growing sorts
Lithospermum diffusum

Milium effusum 'Aureum' (grass)

Oenothera acaulis, missourensis
Origanum amanum, hybridum, rotundifolium
Osteospermum barberae 'Compactum'
Othonna cheirifolia

Pterocephalus perennis

Saponaria ocymoides
Saxifraga x urbium (E)
Sedum (some E)
Sempervivum (E)
Silene
Senecio cineraria maritima
Stachys olympica

Veronica

Zauschnetria californica

BOLD AND/OR ARCHITECTURAL PERENNIAL PLANTS

Acanthus spinosus
Agave americana, 'Marginata' (E)
Artemisia arborescens (Semi-E)

Crambe cordifolia
Cynara cardunculus

Dierama pulcherrimum (E)

Echinops ritro
Elymus arenarius (grass)
Erianthus ravennae (grass)
Eryngium eburneum, giganteum, x oliverianum
Euphorbia characias wulfenii (E)

Ferula communis
Foeniculum vulgare

Gypsophila paniculata

Helictrotrichon sempervirens
Helleborus corsicus (E)

Miscanthus (grass)

Pennisetum (grass)

Stipa (grass)

Zantedeschia aethiopeca 'Crowborough'

var = variegated   arch = architectural

APPENDIX IV
"ANNUALS" FOR SANDY DRY SOIL

HALF-HARDY PERENNIALS

Antirrhinum asarina 6", white flowers 6–9
Arctotis x hybrida 12–18", 'Apricot', 'Flame', 'Pink', 'White',
   'Wine' 6–11

Felicia (see descriptions in text)

Gazania x splendens 6", orange flowers 7–8

Hieracium villosum (see descriptions in text)
Odontospermum maritimum (see descriptions in text)
Othonnopsis cheirifolia (see descriptions in text)

Osteospermum (see descriptions in text)

Pelargonium (a vast choice)

HARDY ANNUALS

Alyssum 'Rosie O'Day', 'Royal Carpet'

Calendula
Chrysanthemum segetum

Dianthus 'Bravo'

Lavatera 'Loveliness'
Limnanthes douglassii
Linum grandiflorum 'Venice Red'

Papaver
Phacelia campanularia

Silene pendula

Tropaeolum (Nasturtium)

HALF-HARDY ANNUALS

Anagallis linifolia phillipsii
Antirrhinum

Begonia

Cleome spinosa

Echium 'Blue Bedder'

Mesembryanthemum criniflorum

Petunia
Portulaca

Tagetes

Ursinia anethoides

Venidium
Verbena

APPENDIX V
ORNAMENTAL GRASSES FOR DRY SOILS

Tufts of the decorative grasses can be very telling in a mixed planting of perennials and shrubs, providing good contrasts of form and colour. They vary in height from a few inches to giants of seven or eight feet. Obviously their flowers are not colourful but they are often exceptionally graceful.

Elymus arenarius 4' x 3'
Very invasive but excellent for binding sand in rough places and handsome with it. Broad blades of a good grey-blue and tall wheat-like flowers of the same colour. N. Hemisphere.

Erianthus ravennae 6' x 3'
"Ravenna Grass" has grey leaves and long spikes of purple-grey flowers on tall purple stems. For warm areas in full sun. Mediterranean.

Festuca glauca 9' x 9'
Compact tufts of narrow powdery blue blades ideal for edging. Full sun. _F. amethystina_ is 18' high and has a brighter colour. Europe.

Helictotrichon sempervirens 4' x 2'
Stiff, narrow, blue grey blades in substantial clumps. Heads of fine light buff flowers on long grey stems. Particularly effective and does not run. SW Europe.

Milium effusum 'Aureum' 15" x 15"
Compact clumps of soft, bright gold blades, "Bowles' Golden Grass" has bead-like yellow flowers on a multitude of slender stems. For shady dry places. Europe.

Miscanthus
A wonderful family of highly decorative tall grasses. _M. sacchariflorus_ has gold striped green leaves. _M. sinensis_ varieties are numerous and include 'Gracillimus' (2' x 2') with blue green leaves, 'Variegatus' (4' x 2') with cream stripes on green leaves and 'Zebrinus' (4' x 2') with yellow stripes across green leaves. Japan, China.

Pennisetum
A genus of half-hardy grasses all of which have ornamental bottle brush flowers. _P. alopecuroides_ (3' x 2') has grey green leaves in a dense clump and feathery, buff-yellow flowers in autumn. Argentina. _P. orientale_

(12" x 12") has narrow, blue-grey leaves and brown-green, bristly flower spikes 5" long on wiry stems in late summer. Abyssinia. *P. setaceum*, "Fountain Grass'", (3' x 18") has rough, mid-green leaves and 12" long spikes of feathery cream-green flowers on stiff stems in late summer. Africa, Arabia, SW Asia.

Stipa

Architectural plants for isolated positions in full sun. *P. calamagrostis* (4' x 2') has compact tufts of grey-green leaves and 12" long plumes of silvery flowers tinged with violet on smooth stems in summer. S Europe. *P. gigantea* (6' x 2') has almost evergreen clumps of narrow grey-green leaves and silver plumes 12" long tinged with purple, resembling pampas grass, on tall stems in June and July. Spain.

References

The publications noted below are simply those I have used in the course of writing this book. Without them it would have been impossible to present the information in any sort of scientific and coherent fashion. In doing so I am aware that I have drawn upon a deep well of recorded knowledge which started with the Greeks of Homer's time in the 8th c. BC, and continued unchecked through the annals of ancient Rome, Persia, Islam and the European monastic foundations. However, it was not until my fellow London medical practitioner, John Gerard, published his *"Catalogue of Plants"* in 1596 that anybody had attempted to record what they were actually growing in their gardens. Gerard excused his enjoyment of gardening by stressing the medicinal use of his plants. John Parkinson was the first to record purely decorative *"Pleasant Flowers"* in 1629. Since then there has been an unbroken succession of gardener-authors, many of the greatest distinction, all contributing to a tradition which has made British horticulture the envy of the world throughout the best part of four centuries. Every one of them I salute with utmost humility.

BISSON, Mike, *Islands in Bloom*, Michael Stephen, Jersey, Channel Islands, 1988.

BONNARD, Brian, *Flora of Alderney*, Brian Bonnard, Alderney, Channel Islands, 1988.

BEALES, Peter, *Classic Roses*, Collins Harvill, London, 4th edition, 1989.

CHATTO, Beth, *The Dry Garden*, Dent, London, 1988 (Reprinted)

COATS, Alice M., *Garden Shrubs and their Histories*, Vista, London, 1963.

COATS, Alice M., *Flowers and their Histories*, A. and C. Black, London, 2nd edition, 1968.

EVISON, J.R.B., *Gardening on Lime and Chalk*, Cassell Educational for the RHS, London, 1986.

FISH, Margery, *Cottage Garden Flowers*, Faber and Faber, London 1985 (Reprinted)

FOX, Robin Lane, *V. Sackville West, The Illustrated Garden Book* (anthology), Michael Joseph, London, 1989.

GREY-WILSON, Christopher, *A Manual of Alpine and Rock Garden Plants*, Helm, Bromley, England, 1989.

INGWERSEN, Will, *Alpine and Rock Plants*, Dent, London, 1983.

KELWAY, Christine, *Gardening on Sand*, Collingridge, London, 1965.

KELWAY, Christine, *Seaside Gardening*, Collingridge, London, 1962.

KING, Ronald, *Tresco, England's Island of Flowers*, Constable, London, 1991.

LATYMER, Hugo, *The Mediterranean Gardener*, Frances Lincoln in association with The Royal Botanic Gardens, Kew, London, 1990.

LLOYD, Christopher, *Clematis*, Viking, London, 4th edition, 1989.

MARTIN, Laura C., *Wildflower Folklore*, The East Woods Press, Charlotte, N. Carolina, USA, 1984.

POLUNIN, Oleg and Huxley, Anthony, *Flowers of the Mediterranean*, Chatto and Windus, London, 1987.

ROSE, Peter Q., *Climbers and Wall Plants*, Blandford, London, 1990.

SHEPHERD, F.W., *Seaside Gardening*, Cassell Educational, London for the RHS, 1990.

STUART, David and Sutherland, James, *Plants from the Past*, Penguin, London 1989.

SYNGE, Patrick M., *Collins Guide to Bulbs*, Collins, London, 2nd edition, 1971.

THOMAS, Graham Stuart, *Plants for Ground Cover*, Dent, London, 1970.

THOMAS, Graham Stuart, *Perennial Garden Plants*, Dent, London, 3rd edition, 1990.

WORKS OF GENERAL REFERENCE

BEAN, W.J., *Trees and Shrubs Hardy in the British Isles*, Vol. I-IV and Supplement, Murray, London, 1980 (Reprinted)

COOMBES, Allen J., *Guide to Plant Names*, Hamlyn, London, 1992.

GOODE, Patrick and Lancaster, Michael, *The Oxford Companion to Gardens*, Oxford University, 1991.

HESSAYON, D. G., *The Flower Expert*, pbi, Waltham Cross, England, 1984.

PHILIP, Chris, *The Plant Finder*, Headmain, Whitbourne, England, 6th edition, 1992.

Reader's Digest Encyclopaedia of Garden Plants and Flowers, Reader's Digest, London, 4th edition, 1987.

The Hillier Manual of Trees and Shrubs, David and Charles, Newton Abbott, England, 6th edition, 1991.

The Royal Horticultural Society Gardeners' Encyclopaedia of Plants and Flowers, Dorling Kindersley, 1989.

SWANN'S WAY

TYROLEAN, TWEED, TARTAN
TOWN & COUNTRY CLOTHES
FOR LADIES GENTS & CHILDREN
SMALL AND LARGE SIZES

SCHNEIDERS [§] GIESSWEIN

55 HOLLYWOOD ROAD, LONDON SW10 9HX
0171 351 7907
WEEKDAYS 10.30 – 6.30 SAT 11.00 – 5.00

With best wishes

eurodis electron

Eurodis Electron PLC
Reigate, Surrey

ALDWICKBURY PARK GOLF CLUB
HARPENDEN, HERTS

wishes Richard Mortimer the best of luck with his
seaside gardening book
Aldwickbury would be an ideal venue to read this
fascinating book. You can have a splendid day out golfing
with friends or business associates in the
Hertfordshire park land

PHONE ALLAN KNOTT ON 01582 765112 FOR DETAILS
A WARM WELCOME AWAITS YOU

ALAN and TARA ELLIOT

congratulate RICHARD MORTIMER

on the publication of his book "THE SEASIDE GARDENER".

They offer their good wishes to

THE IBIS TRUST

and wish the Trust luck in all its fund raising activities

and in the continuation of its valuable work.